MW00721500

Trails to Gold

Volume Two

Roadhouses of the Cariboo

by

Branwen C. Patenaude

Heritage House

Canadian Cataloguing in Publication Data
Patenaude, Branwen C. (Branwen Christine) 1927–
Trails to gold

Volume 2 published by Heritage House
Includes biographical references and index.
Partial contents: Vol. 2, Roadhouses of the Cariboo.
ISBN 0-920663-35-4 (v. 1) — ISBN 11-895811-09-0 (v. 2)

     1. Taverns (Inns)—British Columbia—History—19th century.
2. Roads—British Columbia—History—19 century.   3. Cariboo
(B.C.: Regional district)—History.   4. Cariboo (B.C.: Regional
district)—Gold discoveries. I. Title
FC3822.5.P38 1995   971.1'7   C95-910280-9
F1089.C3P38 1995

First Edition – 1996

Cover photograph and design by Leif and Eva Grandell.
Chapter-head drawings by the author.
Maps designed and drawn by Cecilia Hirczy Welsford
from information furnished by the author.
Design and Typesetting by Cecilia Hirczy Welsford.

Cover: Moffat House, Alexandria BC, "Waiting for the Stage"
       Studio Grandell, Quesnel BC

Heritage House Publishing Company Limited
Unit #8 – 17921 55th Avenue, Surrey, BC   V3S 6C4

Printed in Canada

Acknowledgements

Over the many years of researching roadhouses in the Cariboo, I failed to record the names of all who helped, but there are a few I cannot forget as having gone out of their way to assist:

Geoffrey Castle, retired Custodian of Maps, and Frances Gundry, Head of the Manuscript Division, Provincial Archives of British Columbia;

Jim Wardrop, Royal British Columbia Museum;

Anne Yandle, retired from the Special Collections Library of the University of British Columbia;

Barbara Walters of Clive, Alberta;

Nellie Rankin of Morgan Creek;

Jim and Joan Rankin of Soda Creek;

Kathryn Moffat of Alexandria;

Don and Carrile Yorston of Australian;

Katherine Yorston of Australian;

Molly Forbes of Lac La Hache;

Archie Boyd of Metairie, New Orleans;

Ann Barlow of Quesnel; and,

Sharon Pease of Kamloops.

Heritage House appreciates the support of Canadian Heritage and the Cultural Services Branch of the British Columbia Government.

All photos except those from the collection of the author or the publisher are accredited individually below the image. Primary sources include the British Columbia Archives and Record Service (BCARS) and the Quesnel and District Museum and Archives (QDMA).

Author's Note: Quesnel was known at various times in the 1800s as Quesnelle, Quesnelle Mouth and Quesnellemouth. Spellings used within have been derived from research documents as they apply to specific events and dates and are used interchangeably. Quotations are presented in their original format.

Dedication

In memory of the pioneers who contributed so much to
the Cariboo roadhouse stories, but who have since passed on:

Roddie Moffat of Alexandria.

Jack (John) B. Yorston of Australian.

Jean (Yorston) Kelly of Chilliwack.

Georgina Lyne of Lac La Hache.

Tom Windt of Alexandria.

Louise (Lal) Marie Aiken of Alexandria.

Alec Barlow of Quesnel.

Ceal Tingley of Quesnel.

Laura (Locke) Livingstone of Quesnel.

Bessie (Locke) Butterfield of Quesnel.

Chris Staebler of Quesnel.

Contents

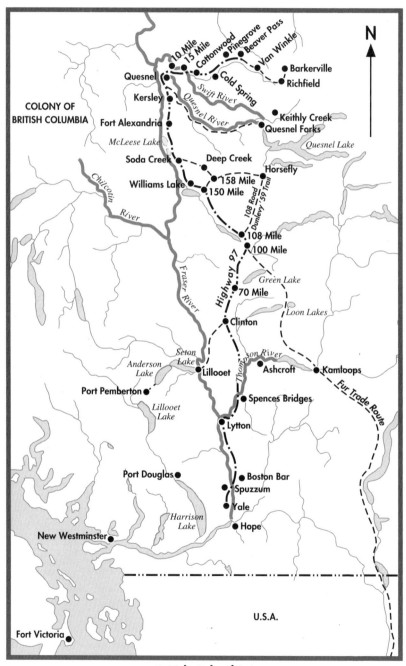

**British Columbia's
Cariboo Wagon Road of 1865**

Foreword

The years 1862 and 1863 marked the height of the Cariboo gold rush and saw the building of key sections of the Cariboo Wagon Road from Lillooet and Yale to Clinton and north to Alexandria on the east bank of the Fraser River. Along these routes travelled thousands upon thousands of would-be prospectors, all responding to tales of fabulously rich finds of gold in the Cariboo in 1861. The travellers came from all over the world — from eastern Canada, the United States, the British Isles, China, Australia, Germany, and Russia.

The continuation of the wagon road north of Clinton in the summer of 1862, and the influx of a large population heading for the goldfields, resulted in the building of as many as thirty new roadhouses in that year alone. And, as with all mass human migrations, it was the hostels and farms that survived the ups and downs of the uncertain economy.

Roadhouses were constructed near roads, real or anticipated, and in the Cariboo, their success or failure was tied both to the construction schedule and charted route of the road. Both on the southern portion, where two routes from Yale and Lillooet were to converge at Clinton, and north of Clinton en route to Barkerville, it was the competence or complacency of individual contractors who determined the fate of every roadhouse and its keepers. Among the road builders no name was better known than that of Gustavus Blinn Wright.

G. B. Wright was both competent and wily. He completed his contracts through Cut-off Valley, fifty miles east of Lillooet, to Clinton in

August 1862, and, a year later, while others were still struggling to finish the alternate route from Yale through the Fraser Canyon to Clinton, Wright was further north completing the road to Alexandria. Due primarily to Wright's own agenda, it was two more years before the next thirty-mile stretch to Quesnelle Mouth would see a road bed. When the government put out tenders for this contract, no one applied — certainly not the astute Gustavus and his associates who, with no viable road, offered the best alternative to anyone headed to Barkerville. They were enjoying the profits from the operation of the first sternwheel steamer on the upper Fraser River, the *SS Enterprise*, launched at Four Mile Creek in May 1863.

With Wright's steamer originally expected on the upper Fraser River as early as June 1862, the colonial government planned to build a trail linking the mouth of the Cottonwood River to Van Winkle on Lightning

G. B. Wright (COURTESY BCARS)

Creek, the scene of recent rich gold strikes. By May 1862, with Wright preoccupied by the Lillooet-Clinton connector and no sign of the steamer on the upper Fraser, pressure from freighters, merchants, and the general public forced the building of an alternate trail starting four miles up the Quesnel River. The trail was completed in June, with a rope ferry operating across the river at Four Mile Creek.

By the following year, a trail built from Quesnelle Mouth to Cottonwood bypassed the Four Mile Creek trail. In 1864, when the government called for tenders to build a full-blown wagon road from Quesnelle Mouth to Richfield, G. B. Wright returned to the construction business. He received an $85,000 contract to build the first twenty-six miles to Cottonwood. Under a separate contract for $9,000, Wright also built a toll bridge across the Cottonwood River. Between Cottonwood and Richfield, the Royal Engineers (RE) revised the route of the wagon road no less than three times, putting several roadhouses out of business when their premises were bypassed. Meanwhile, another Cariboo contractor, Pegleg Smith, was building the thirty-mile stretch between Alexandria and Quesnelle Mouth that Wright had passed on.

In April 1865, Malcolm Munroe of Victoria, upon his guarantee that the work would be finished by October, won a contract to complete the wagon road to Richfield according to the final Royal Engineers revision. On reaching Van Winkle, Munroe's efforts were plagued with bad weather, but when he wrote to Joseph Trutch, Chief Commissioner of Lands and Works, for an extension, the latter refused. By this time, Munroe was badly in debt to both his employees and to local merchants. Because of his mismanagement, he served time in the penitentiary at New Westminster and ended up bankrupt. The road to Richfield was completed in 1865 by James Duncan, who billed the government for $509.63.

Malcolm Munroe was not the only contractor to succumb to the forces of nature. All contractors chartered to build road sections from Yale had been on schedule with the exception of the partnership of Charles Oppenheimer, Walter Moberly, and Thomas B. Lewis. In May 1862, these partners started the twenty-one miles of road between Lytton and Cook's Ferry (Spences Bridge). For a time all went well but by the end of June, progress fell off dramatically when hundreds of workers defected to the gold rush in the Cariboo. Large gangs of Oriental and Native peoples were hired but soon they were decimated by an attack of smallpox. By fall, with the road unfinished, Oppenheimer and partners lost their contract. The road to Clinton was not completed until the fall of 1863.

Meanwhile, following the signing of papers awarding him a contract to build the wagon road to Alexandria, G. B. Wright quickly left Clinton behind and travelled by buggy, checking on the progress of his advancing road crews. Triumphant over the completion of forty-seven miles of road through difficult terrain southwest of Clinton, Wright was, at the same time, under extreme pressure to finish linking the 130 miles of trail south of Alexandria. The entire road was to have been completed by November 1862 and that winter impatient roadhouse keepers struggled to survive until spring. It was largely due to skill and ambitions of Gustavus Wright that the project finally reached its destination in August 1863.

So it was as bureaucrats and engineers responded to the human onslaught with ever-changing trails to gold, trails that determined the fates of the Cariboo's most intriguing structures—the roadhouses.

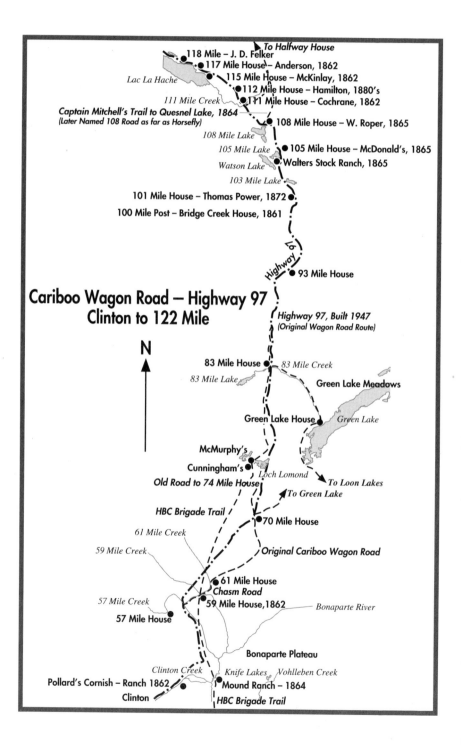

To Halfway House
118 Mile – J. D. Felker
117 Mile House – Anderson, 1862
Lac La Hache   115 Mile House – McKinlay, 1862
                      112 Mile House – Hamilton, 1880's
111 Mile Creek   111 Mile House – Cochrane, 1862
Captain Mitchell's Trail to Quesnel Lake, 1864
(Later Named 108 Road as far as Horsefly)   108 Mile House – W. Roper, 1865
108 Mile Lake
105 Mile Lake   105 Mile House – McDonald's, 1865
Watson Lake   Walters Stock Ranch, 1865
103 Mile Lake
101 Mile House – Thomas Power, 1872
100 Mile Post – Bridge Creek House, 1861

Highway 97

93 Mile House

Cariboo Wagon Road – Highway 97
Clinton to 122 Mile

Highway 97, Built 1947
(Original Wagon Road Route)

N

83 Mile House   83 Mile Creek
83 Mile Lake   Green Lake Meadows

Green Lake House   Green Lake

McMurphy's
Cunningham's
Loch Lomond
Old Road to 74 Mile House   To Loon Lakes
                                   To Green Lake
HBC Brigade Trail
                        70 Mile House
61 Mile Creek
59 Mile Creek   Original Cariboo Wagon Road

                        61 Mile House
                        Chasm Road
57 Mile Creek   59 Mile House, 1862   Bonaparte River
57 Mile House

                        Bonaparte Plateau
Clinton Creek   Knife Lakes   Vohlleben Creek
Pollard's Cornish – Ranch 1862   Mound Ranch – 1864
Clinton   HBC Brigade Trail

CHAPTER ONE

Clinton to the 108 Mile House

POLLARD'S CORNISH RANCH AND ROADHOUSE, 1862
Lots 245, 246, 247 and 248, G.1., Lillooet

While hundreds of additional prospectors reached the Cariboo goldfields in 1862, others, who had tried and failed, saw a brighter future in settling the land. One such man was John Pollard, a pioneer rancher and roadhouse keeper in the Clinton area. Leaving his home in Cornwall in 1849, Pollard first travelled to California, where he mined for gold with some of his countrymen, including John Butson and John Churchill. Following the "rush" to British Columbia and the Fraser River in 1858, John and his companions moved upriver to Lillooet, where they worked at Texas Spring and Canada Bar for two seasons with a company of miners, one of whom was an Englishman known as Billy Barker. Late in the fall of 1860, Pollard and his associates moved north to the Quesnel River, where they took part in the fantastically rich gold discoveries at Keithley Creek. Too late to find ground on Antler Creek, they were among the discoverers of Williams Creek; they were with "Barker & Co." when it staked claims on Williams Creek. During that first season, the creek yielded only small amounts of gold; and, in September, when the miners left for Victoria, they were calling the creek "a humbug." Still skeptical of the mining opportunities, Pollard accompanied his friends on their return to the Cariboo the following spring. Travelling by way of Lillooet[1] and Pavilion Mountain, Pollard noticed the several tracts of good farming land being developed in the Cut-Off Valley area and, in particular, some rich bottom land on the northeast end which was still open for pre-emption. By midsummer, with little to show for their hard work, Pollard and his associates, John Butson and John Churchill, left the goldfields and travelled south. Finding the land in Cut-Off Valley still open, the three men pre-empted 160 acres each "about 50 miles from Lillooet and opposite Wasley's farm," in July and August 1862.[2]

That same year, after improvements were made and registered, Pollard bought out Butson, Churchill, and Wasley, acquiring 640 acres. Many more acres were added later. By fall, several log cabins appeared on Pollard's pre-emption, through which the new wagon road passed. The largest of these, built essentially as a cookhouse for ranch hands, soon became a popular roadhouse — more popular even than Watson's Clinton Hotel less than a mile away. Frequented by passing freighters and miners who appreciated a good plain meal, the Chinese cooks were kept busy all hours of the day and night.

Twenty years later, as a well-established rancher in the area, John Pollard, at nearly sixty years of age, began to think seriously of marriage. Through his family in England he arranged to marry a young woman, Kezia Truan of Kenwyn Parish, Cornwall. In anticipation of the coming event, Pollard built a two-storey log house on his ranch, close to the original buildings. It was fall of 1887 before he travelled across the seas to England, where he and young Kezia were married in the little parish church at Kenwyn. On their return to British Columbia and the Pollard Ranch, the plucky young bride settled in, accepting her role as a pioneer wife in a strange, new land. Her positive attitude and her willingness to share in the work brought success to the family enterprises. Along with the ranch chores, Kezia fed and housed many a passing traveller at her home beside the wagon road. In that house, seven children were born, and while she raised them, Kezia employed numerous Chinese cooks to work at the roadhouse. Fortunately, the four boys and three girls were all healthy and, when of age, attended the little school at Clinton. This ideal life continued until 1901, when John Pollard passed away, leaving his wife and young family to carry on with the enterprises he had started.

Kezia was not entirely alone in her task. Aware of his impending death, Pollard had arranged for his ranch foreman, Jack Arthur, to operate the ranch until their sons were of a responsible age. Kezia's roadhouse business was a financial success and her three-storey frame house, built in 1908, was considered to be a mansion. Nicknamed the Big House, the combination roadhouse and family residence featured a bathroom on every floor, with water closets and running water. These conveniences were made possible by a large gravity-fed storage tank in the attic of the house and a ready supply of water from a nearby spring. Another modern feature of the Big House were the folding doors which divided the sitting room from the dining area; on the occasion of a large gathering, these doors were folded back, allowing room for people to dance to music provided by a player-piano. The grand opening of the new house was timed to coincide with the twenty-first birthday of Charles Pollard, the eldest son, and with Jack Arthur's departure for his home in eastern Canada. The whole community attended the party given by Kezia Pollard. Throughout the years, Kezia was very generous with her facilities, frequently opening her home to the young people of the area.

By the time of the First World War, John, the third Pollard son, had taken over the family ranch, while his mother and two younger sisters operated the roadhouse. With the advent of cars and trucks on the highway after 1910, and with a shortage of hired labour during the war, the roadhouse business fell on lean times. To compound this, Kezia Pollard, now well into her seventies, passed away at home in 1923.

During the late 1920s, the Pollard family met the challenge of changing times by opening one of the first guest ranches in the Cariboo. It was here, at Pollard's Three Bar Ranch (their cattle brand), that city folks with a desire to experience the workings of a real cattle ranch spent their holidays. Once more the Big House buzzed with activity, as dozens of summer guests filled it with laughter and gaiety. During the fall and early winter, the house catered to yet another set of guests, as John Pollard the Second and his sons guided hunters into the nearby hills, where ranged some of the largest moose the region had ever seen. These traditions continued for many years, long after the death of John Pollard the Second in 1961.

Today, although no longer owned by the Pollard family, and bypassed by Highway 97, the Cornish Ranch continues as a working guest ranch, with visitors being accommodated in the roadhouse built for Kezia Pollard in 1908. In settling the land in 1862, John Pollard did indeed provide his family with a lasting legacy.

THE 59 MILE HOUSE, 1962
Lot 384, G.1., Lillooet

As G. B. Wright's road crew worked its way north out of Cut-Off Valley in the early summer of 1862, the land rose sharply for about three miles to a high plateau, 3,200 feet above sea level. Here the road crossed the old Hudson's Bay Company brigade trail and swung east along the rim of spectacular Painted Chasm, whose colourful lava walls extended 800 feet up from the creek bed.

At work on Wright's road-building project were two entrepreneurs, Isaac Saul and William Innes, who pre-empted land at the head of the chasm, where they established the 59 Mile House (and later, a bit further up the road, the 61 Mile House). It was a logical site for a roadhouse, not only because of its unusual view, but also for practical reasons. As the first roadhouse north of Pollard's ranch, it was a welcome refuge for freighters and their teams, who sometimes spent all day moving their wagons up the steep hill out of the Cut-Off Valley.

The partnership of Saul and Innes lasted until 1867 when John Saul bought Innes out; the firm then became Saul & Company. Isaac Saul and his brother John had arrived in the Cariboo from Ontario at the start of the gold rush and, by the 1870s, acquired considerable real estate between Clinton and Lac La Hache. On maps tracing the route of the Collins Overland Telegraph in 1866, the 59 Mile House is noted as "Saul's House," a name also mentioned in the diaries of early travellers on the Cariboo Wagon Road (hereafter referred to as the Cariboo Road). One of these early travellers was Harry Jones, the youngest of a group of twenty-six Welsh miners on their way to the Cariboo in July 1863. On

The 59 Mile House, Cariboo Wagon Road. (COURTESY BCARS)

reaching the "green timbers" on the plateau north of Clinton, several of the men took a wrong turn and, after several hours of wandering around, came out of the woods at the 59 Mile House. "The proprietor was very kind," wrote Harry in his memoirs, "furnishing them with a good meal and sending them off to bed for a few hours."[3]

As it was with most roadhouses, the 59 Mile House was a business investment, owned and operated by many individuals over long periods of time. During the 1890s, the roadhouse was owned by Peter Eagan and managed by Arthur Switzer. At this time, the property was surveyed and a Crown Grant issued. (A Crown Grant transferring title to the land was issued once all the requirements of the Pre-emption Act had been met.)

Perhaps the most interesting and comprehensive account of the 59 Mile House, its owners, and the many stage drivers and freighters on the road prior to the First World War was written in 1976 by Angus Ryder of Mount Lehman, British Columbia. Angus's father, James Ryder, had bought both the 59 Mile House and the 61 Mile House in 1910. The move from the Fraser Valley to the Cariboo and the 59 Mile House entailed quite a change in lifestyle for James's wife, whose first concern was to establish a school for her four children. Fortunately, their nearest neighbours, the Bishops, at the 57 milepost,[4] also had several offspring who were eligible to attend school. Between them, the two families made up the required number of pupils and, after much letter-writing, the government hired a Miss Renouf of Brunswick as their first teacher. Classes were conducted in a small, log building on the roadhouse property.

59 Mile House engulfed in flames, June 30, 1948. (COURTESY EARL CAHILL)

Described as a two-storey log building with two dormer windows and two chimneys, the 59 Mile House stood on an open flat of land facing the Painted Chasm. The house had many bedrooms and could accommodate twenty guests at a time. A full-length porch sheltered the front entrance from winter storms and shaded the parlour from the hot summer sun. Lumber siding was added to the exterior before the turn of the century. In a barn across the yard from the house were fifty stalls, built during the 1880s and 1890s to accommodate the horses used by the British Columbia Express Company, (the "BX" Co.).

When the decision was made to sell out in 1914, the property was purchased by George Fairburn and John Harvey who operated the roadhouse for a year. Molly (nee Barton) Forbes, originally of Clinton, recalled: "Fairburn did the cooking, but never took his pipe out of his mouth."[5]

On the departure of his parents in 1914, Angus Ryder remained to work at the 59 Mile House for part owner John Harvey. In his reminiscences, Angus recalled: "Fairburn sold the roadhouse in 1915 to Tiny Bray, a BC Express Co. manager in Prince George. Tiny immediately went overboard, adding eight bedrooms and a barroom to the house. He furnished the rooms in fine fashion from the Hudson's Bay Co. Then Tiny got into difficulties with the BC Express Co. and ended up losing everything."[6]

In 1947, while the roadhouse was owned by Ross Mark and his wife, the site of the 59 Mile House was bypassed by Highway 97 but was still accessible by way of Chasm Road. On 30 June 1948, a year after the road had been changed, the 59 Mile House burned to the ground in a spectacular fire, thought by some to be "an insurance fire." A snapshot of the burning building was taken by Earl Cahill of Clinton, who happened to be there at the time. Today, a provincial park surrounds the area of Painted Chasm, affording visitors a pleasant picnic spot from which the chasm, the original 1862 wagon road, and the site of the historic 59 Mile House may be seen.

THE 70 MILE HOUSE
Lot 227, G.1., Lillooet

As August 1862 drew to a close, Sergeant John McMurphy's diary reflected a mood of optimism, generated no doubt by the recent visit of the road contractor G. B. Wright. Having built seven long miles of road uphill from the Cut-Off Valley, McMurphy's crews of over 200 roadmakers spread out between the 57 milepost and the 69 milepost

Built in 1862, 70 Mile House derived its name based on the measured distance from Lillooet. (COURTESY BCARS)

worked with renewed vigour and enthusiasm. Where large numbers of men laboured there were frequent illnesses and the occasional death: "I attended the funeral of one of our men who took ill on Friday night and died this morning," reported McMurphy, "he could not be kept any longer as the smell from his body was strong."[7]

In describing the road built across the plateau, McMurphy wrote: "It is a very nice piece of road leading through a thickly timbered country, and where possible it is cut as straight as a bee line."[8] Although the workers found the plateau easy ground for road making, this area, which extended north for almost forty miles, was described as dreary and generally worthless. Covered with pine, and dotted with smal alkali ponds and swamps, its one redeeming feature was that it provided extraordinarily good hunting for wild ducks, grouse, and geese.

On 11 September 1862, McMurphy notes in his diary: "Where I am encamped at present the land is pre-empted, and a good log house going up ... The owner has cut about twenty tons of hay."[9] The good log house mentioned by McMurphy had been constructed by Charles Adrian, who pre-empted that land in September 1862. The house was built of hand-hewn, squared timbers which extended the full length of the structure and were pinned together at the corners with steel bolts.

During that first season, the 70 Mile House served as a hostel for G. B. Wright's road crews, and sold to Wright in April 1863. As the crews moved north, the house was leased to various proprietors. In 1865, when the telegraph line went through, it was known as "Graham's House," after Robert T. Graham, owner of Green Lake

House. During this early period, the 70 Mile House was a crude, one-room log structure, as were most wayside houses of that era. One traveller in 1863 compared it to a robber's cave, where the landlord slept on the liquor counter to guard the miners "pokes," which were said to be cached in a secret panel of the bar. In comparison to this is Sarah Crease's description of the same roadhouse nearly twenty years later:

> *"Soon entered the "green timbers," an uninteresting road of twenty three miles [from Clinton] ... Reached "Saul's" 70 Mile House at 5.00 p m, sun warm and bright. Henry and Evans [her husband and the groom] went after some ducks, but returned with nothing but a ducking! Had excellent supper, delicious bread, butter, and cream. Mrs. Saul quiet and thoughtful woman with small children. Rooms clean, beds wide, but blankets smelled of cats!!"[10]*

The Sauls of Saul & Company, 1875

By the mid-1870s, the 70 Mile House and ranch had seen several changes of ownership. In 1864, Wright, who was constantly juggling his assets to finance further enterprises, mortgaged the property to Francis Tarbell and Edgar Marvin. Regaining the title in 1867, he sold the roadhouse to J. M. Rodgers and Edward Fisher in 1869.

By May 1875, the 70 Mile House had been transferred to the Saul brothers, John and William, of Clinton, who operated the house and ranch for the next ten years. Almost immediately upon taking possession, a second storey was added on to the original house, and a two-storey "L" was built on to the east (the rear) of the house. With these additions, the house now contained a dozen bedrooms. By purchasing a herd of dairy cows, which were pastured on the Green Lake Meadows several miles to the northeast, the Sauls were able to produce their own dairy products, adding variety to the meals served at the roadhouse.

William Boyd

Described as a good-hearted and honest Irishman, William Boyd had arrived in the Cariboo with the Canadian Pacific Railway worktrains of the 1870s. Moving to Clinton, he became district road superintendent and married Mary Nicolson, a niece of Ewan Bell of Clinton. By the 1880s, and with a family of several children, Boyd tired of the constant travel his job required and bought the 70 Mile House from Saul & Company. The Boyd family operated the roadhouse for the next twenty years, including the dairy farm at Green Lake Meadows. A Crown grant respecting the property at the 70 Mile House was issued to William Boyd in 1897. During the early 1900s, the Boyds also enlarged the facilities by adding a single-storey freight shed on to the north end of the roadhouse, which eventually contained twenty-eight rooms.

During the 1890s and early 1900s, when they were of school age, five Boyd children were taught by a tutor in a room on the second floor. Whenever a stagecoach arrived during school hours (a fairly frequent occurrence), lessons were forgotten while the boys helped their father unload the freight and luggage. In winter, as traffic approached the 70 Mile House, the steady crunching of horses' hooves on the crusted snow, along with the sound of sleigh bells, could be heard for miles. In summer, one had only to watch the behaviour of Boyd's dog to detect the imminent arrival of traffic. Sitting patiently out in the middle of the road, the dog's ears would go up and his tail start to wag as soon as he heard the familiar sounds, which, of course, was long before human ears could detect them.

Over the years, many well-known personalities in British Columbia's early history stayed as guests at the 70 Mile House, including Judge Matthew Baillie Begbie, the poet Pauline Johnson, and the packer Jean Caux (more familiarly known as Cataline). During his stay, Cataline's pack-train of many mules was always unloaded out in the yard, to one side of the roadhouse. There the freight remained all night, and nothing was ever stolen.

Following a hunting accident in August 1905, William Boyd died on the operating table in a Vancouver hospital at the age of fifty-seven. In spite of her great loss, Mary Boyd, with the help of her four sons (James, William Jr, Jack, and Ira) and one daughter (Dorothy [Tottie]), operated the 70 Mile House until 1917. The entire ranch except for the Green Lake Meadows was sold to R. D. Cumming of Ashcroft. Cumming only kept the 70 Mile House for six years before selling out in May 1920 to Charles Matthew Porter.

The Porters: Matt and "Ma"

Originally from eastern Canada, Matthew Porter's financially comfortable family had settled on a ranch on the North Bonaparte River in the early 1900s. Never having faced adversity or assumed serious responsibility, young Matt and his brother Bill drifted from one failed scheme to another. Unmarried and without a family to assist him with the work, Matt had to hire all his help, including a housekeeper, when he bought 70 Mile House.

The cook at the 59 Mile House at this time was Isobel McConnell, a widow with two sons. "Ma," as she was affectionately known, was an excellent cook and an untiring worker. A large, raw-boned woman with an equally large heart and a good sense of humour, Ma hailed from the Red River District of Oklahoma. With her hard-working, rancher-cum-freighter husband, David McConnell, she arrived in the Cariboo in the early 1900s. It was here that Dave got his start feeding cattle for Bill Parker at the Big Lake Ranch. With careful management, the McConnells were soon able to afford their own small ranch near Lac La Hache. Just as things were looking up, Dave McConnell fell ill and died, leaving his wife and sons to fend for themselves.

Needless to say, when Matt Porter offered Isobel McConnell twice the going rate to cook for him at the 70 Mile House, she took the job. This worked out very well, until Ma began to feel uncomfortable living under the same roof as a bachelor. Issuing an ultimatum, Ma threatened to leave unless Matt married her. By this time, Matt knew he needed Ma, and so the knot was tied.

As land on the North Bonaparte River was being settled during the late 1920s, the 70 Mile House became an important supply centre and distribution point for the area. With the services of a post office and a telephone, established in 1908 and 1909 respectively, it had also become the social centre of the area, where ranchers and their wives drank Ma's powerful coffee and ate her delicious baking while catch-ing up on the latest gossip. By the early 1940s, Ma's grandson, "Sonny" David McConnell, looked after the ranch while she ran the roadhouse. Matt Porter operated the post office and mail route which encompassed a large area along the North Bonaparte River. As a result, Matt, driving a Pierce Arrow sedan, was gone from home for many hours on mail days.

At his best, Matt was a mild-mannered man of small stature with a talent for anything mechanical; but, during his bachelor years, he had developed a weakness for the bottle. Especially hard to resist were the many offers of "a swig" wherever he stopped along the mail route. Almost always, by the time he got home, he was stewed to the eyeballs. Ma managed in her congenial, self-assured manner and ruled the roost at the roadhouse. It was just as well she did, for business would have failed without her. During the 1940s, Ma not only looked after at least half a dozen "regulars" at the 70 Mile House, she also fed and housed fifteen men of the Dawson & Wade Company road crew during the building of a new highway between the 59 Milepost and the 70 Milepost. This was history repeating itself, for in 1862, G. B. Wright's men had been housed here. Ma, who must have been in her sixties by this time, was up each morning at 4:00 a.m. to light the fire in the large kitchen range, where she began the day by cooking an enormous breakfast consisting of porridge, hot cakes, bacon and eggs, mountains of toast, and gallons of strong coffee. It was often after 11.00 p.m. before she climbed the stairs to her bed in a small room on the second floor.

In the kitchen of the roadhouse, located in the northeast corner, the only modern convenience was a sink and a cold-water tap, which meant that while the dishes could be washed in the sink, all the water had to be heated on the cook stove and in the copper reservoir. In the bathroom, a small room just off the kitchen, was a large antique bathtub, used occasionally by serious bathers. Filled by hand, the heavy cast-iron tub absorbed all the heat, and, by the time there was enough water for a bath, it was almost cold.

Ma was constantly battling with Matt (whom she always referred to as Porter) over his drinking. As long as he was quiet and kept out of the way of her guests, she was only mildly critical. One night, just as she was getting ready to serve supper to a house full of people, Matt, in a state of extreme intoxication, arrived back from his mail route, making a loud and obnoxious entrance by way of the kitchen. Leaving the cooking to several of her helpers, Ma coaxed Matt upstairs to his bedroom, located directly above the kitchen. For a few minutes her voice could be heard, and then all was silent. Pleased with her success in quieting her drunken mate, Ma returned to the kitchen stove where the last-minute details of preparing a meal were taking place. Suddenly, to everyone's amazement, Ma began to swear. They had heard her swear before, but never like this. At first, what caused the outburst escaped them, but they soon understood. A stream of 98-degree liquid could be seen pouring down through the ceiling onto the range, straight into the mashed potatoes and gravy. Matt Porter had wreaked his revenge on Ma from a corner of his bedroom!

After Matt's death in 1954, seventy-year-old Ma retired and rented the 70 Mile House, first to William Goodrich and then to Jack Parrot.

It was a windy day in May 1956 when, for reasons unknown, the grand old roadhouse, just six years short of a one-hundredth anniversary, burned to the ground. Almost everything was lost in the fiery blaze, but amongst the few items saved was an antique piano, a gramophone, and a buffet. Ma lived on in a cheerful little house, built for her on the site of the old roadhouse, until her death on 11 January 1968. Ma never lost her zest for life; right to the end she loved to tell a good joke, which was always followed by a rousing, infectious giggle, a slap of the knee, and a twinkle of her dark, snapping eyes.

LOCH LOMOND HOUSE, (McMURPHY'S), 1862–65
The 74 Milepost, from Lillooet

As G. B. Wright's road crews continued north across the "green timber" plateau in the last week of September 1862, the weather turned cold, with alternating periods of snow, hail, and rain. In his diary of September 18, Sergeant McMurphy reported an accident–while falling a tree one of the workmen had broken his leg below the knee. A doctor was sent for.

Working at top speed, to build as much road as possible before winter forced their withdrawal, crews of men were spread out at intervals between Bridge Creek and Lac La Hache. By September 23, McMurphy, who had been stationed at the 70 Milepost, mentioned that he had moved his camp: "Shifted camp to the Sergeant's Lake, 4 miles ahead."[11] This referred to the fact that McMurphy had pre-empted 160 acres of land at the 74 Milepost, close to a lake he had already named "Sergeant's Lake," but which he very soon renamed "Loch Lomond." While it has been generally assumed that McMurphy did not take up land until the Royal Engineers disbanded in the summer of 1863, research reveals that he had begun these developments as early as 27 September 1862, when he applied for "160 acres of land situate between the 73 and 75 mileposts on the Lillooet and Mud Lake Road."[12]

In March 1863, prior to the completion of Wright's road, the following advertisement appeared in the *British Columbian*:

Loch Lomond House.
We direct the attention of those going to Cariboo to this House, which is situate at the 74 Milepost on the Lillooet–Alexander wagon road. From our acquaintance with the chief proprietor Sergeant McMurphy, R.E., we can confidently recommend travellers to make "Loch Lomond" a stopping place.[13]

This advertisment indicates that McMurphy's roadhouse was built and that it was ready for business by early spring of 1863. Harry Jones, in his reminiscences about his journey to the Cariboo that summer, mentions "Loch Lomond, where a Scotsman has built a roadhouse at the southern end."[14] The wagon road at that time passed through McMurphy's property on the west side, where the roadhouse stood by the creek, at the entrance to the lake.

In August that first year, McMurphy's cook had a few moments of excitement when two men, suspected of murdering Thomas Clegg at the 141 Mile House, walked through his door and demanded food.[15] Late that fall, following a season of very successful mining on Williams Creek, John "Cariboo" Cameron transported his gold to the Coast with the government-sponsored Gold Escort. (This was a government appointed group of twelve men, mounted and armed, who travelled between the Cariboo and New Westminster, escorting the miners' gold. After two seasons the service failed when the government refused to insure the gold.) En route, the party stopped at the 74 Mile House, where McMurphy was given the responsibility of guarding the gold overnight. Piling the bags of bullion into a heap on the floor, mattresses were placed on top, upon which McMurphy and his son John slept all night. Young John was heard to remark that he "didn't have to go to heaven to sleep on a bed of gold."[16]

John Clapperton, a miner who worked for several seasons on "The Point" claim on Lightning Creek, travelled on foot from Yale to Van Winkle in the spring of 1864. Along the way, he stayed overnight at McMurphy's roadhouse and, in his diary, commented in detail on a very pleasant evening:

74 Mile House, stayed over. Good Scotch songs — much pleased with renditions of 'Friendship's Brought Us Ti'gether,' and 'Ay, she turned the Spinning Wheel.' Had there been bagpipes with the singing, I believe we would all have been dancing.[17]

These remarks indicate the cultured and sociable atmosphere of the McMurphy roadhouse—quite exceptional at that early time. One can just picture a gathering of weary travellers who, having partaken of a hearty meal, would sit about the fireplace singing songs and swapping stories over pipes and "a wee dram" before rolling up in their blankets for the night.

McMurphy's roadhouse did well until 1865 when Cariboo miners and entrepreneurs rushed to the "Big Bend" of the Columbia River, and traffic on the Cariboo Road subsided. Having been settled for such a short time, the roadhouse farm had not yet become self-sufficient; and, without adequate business, McMurphy's enterprise did not survive the short depression. To add to the dilemma, there was a large family of children to support. Recognizing financial disaster, McMurphy applied for work as an engineer on several government-sponsored road projects in the colony, but without success. Considering his military record, his experience as an engineer, and his personal need, it is strange that he was not granted a job. Possibly there was lingering bitterness regarding his involvement in the scandal over G. B. Wright's road bypassing Williams Lake in the summer of 1863. Obviously, McMurphy had sided with Wright, and the very harsh criticisms received by the government may have jeopardized his chances for any future work as an engineer.[18] Late in 1865, when he received a pension for twenty-five years of military service, McMurphy and his family left "Loch Lomond" for New Westminster. Prior to leaving, the property was sold to John and Thomas Buie, entrepreneurs of Barkerville, for $1,500. At New Westminster, McMurphy was forced to work as a clerk in order to augment his meagre pension, while his eldest son, John, left school to work as a teamster on the Cariboo Road. Sergeant John McMurphy died at New Westminster on 5 January 1901. He was eighty-eight years old.

THE 74 MILE HOUSE, (CUNNINGHAM'S), 1891–1966
Lot 570, G.1., Lillooet

Following the departure of the McMurphy family from Loch Lomond House in 1865, the new owners leased it to Edward Trofatter in 1867. The venture was not a financial success, and, as nothing more was heard of this site, it is presumed to have been abandoned. Years later, in 1891, almost the same land was once again pre-empted, this time by Jack Cunningham who was also from Scotland. While awaiting the arrival of his fiance, Margaret Clark, Jack developed a few acres of land and built a comfortable log cabin about half a mile southwest of the site of McMurphy's roadhouse. Following their marriage in Clinton on 12 December 1896, Jack and his bride hired Sandy Innes, an excellent axe man, to build a large, two-storey, squared-log house beside the wagon road.

Where McMurphy's roadhouse had failed almost thirty years before, the Cunninghams began their venture at a more economically viable time. With the arrival of the Canadian Pacific Railway at Ashcroft in 1885, business had improved for northern roadhouses. At the 74 Mile House, where there were always several freight teams staying overnight, along with passengers of the BX Stage, Margaret Cunningham had her hands full.

Cunningham had her hands full.

The next fourteen years were happy ones as the Cunningham's roadhouse made money, their cattle herd grew substantially, and four healthy children were born. To assist Margaret, a Chinese cook and governess were hired. Jack became district road superintendent, and was away often. In his absence, Margaret learned to manage their affairs alone; an experience she would ruefully come to value.

It was late in 1910 when the bottom fell out of Margaret's world. A simple case of measles among the children became tragic when Kenneth, the eldest son, died from a ruptured appendix. Two weeks later, Jack Cunningham died of complications following a bout of pneumonia. In keeping with her Scottish upbringing, Margaret faced these heartbreaking events with courage and fortitude, carrying on with the family business. A foreman, Frank Mills, took over the ranch work, while Margaret raised her children and operated the roadhouse. With an established reputation for excellent meals and clean beds, the 74 Mile House continued to serve passing teamsters and stage drivers. Mindful of the cruel blow fate had dealt Margaret Cunningham, people went out of their way to take business to her door.

During the summer of 1911, the countryside was terrorized by an outlaw, Paul Spintlum, a Native from Canoe Creek accused of murdering a White man south of Clinton. A second man, said to be a witness to the crime, was found murdered soon after. For months, Spintlum and a companion, Moses Paul, hid in the hills behind Clinton, initiating one of the longest manhunts in the history of the Cariboo. For nearly a year the search, involving special police, Native trackers, and many volunteers, searched from Lillooet to Decker Lake without success. In May 1912, when a rider from Pollard's Ranch spotted Spintlum's camp without being seen, he reported his find to Constable Alex Kindness at Clinton. Kindness formed a posse but when they reached the hideaway, Spintlum was waiting on the trail, hidden by a windfall. Almost at blank range, Spintlum rose up and shot Constable Kindness dead. Although members of the posse shot back, Spintlum got away. One of the deputized policemen in the posse was young Roy Eden, a hostler for the BX Stables at 74 Mile House. Upon Roy's return to the roadhouse, the search for Spintlum became very real to the Cunningham children; in fact, the whole countryside was nervous. The Cunningham family had always been on friendly terms with the local Native people. Now, with Spintlum on the loose, the children began to fear all Native people and took to hiding under the stairs when the locals came to buy groceries and exchange news. It was eighteen months later with the winter of 1912 fast approaching that Spintlum and Moses Paul turned themselves in. At a trial in Kamloops, both men were found guilty. Spintlum died on the gallows, and Paul died in jail, having served but one year of a life sentence.

By 1920, cars and motorized freight carriers had become a common sight along the Cariboo Highway. One of the first was the Interior Transportation Company, better known as the IT Stage Line, whose drivers stopped for meals at the 74 Mile House and sometimes remained overnight. Other guests included families from Vancouver and Seattle, who enjoyed getting away from the city.

The Cunningham children gradually took more responsibility for running 74 Mile House. Norman, while still a teenager, ran the ranch with the help of one hired man, while Margaret, the youngest, helped with the housework and cooking at the roadhouse. Rita, the elder daughter, worked with horses. During the 1920s and 1930s, her name became synonymous with competitive horse racing in the Cariboo.

Margaret Cunningham's woes were not over. Her family was totally unprepared for the devastating fire that consumed the 74 Mile House in December 1923. However, with the aid of family and friends, a new roadhouse was built on the same site within the year.

By the late 1930s, most Cariboo roadhouses were closed. The survivors turned to dude ranching and the astute Cunningham family decided to cater strictly to teenaged boys from urban areas. For many years, up to twenty boys from Vancouver and Victoria spent summer holidays at the 74 Mile House ranch. Housed in cabins, they ate their meals at the roadhouse. So popular was the facility that it was impossible to accommodate all applicants. In fall, when the roadhouse returned to its normal schedule, guests of long standing arrived to take advantage of the excellent duck hunting in the area. During the Second World War, Margaret Cunningham cared for two children sent to Canada to escape the bombing of London. And often, Canadian Air Force personnel stationed nearby boarded at the 74 Mile House.

In 1948, when the Cariboo Road was relocated between the 70 and the 83 mileposts, bypassing the 74 Mile House, Margaret realized she had reached the end of an era. With the new highway more than a mile east, few, if any, passersby would call at her roadhouse. Having overseen the 74 Mile House for over fifty years, Margaret was ready to rest. She lived with her son, Norman, his wife Molly, and their family at the 74 Mile House, the house she loved so well, until her death

THE 83 MILE HOUSE AND RANCH, 1862
Lot 350, G.1. Lillooet.

We return now to Sergeant McMurphy's diary of 30 September 1862, when he moved his camp nine miles north to the 83 Milepost. By this time, the weather had turned colder, with daily showers of hail and sleet. To speed up the road-building project, the approximately 200 workers had been offered a four-dollar-a-month raise to work on Sundays. For White men, the wages were fifty-four dollars a month, and for Chinese men they were forty-six dollars a month. Subcontracts were also being given to the "Overlanders", a hardy group of 250 who trekked from Ontario to the Cariboo to join the gold rush. Arriving at Quesnelle Mouth in September they were making their way south for the winter when opportunity presented itself: "A party of Canadians has taken a contract for $2^1/2$ miles of road at Bridge Creek," wrote McMurphy, "they get $450.00 per mile."[19]

McMurphy was quite impressed with his camping spot at the 83 milepost, where 480 acres of land had been pre-empted by three road-makers: "This is a beautiful place, a lovely meadow with here and there a Beaver dam, which causes the water to lay, but with very little trouble in cutting the dams, there is lots of hay."[20]

Richard, Thomas, and John Walters

Originally from Haldimand County, Ontario, two brothers, Thomas and John Walters, left home in 1856 and headed for California. Although John had been trained as a surveyor, he and Thomas took up farming in the Marysville area with the intention of selling their crops to the miners. Both John and Thomas were married, John in 1859 to Margaret McDonald, a Scottish woman he had known in Ontario, and Thomas in 1861 to Mary Flanders, a member of the Studebaker family of California. The farming venture proved to be a failure when, for three successive years, their crops were flooded out, not due to natural causes but to miners releasing reservoirs of water into the Sacramento River which flowed through the Walters property.

In the meantime a third brother, Richard Walters, younger than the others and thought to be sickly, had left home and headed for the gold rush in British Columbia. By 1862, Richard was working his way north to the Cariboo as a member of G. B. Wright's road crew, and, on 11 October 1862, he and his companions, John Saul and Robert Beard, "pre-empted 160 acres of adjoining land between the 83 and 84 mileposts on the Lillooet to Alexandria Wagon Road."[21]

"pre-empted 160 acres of adjoining land between the 83 and 84 mile-posts on the Lillooet to Alexandria Wagon Road."21

Leaving California late in 1862, Thomas and John Walters also travelled to the Cariboo where they joined their brother Richard on his ranch at the 83 Milepost. Taking over Saul and Beard's pre-emptions, they began building a roadhouse. The Overlander, Robert B. McMicking, in his diary of 5 November 1862, mentions the Walters ranch, as did a reporter for the *Victoria Colonist*: "Mssrs. Walters & Co. are building a large hotel, 24' x 48' at the 83 Mile."22

Over the next several years, the Walters brothers enlarged their acreage at the 83 Milepost and established other roadhouse farms at the 93, the 105, and the 122 Mileposts as well as a stock ranch on Horseshoe Lake, west of the 105 Mile House ranch. Little more is known of Richard Walters, except that he died in early January 1867, while returning from Lytton. He was buried behind the 105 Mile House beside Mary, the infant daughter of John and Maggie Walters.

In 1865, when a son, Henry Lincoln Walters, was born to Thomas and Mary Walters at the 83 Mile House, the baby was said to have been the first White male child born in the Cariboo. That same year, the Collins Overland Telegraph Company, a branch of the Western Union, reached the 83 Mile House, with Albert Crysler as operator and lineman. Crysler bought the 83 Mile House from the Walters brothers in 1866. The Walters family left British Columbia in 1870 and returned to Ontario, where their mother had died and their father had gone blind. John and Thomas Walters did not return to

The 83 Mile House, built by the Walters Brothers in 1862.
(Courtesy Vancouver Public Library)

British Columbia, but the sons of the latter, Henry L. and Thomas H. Walters, settled in the Horsefly area of the Cariboo early in 1900.

Albert Crysler, 1866–68

With good meadowland for pasture, and an adequate supply of hay and oats for winter feed, the 83 Mile House became a very popular stop for teamsters and pack-train operators during the latter part of the 1860s. As soon as spring allowed, and until late fall, there were often a dozen or more "outfits" on the wagon road each week between Yale and Barkerville. By November, however, when cold weather settled in, there was no way of ploughing the heavy falls of snow that usually came soon after the New Year. During this time, almost the only traffic on the Cariboo Road consisted of Barnard's Express Company stage-coaches, (forerunners of the BC Express Co.) whose drivers often had a very hard time getting through. In January 1867, when J.B. Leighton was one of ten passengers travelling south from Barkerville with driver Steven Tingley, the stagecoach reached the 150 Mile House at noon, where it met with heavy drifting snow and cold temperatures. From there it took three days to reach the 83 Mile House, almost the highest point on the road. Long overdue, the driver and passengers found Albert Crysler, still waiting for them and offering a hot meal and warm beds.

Murdoch Ross, 1868–89

By 1868, Crysler had sold the 83 Mile House to Murdoch Ross, a Cariboo miner who continued to operate the house until 1889, when Steven Tingley, owner of the BC Express Co., leased the property.

Steven Tingley, 1897–1905

When Tingley bought the 83 Mile House in 1897, he had the property surveyed and was issued a Crown grant. On taking over the BC Express Company, (BX) and upon moving its headquarters from Yale to Ashcroft in 1886, Tingley made many changes to its policies and scheduling. The result was a much more efficient company. For the first time it became possible for a letter to reach Barkerville from Ashcroft in four days. At this time, the 83 Mile House was completely renovated and enlarged, and it became one of the main stations on the stagecoach line. While operating more efficiently, the 83 Mile House retained the same prices it had always had — fifty cents for a bed or a meal. Out in the yard behind the roadhouse, a large horse-barn, built

by Sandy Innes, accommodated fifty horses. This was the heyday of
the 83 Mile House.

David A. Stoddard, 1905–15

By the early 1900s, Steven Tingley was ready to retire and, in
1905, the 83 Mile House was sold to David Stoddard, a Clinton tinsmith
who represented Lillooet in the 1890 provincial legislature. Under his
efficient management, the roadhouse, for the first time in its history,
became a financially successful business. While Stoddard gave free
drinks to the stage drivers and always set a good table, he didn't
encourage any unnecessary spending. In fact, some accused him of
being downright miserly. Over the years, stories circulated about how
he never gave his guests any more than half a candle to see their way
to bed, and about how he always lit all the candles on one match.
Following the First World War, Stoddard, wise businessman that he
was, could see changes coming, with the building of the Pacific Great
Eastern Railway from the coast. Knowing the new train would affect
traffic on the Cariboo Road, Stoddard sold out. The property was purchased by the government-sponsored Soldier Settlement Board, which
placed two veterans, Tony Orford and Jack Templeton, in charge of the
83 Mile House. At a time when trucks and cars were crowding the
horses off the road, these inexperienced bachelors did their best to
cope. In any case, before their inadequacies could become evident, the
83 Mile House burned to the ground in the fall of 1922, supposedly as
the result of a faulty stovepipe.

During the 1930s, the 83 Mile House was rebuilt by a druggist
from Williams Lake, and the restaurant was kept busy serving meals to
Clarence Stevenson's IT Stage passengers. Following the changes made
to the Cariboo Road in the 1940s, which caused it to bypass the 83 Mile
House, the owners put up the Four Star Motel and Restaurant beside the
new road. Today, with the building of an excellent highway between the
93 Mile House and Clinton, the proprietors of the present 83 Mile Gas
Station and Restaurant are still offering their facilities to the travelling
public — a tradition established 130 years ago.

THE 93 MILE HOUSE, 1865

From his camp at "Robertson's Ranch," which became the 90
milepost on the wagon road from Lillooet, on 17 October 1862
Sergeant John McMurphy noted in his diary not only the progress of
the roadmakers, but also the exodus of large numbers of the mining

Mountain with a severe fall of snow, which fell without ceasing to the depth of 5ft. in drifts."[23] Despite winter's early arrival in the "high country," some pack-trains were still on their way north from Lillooet: "Sunday, all the men at work, two large wagons came in from Lillooet, one with eight yoke of oxen drawing 10,200 lbs., the other with six yoke drawing 7,000lbs., their cargoes are provisions and dry goods."[24]

While, in 1862, the area of the 93 milepost had been part of Robertson's ranch, by 1865 the land had been abandoned. At that time, the Walters brothers, Thomas, John, and Richard, built a stopping house beside the road at the top of the long hill from the 100 Mile House. On its completion, the 93 Mile House was advertised in the *Cariboo Sentinel* of 12 June 1865:

> *93 Mile House, Cariboo Road.*
> *Walters Bros. Proprietors.*
> *Have opened the above House for the reception of travellers;*
> *the table is well kept and the liquors cannot be surpassed;*
> *Beds are clean and comfortable.*
> *Stabling for horses; hay and oats at moderate rates.[25]*

"Walters House," at the 93 milepost, also appears on a map published in 1866 by the Western Union Telegraph Company. While the 93 Mile House was much appreciated by teamsters travelling south up the long hill from the 100 Mile House, it did not prove as popular as did several of the other roadhouses operated by the Walters brothers. Logically, considering the success of the 83 Mile House, another house ten miles north should also have done well as ten miles was a day's journey for many horse driven vehicles. And until 1867 it did; but then business on the Cariboo Road dwindled due to miners leaving for other gold rushes in the Columbia River, Kootenay, and Bridge River districts of the province. Subsidized by the operations of their more successful roadhouses, the Walters brothers continued to operate the 93 Mile House until late in 1870, when the whole family left the Cariboo.

This area of the Cariboo Road did not assume any permanency until the late 1930s, when homesteaders and farmers of Lone Butte and Bridge Lake needed a connecting point on the main highway. It was in June 1936 when Ray and Emma Flaherty built a depot at the 93 milepost for passengers and freight on the IT Stage Line. Four years later, in 1940, Flaherty built a gas station and cafe on the upper side of the highway. Today, the 93 milepoint on Highway 97 is a regular Greyhound bus stop.

BRIDGE CREEK HOUSE, 1861
100 Mile House Ranch and Roadhouse, 1880–1937
Lots 31, 32, and 33, G.1., Cariboo

The valley of Bridge Creek, endowed with ample water and pastureland, had long been a favourite campground of the fur traders along the Hudson's Bay Company's historic Brigade Trail.

With the start of a goldrush in the Cariboo, the first cattle to arrive were driven in by Joel Palmer in 1859 and, in 1861, by the Jeffries brothers (John and Oliver) of Alabama who drove a herd of cows in from Oregon to Bridge Creek where they settled that year. Although it was Thomas M. Miller who first pre-empted the land on which Bridge Creek House was built, research into the chain of ownership shows that Miller, the Jeffries brothers, and their partners, J. E. Johnstone and Reinhardt, were continually conveying the land back and forth between them. This process went on until August 1864, when the 100 Mile House property was sold to Uriah Nelson.

First advertised in Victoria's *Colonist* of 21 February 1862 (which published a list of roadhouse accommodations for travellers) Bridge Creek House was built in the summer of 1861. Known as "Jeffries store," the single-storey, squared-log structure contained a bar-room, kitchen, and, in the attic, a sleeping area. Bishop Hills, in his diary entry of 10 July 1862, describes his visit to Bridge Creek:

> *At Bridge Creek was a band of cattle driven in from Oregon by the brother of Jeffries. He places at various points droves of cattle. Here one of them keeps a store. Mr. Knipe and I had dinner there today. For a beefsteak and coffee the charge was a dollar & half. I also bought for my party 10lbs of beef at 45cts a lb. We camped about a mile south of the House, and sent our horses across the stream to a bench where was an excellent feed of Bunch grass.[26]*

It was not long before increased business made it necessary to add two lean-to structures onto the north and south ends of the road-house. A newspaper correspondent passing through the area in May 1863 mentioned the new accommodations and the unusual fact that they included "bedrooms, rather a novelty in a land where everyone sleeps on the ground."[27]

In the later 1860s, while the roadhouse and ranch at Bridge Creek was operated by Mard Nelson and his partner, Charlton, the facilities and accommodations were again enlarged with the addition of a single-storey residence (with bay window) and two substantial two-storey, squared log houses, one on each end of the originals. Thus, by 1867, Bridge Creek House had become a line of five adjoining buildings. The original of these contained a store and telegraph key, operated by H. Carters. The main kitchen contained a massive French range. Having several different floor levels and ceiling heights, the interior of the Bridge Creek House was quite irregular, and it was said that some of its sixteen bedrooms were without windows. While the roadhouse provided accommodation for many guests, there was no insulation in the walls. George Sargison, travelling from the Coast by stage on his way to Barkerville in December 1871, commented as follows:

Cold day, 25 to 30 below zero. Reached 100 Mile House at 8 30 p m chilled thoroughly. Thermometer frozen — mercury gone out of sight. Slept in cold room. Ice formed on bed clothes. Temperature same inside as out! By morning House cold beyond expression — only Bar Room warm — kept my overcoat on in House. Brandy frozen in sleigh.[28]

By 1872, Nelson and Charlton had sold the 100 Mile Ranch and roadhouse to Charles M. Beak, cattle rancher, butcher, and businessman who first arrived in the Cariboo in 1862. Beak, who later owned the 105 and 108 ranches, operated large dairies and ran herds of cattle on his land, the products of which were sold in his shop at Barkerville.

100 Mile House is shown about 1868 when owned by Uriah and Mard Nelson. It was built in 1861 by Jefferies Brothers (COURTESY BCARS)

David Pratt and his half brother, John Wright, of the 127 Mile Ranch were hired by Beak to manage these dairies. In 1873, Pratt exchanged his interest in the 127 Mile Ranch for the 100 Mile property. Pratt and his vivacious young wife operated the ranch and roadhouse until his death in 1878. Mrs Pratt, with the assistance of her brother, Lindsay, continued the business until her marriage in 1880 to a Mr Develin. The honeymoon consisted of a trip back east, and, while the happy couple were gone, Lindsay was left in charge.

It was in September 1880, while Mrs Develin was away, that Sarah Crease remained overnight at Bridge Creek House. Although she referred to the house as "rough and dirty," she was quite delighted with the talents of the Chinese cook, Ah Fou, who served a delicious meal complete with bread, cream, butter, and jam — all products of the ranch. Also mentioned were the twenty-seven pounds of butter, which were made daily from the milk of seventy cows. Prior to her final departure from the Cariboo in 1881, Mrs Develin sold the 100 Mile Ranch and its various enterprises to Thomas Hamilton, a brother of Gavin Hamilton, owner of the 150 Mile House ranch. A Crown grant was issued to Thomas Hamilton on land at the 100 Mile House in 1882.

During the early 1890s, William Allen, a land surveyor from Scotland, owned the 100 Mile House property. Allen soon found the enterprise more than he could handle and sold out to the Stevenson brothers, Frank and Sydney. Said to be related to the inventor George Stevenson, the brothers established a sawmill at the 100 Mile Ranch near Bridge Creek Falls. Under development at this time were over 3,000 acres of land, where more than 700 head of cattle ranged, and where a large herd of dairy cows pastured on three separate ranches. It was the Stevensons who built the very large barn which, until very recently, stood beside the highway in the community of 100 Mile House. Bad luck befell the Stevensons when Sydney was suddenly killed in a shooting accident. Heartbroken over his loss, Frank sold the ranch to the Marquis of Exeter in 1912. Charles G. Cowan, a Kamloops real-estate agent, managed the ranch until the Marquis's son, Lord Martin Cecil, came of age and moved from his home in England to the Cariboo. Prior to his arrival, a new home was built for him. While the original buildings were of historic interest, they were infested with bedbugs and lice. Roddy Moffat, a freighter on the Cariboo Road in the early 1900s, noted that the ceilings of the bedrooms in the old house were spattered with blood from the bugs that had been killed. Even more objectionable was the peculiar, pungent odour of the bedbugs. It was just as well, then, that Bridge Creek House, a row of uniquely irregular buildings with crooked doorways and rickety staircases, burned to the ground in the spring of 1937. At the time, Lord Martin Cecil was heard to remark on the terrible loss of life — none of which was human.

THE 105 MILE HOUSE, 1863
Lots 358 and 80, G.1., Cariboo

As the building of Wright's wagon road progressed north from the valley of Bridge Creek, it climbed steadily for a mile, then ran through a short flat of heavy timber to where it began sloping downwards to Lac La Hache — a distance of approximately fifteen miles. The lower altitude made a vast difference in climate and growth. Where heavy stands of pine had dominated the scene, there were now gently rolling hillsides bedecked with small groves of aspen and cottonwood. The many creeks running through wide expanses of pastureland harboured a myriad of waterfowl. In July 1863, Harry Jones, a young Welsh miner travelling through the area on foot, commented: "In the short grass we found great patches of wild strawberries ... and spent many hours picking and eating these berries each day."[29]

That spring, John I. McDonald had pre-empted 160 acres of land between the 105 and 106 mileposts on 25 April 1863. Here, McDonald built a roadhouse which was still operating beside the wagon road in 1866 when he sold out to the Walters brothers. The Walters brothers, Thomas and John, had a stock ranch to the west of the 105 Mile Ranch, in the vicinity of Horseshoe Lake where they pastured dairy cows for Charles Beak of the 108 Mile House. When the Walters family left the Cariboo in 1870, they sold both the 105 Mile House and the Horseshoe Lake Ranch to Charles Beak. In the 1870s, when Beak also left the Cariboo, he sold the 105 Mile Ranch and roadhouse to Thomas Power, who owned many acres of arable land between the 101 and 108 mileposts on the Cariboo Road. During the late 1880s, Power sold the 105 Mile Ranch to Mrs Simon Philipine, a sister of Mrs Moses Pigeon of the Meadow Lake Ranch. To begin with, the 105 Mile House had been a crude single-storey log building, but at this time a new two-storey, frame house appeared on the upper side of the wagon road where Mrs Philipine catered mostly to freight-wagon operators. One of these teamsters was Benjamin Harrison McNeil, who bought the ranch from her in 1895.

Ben McNeil and his brother Lester, both born in Minnesota, were young boys in Seattle in the early 1890s, where an older brother had arranged for them to cook on a railway construction job. Tiring of the never-ending sequence of dishes and meals, the two teenagers teamed up with an older acquaintance, Dick Foss, and used their savings to outfit a ten-horse pack-train to travel north by way of the Okanagan to the Cariboo, where they hoped to find gold.

Arriving in the Bridge Creek area in the fall of 1893, the McNeil brothers changed their minds about mining and turned to trapping. By 1894, Lester had returned to Seattle, and Ben was freighting goods, with a ten-horse outfit between Ashcroft and Barkerville. When Ben took over the 105 Mile House, he hired a Chinese cook. As it turned out, this man was a hard worker, cooking for the freighters, milking several cows, and turning a profit in butter sales. A year later, while Ben's brother Lester and his family were visiting, the roadhouse caught fire and burned to the ground. Ben lost no time replacing it, but this time the exterior of the building was covered with sheet-metal siding, and, in the interior, each room had an embossed metal ceiling.

Ben McNeil remained a bachelor for many years. He had already met the love of his life in 1901 when Laura Blackwell of Ontario taught school at Lac La Hache for two years. But Laura was not ready to marry the rough, outspoken American who enjoyed drinking and gambling. Ten years later, however, in 1912, Laura gave up teaching, married Ben, and spent the rest of her life in the Cariboo. At heart, Ben

The second 105 Mile House was built in 1908–09.
(COURTESY BIG COUNTRY CARIBOO, HELDOR SCHAFER, QUESNEL, BC)

Ben McNeil, builder of the second 105 Mile House and his wife Laura.
(COURTESY BIG COUNTRY CARIBOO, HELDOR SCHAFER, QUESNEL, BC)

was a farmer, and from the early 1900s had begun to clear land at the bottom end of Canim Lake, a few miles southeast of the 105 Mile House. In 1916, when Ben sold the 105 Mile Ranch to the agents of Lord Edgerton, he and his family had become full-time farmers at Canim Lake. In 1948, when estate duties forced the sale of the 105 Mile Ranch, it was purchased by Fred Davis. By the 1970s, the property had become a dude ranch, operated by R. M. Monical. When a new highway threatened the existence of the 105 Mile House in 1979, the building was moved to the 108 Mile House area where it was completely restored and became the focal point of a historic park.

THE 108 MILE HOUSE, 1863–1900
Lot 76, G.1., Cariboo

A roadhouse built by James Roper stood beside the Cariboo Road at the 108 milepost in 1863. Born in Dorsetshire, England, in 1841, where he was educated at Sherbourne College, Roper sailed for the New World in 1862, arriving in Victoria, British Columbia, by way of Panama and San Francisco. The following spring found Roper at Lillooet, where he mined for gold and freighted goods to the Cariboo. It was during his first trip north, when he caught sight of the soft rolling landscape of the 108 Mile country, that Roper was reminded of his old home in England. Thinking he might settle down at this site, he pre-empted 160 acres on 23 November 1863. At that time, a fair proportion of the traffic heading for the Quesnel River went by way of the Horsefly trail and "Roper's

House," situated beside this trail, catered to these travellers. The house, pictured as a large, two-storey log structure, featured an encased stone and mortar chimney on the north wall. Despite the many opportunities of the time, William Roper did not make a success of his enterprise at the 108 milepost, and before returning to the more lucrative business of freighting in 1868, he sold out to Charles M. Beak. Beak and his wife operated the roadhouse, ran cattle, and started a herd of dairy cows on the 108 Mile Ranch, shipping large amounts of butter to Barkerville by way of the BC Express Company.

Leaving home in England in the 1850s, Beak spent some time in association with a vigilante group in the goldfields of California, where he mined along the Sacramento River. In 1862, in association with two other drovers, Beak herded 300 head of cattle north to British Columbia, selling meat en route to the Cariboo. On his next trip, with his partner James Doyle, Beak drove a very large flock of sheep to Barkerville, where he opened a butcher shop and sold mutton at forty cents a pound and candles of mutton tallow at fifty cents a pound. By 1866, and due to increased competition, Beak was forced to close his shop in Barkerville and return to the United States.

In Oregon, during the winter of 1867, Beak married sixteen-year-old Marie Johnson of Glencoe, Oregon. Returning with his bride to the Cariboo the following spring, Beak purchased the 108 Mile House and ranch.[30] While the Beaks operated the roadhouse, store, and telegraph key, they also worked in cooperation with neighbouring ranchers in the

Charles M. Beak, entrepreneur of the 1860s and 1870s, who owned several roadhouse farms between the 100 Mile and 127 Mile posts. (COURTESY HUMPHREY BEAK)

100 Mile and Lac La Hache areas to increase the number of cattle in the region; as a result, they were able to reopen a retail butcher shop in Barkerville. In addition, Beak provided the financial means to establish several dairies at the 100, 105, 127, and 137 Mile ranches, the products of which were also sold in Barkerville. While Beak operated his retail outlet in the gold-rush town, he left his associates, David Pratt and his stepbrother, John Wright, to maintain the several dairies.[31] Unfortunately, Beak's second attempt to establish a retail market in Barkerville did not succeed. Due to marauding bears and wolves on Bald Mountain, where stock was held for butchering, by 1870 Beak was once again forced to withdraw. For a few years, he and his wife Marie continued with their various operations at the 108 Mile House, maintaining herds of cattle on their several ranches in the Lac La Hache area. These were driven to Barkerville and sold to the butchers Von Volkenburgh and Company. Convinced by this time that the Cariboo was not suited to raising beef, Beak sold off his properties, and, by 1878, he had relocated to the Upper Nicola River, where he became one of the founding members of the Douglas Lake Ranch.

William Walker and his wife Emily bought the 108 Mile Ranch from Charles Beak in the 1870s. Walker was another of the Cariboo's early entrepreneurs, owning or having an interest in various properties from the early 1860s until his death in Kamloops in 1905. Besides

This photo shows the site of 108 Mile House in the 1980s.
(COURTESY MARY PATENAUDE)

108 Mile Ranch, late 19th century. (COURTESY BCARS)

keeping a large herd of cattle at the 108 Mile Ranch, the Walkers operated the roadhouse, store, and telegraph key until 1889, when they sold out to Steven Tingley, owner of the BC Express Company, for $2,500.

Tingley kept many horses on the fields of the 108 Mile Ranch, where he installed his son Clarence as agent and storekeeper of the BC Express Company. At this time, a very large horse-barn was built at the 108 Mile Ranch, and it still stands today. Clarence Tingley's operations at the 108 Mile Ranch ended in the early 1900s, when his father retired from business. The ranch, which at this time included 1,000 acres of land, was sold to Captain Geoffrey L. Watson, an English army officer. Watson also kept a herd of cattle, but his personal interest was in fine horses. At this time, the roadhouse was closed, but it continued as a residence for Watson until a very fine mansion was built for him on land that, in the 1860s, had been the Walters brothers stock ranch. This mansion was located near Horseshoe Lake, which was later renamed Watson Lake.[32]

Notes to Chapter 1

1. The mileage on this route starts from Lillooet.

2. GR 827, John Pollard, 16 July 1862, Lillooet Land Records, vol. 1, British Columbia Archives and Records Service (hereafter referred to as BCARS).

3. Louis LeBourdais, "Harry Jones Story," addit. MSS 676, vol. 7, p. 13, BCARS.

4. Branwen Patenaude, *Trails to Gold* (Victoria: Horsdal & Schubart 1995), xix, 122, 123.

5. Molly Forbes, "Some Old Roadhouses: Cariboo Calling," *100 Mile Free Press*, 1973.

6. Angus G. Ryder, "Recollections of the 59 Mile House," MS 1069, BCARS.

7. Sergeant J. McMurphy, RE, Diary, 31 August 1862, E/B/M221, BCARS, 18.

8. Ibid.

9. McMurphy, Diary, 11 September 1862, 20.

10. Sarah L. Crease, Diary, 11 September 1880, A/E/C86, BCARS, 7.

11. McMurphy, Diary, 23 September 1862, 21.

12. GR 827, 27 September 1862, record no. 92," 160 acres of land situate between the 73rd. and 75th. mileposts on the Lillooet to Mud Lake Road."

13. *British Columbian* (New Westminster), 14 March 1863, 3.

14. LeBourdais, "Harry Jones Story," 13.

15. *British Colonist,* (Victoria), "74 Mile House," 31 August 1863.

16. John McMurphy Jr, undated and unidentified newspaper. Interview with J. Mahoney. Royal Engineers Museum, Chilliwack, BC.

17. John W. Clapperton, Diary, 1864, E/C/c53.3, BCARS.

18. See *Trails to Gold,* 134–36.

19. McMurphy, Diary, 25 September 1862, 23.

20. Ibid., 1 October 1862, 23.

21. GR 1069, Lillooet Pre-emptions, record no. 101, 11 October 1862, BCARS.

22. *British Colonist* (Victoria), 25 November 1862.

23. McMurphy, Diary, 17 October 1862, 25.

24. Ibid., 5 October 1862, 23.

25. *Cariboo Sentinel,* 12 June 1865.

26. Bishop George Hills, Diary, 10 July 1862, Anglican Provincial Synod of British Columbia Archives, Vancouver.

27. *British Colonist* (Victoria), 29 May 1863, 3.

28. George Sargison, Diary, December 1871, E/C/Sa7, BCARS.

29. LeBourdais, "Harry Jones Story," 15.

30. *Cariboo Sentinel,* 12 June 1865.

31. Ibid. 3 June 1869, 2.

32. *Williams Lake Tribune,* 24 December 1983.

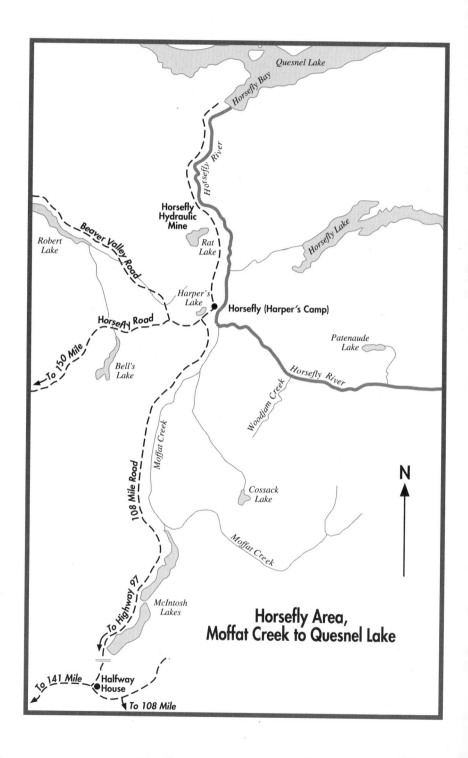

**Horsefly Area,
Moffat Creek to Quesnel Lake**

CHAPTER TWO

Halfway House to Horsefly, 1859–1945

The intriguing history of a trail used by miners in 1859 includes the almost forgotten site of an early roadhouse. References to the trail began with the Peter Dunlevy party, a group of five miners guided by a Shuswap, Baptiste, from the southeastern end of Lac La Hache to Little Horsefly Creek (near Horsefly Lake) in June 1859. This journey led to the discovery of the first big gold strike in the Cariboo.[1]

In his story of the Dunlevy party and the first gold strike, Alexander P. McInnes's *Chronicles of the Cariboo* describes the journey along what is today known as the 108 Mile Road.[2] Branching off the 108 milepost on Highway 97, the road heads north past Spout Lake and the McIntosh Lakes to Moffat Creek, the Horsefly River, and Quesnel Lake. According to Alex McInnes, Baptiste knew the country well, for the trail had been used by Native peoples for centuries. During their journey, one of the partners, Thomas Moffitt, who was more of a gambler than a miner, became convinced that a certain creek along the way was rich in gold. Although his companions tried to dissuade him, Moffitt delayed the journey for a whole day while he prospected. For this reason, the partners named the creek after him (it is now known as Moffat Creek, a corruption of the original).[3]

Five years later, in 1864, Captain Isaiah Mitchell, builder of a bridge across the North Fork of the Quesnel River and operator of a ferry across Quesnel Lake, was constructing an improved trail on the same route taken by the Dunlevy party.[4] Mitchell hoped the government would endorse his trail as the route of a wagon road to the mines of the Cariboo. So popular was this route that soon there were several different branches of it: at the 111 milepost, the 122 milepost, and Knife Creek at the 141 milepost.

In 1865, this route was travelled by a reporter from the *Cariboo Sentinel* who wrote an article describing the countryside through which it ran. Starting from the 111 milepost, the fifty-two miles to Mitchell's bridge was described as being "definitely shorter than [was] the wagon road, but the steep hills, swamps and lingering snow on the high mountains made it impractical."[5] Also mentioned in the article was the "one House of accommodation along the way," where William Moore had pre-empted some meadowland in November 1862 and on which he built a stopping place known as "Halfway House."[6] Needless to say, Captain Mitchell's trail of 1864, given all its deficiencies, was not developed at this time.

A new era of popularity for the route began in the mid-1880s, following the arrival of the Canadian Pacific Railway at Ashcroft, when English money paid for the development of hydraulic mines on the Horsefly and Quesnel rivers. At this time, a program (sponsored, in part, by mining companies) to improve the trail got under way. Besides clearing brush and widening the trail, the many miles of swampland were "corduroyed." This involved placing logs the width of the trail, side by side, across the swamp. Finally, dirt was piled over these logs, making a bed for the road, and only then were horses with loaded wagons able to travel the trail without being mired down. In the late 1880s, with the resurgence of traffic through this route, John P. McIntosh (originally of Ontario) took up a homestead on land between Spout Lake and what later became known as McIntosh Lakes. During this time, McIntosh's home, on the site of the original "Halfway House," continued the tradition of accommodating travellers on their way to Horsefly. The McIntosh family (John P., his wife, and their two sons, Allan and Duncan) lived and farmed at this site until John's death on 5 June 1897.[7]

HARPER'S CAMP, 1892–1921

During the 1890s, Harper's Camp (a mining community beside the Horsefly River, forty miles northeast of Williams Lake) supported two hotels. Although in the past, crude mining methods had proved unable to reach the more inaccessible ground of the Cariboo, the arrival of the Canadian Pacific Railway at Ashcroft in the mid-1880s allowed for the shipment of heavy machinery from eastern Canada and the United States. As a result, several British and American syndicates were willing to provide the financial backing to develop mining properties in the Horsefly River area.

Following the first rich strike on Little Horsefly Creek in 1859, gold deposits on the Horsefly River continued to attract miners during the 1860s and 1870s. The gold that was found was embedded in a sticky blue clay, which was hard to wash off. A steadily increasing community of White and Chinese miners lived in cabins on the flat north of the confluence of Moffat Creek and the Horsefly River.

This was more or less the situation in 1884, when Thaddeus Harper of the Harper brothers (Cariboo entrepreneurs) acquired several mining leases on land that later became part of Harper's Camp, adjoining the Chinese-owned Horn King Mine. By 1887, Harper had acquired the Horn King claims and was employing a large crew of men to test the ground. One of the first hydraulic mines in the Cariboo began operation at this site, the results of which sparked a new rash of prospecting in the area.[8] In spite of his heavy investments, Harper was unable to make a profit, and, by 1891, his claims were taken over by the Horsefly Gold Mining Company, which was managed by Robert T. Ward. In the meantime, as a result of extensive prospecting in the spring of 1887, Dan McCallum and his associates, Brodie and Chambers, made several worthwhile finds five miles downstream from Harper's Camp. These men formed a partnership known as the Discovery Company, and, in 1892, the Canadian Pacific Railway sent engineer John B. Hobson to examine their finds. Within the year, their property had been leased by the Horsefly Hydraulic Mining Company, which was managed by Hobson. With start-up capital of $100,000, the labour force hired to prepare the site for development included thirty Whites and an equal number of Japanese. Although the original route to Horsefly River by way of the 108 Milepost trail was still in use, the machinery and supplies needed to set up Hobson's mine were hauled from Ashcroft, by way of the 150 Mile House, over a road built in the winter of 1892.[9] The large camp built at the site of the new mine covered several acres and included a sawmill, a store, and (in 1895) the first post office in the area. By 1897, a third large mining operation, developed by the Miocene Gravel Mining Company under the direction of Senator R. H. Campbell, was working on the flat at "Harper Bar."[10] These several large developments brought about a significant increase in population. By the mid-1890s, Harper's Camp had become a frontier town of several hundred inhabitants, and, in 1896, it opened its first hotel.

MEISS'S CITY HOTEL, 1896–1945
Lot 348, G.1., Cariboo

Born in Victoria, British Columbia, in 1864, Alexander Meiss spent his early years freighting goods from Ashcroft to the mines of the Cariboo. It was during one of those trips, while waiting over at Clinton, that Alex had a tragic accident. As he sat cleaning a rifle, the gun went off, shattering his left knee. Dr Sanson, the attending physician, decided to amputate, and an operation was performed on the dining-room table of the Thomas Barton home in Clinton. Jessie, (Mrs Barton) nursed Alex through many weeks of convalescence while he lay flat on his back, feeling totally useless. Following his recovery, Alex never forgot the kindness shown him by the Barton family, and he spent the rest of his life trying to repay them. Fitted with a wooden leg, Alex hobbled around Clinton for a while, where he met the Gaspard girls from Dog Creek, who were working as cooks at the hotel. The father of these girls, Isadore Versepeuch, a French count, had settled in the Dog Creek Valley in 1860.[11] Realizing that most people found the word "Versepeuch" too difficult either to pronounce or to spell, the count adopted Gaspard as a surname.

Alex Meiss and Matilda Gaspard were married at Williams Lake on 1 March 1897 and settled at Harper's Camp, where Alex had started his store and restaurant the year before. Matilda immediately took over the operation of the business, while Alex freighted supplies in from Ashcroft. Having lost her mother while still quite young, Matilda had learned very early how to cook and keep house for her family at Dog Creek. At Harper's Camp, she also learned how to maintain peace and order amongst the rowdy miners who frequented her restaurant.

The land pre-empted by Alex in 1897, and on which his first cabin was built, later became the centre of the little community. In 1898, encouraged by the expanding activities of the local mines and the increasing population, the Meisses built a good-sized, two-storey squared-log house, which they named the City Hotel. Measuring about thirty-five feet square, the ground floor of the structure contained a front entrance and lobby, a kitchen and dining room, a combination

Alex Meiss, peg leg prominent, rests in a wagon while Matilda Meiss stands to his left. A blowup of this photo is displayed in the Horsefly Museum.

saloon and store area, and one bedroom with an attached private sitting room. A flight of hand-carved wooden stairs, situated just beyond the front door, led to several bedrooms in the upper storey. In a photograph of the City Hotel taken in the early 1900s, a second door is seen in the upper storey directly above the front door. A second door was quite common in log buildings of the time, serving both as a fire escape and as a way of getting furniture into the upper storey. Both doorways were decorated with narrow panels of stained red and blue glass. In the morning sunlight, these panels reflected rays of purple lights along the interior walls. Out in the small fenced yard surrounding the hotel, the pathway leading to the garden gate was bordered with old bottles, turned neck down in the dirt. Close by was a small oak tree, planted by the Meisses, which eventually grew to cover the front entrance of the hotel.

In the saloon of the City Hotel, a rather dark and sombre place between the kitchen and the dining room, as many as twelve men could stand shoulder to shoulder in front of a long bar, behind which were many shelves filled with every conceivable brand of liquor. Here also, to one side and on racks hanging from the ceiling, were clothing, boots, camping gear, canned goods, biscuits, and confections. To encourage his customers to buy more, Alex issued twenty-five-cent tokens. The floor of the barroom, built of twelve-inch wide boards, eventually became so worn from the constant scuffing of hobnailed boots that the knots fairly stood out from the wood. Around the room were small tables and bar-room chairs, where the miners sat up half the night drinking, playing poker, smoking, chewing tobacco, and spitting on the stove. The men respected Alex Meiss, but there were nights when things got rough. It was quite common for Alex to have to escort an offending patron outside, and, one night, when two miners had a serious quarrel, a gun was pulled. Fortunately, Alex was there with his six-shooter to intercede.

The hydraulic mining operations at Horsefly did not last long, and by 1905 the rich deposits of gold seemed to be exhausted. As the big companies pulled out and large numbers of labourers moved on, the merchants and hotel keepers at Harper's Camp suffered a severe slump in business. There was, however, a general feeling of optimism amongst the more permanent residents. Although the big employers were gone, there were still a number of small placer mines in the area. Rather than moving on, some of the men who had worked in the mines remained to take up ranch land on which to raise their families. Trapping was also a common occupation.

Perhaps for all these reasons, Alex and Matilda Meiss continued to enlarge their hotel at Harper's Camp. In 1904, a second large, single-storey log house of saddle-and-notch (round logs, rather than squared) construction was built, close to the City Hotel. Originally, it had been intended as a bunkhouse — an addition to Alex's original cabin (which had been relegated to that site when the hotel was first built). There always seemed to be a shortage of accommodation, especially for single men, who came from the north to winter at Harper's Camp. Before long, the space between the two buildings was filled in by yet another addition; this one was similar to the first, except that it had two attic bedrooms (each with a dormer window) facing the road. This last and final addition brought the total length of Meiss's hotel to about 100 feet. At this time, a new main entrance was built in the most recent addition, and the space that had been the front hall became the lobby and, later, a post office, where a telephone was installed in 1912. The narrow, stained-glass panels from around the original doorway remained, still making purple reflections on the walls on sunny mornings. In one corner of this room stood a large, roll-top desk with many pigeon holes, and, along the wall were wooden slots which held the Harper's Camp mail. Also in this room was a well-upholstered barber's chair. Seldom used as originally intended, the chair more often served the victims of toothache or those needing first aid. Due to the absence of qualified doctors or dentists in this rural community, Matilda, who was a competent midwife, served as nurse and, on occasion, as doctor.

In the case of unbearable toothache, the patient was given several doses of overproof rum and, when adequately numbed, was placed in the barber chair, where a pair of forceps soon removed the problem.

Matilda Meiss, a woman of many talents, not only raised a good vegetable garden each year, she also grew many luxurious house plants inside the hotel. Along the window sills in the lobby were bright red geraniums, so tall they reached the ceiling, with stalks an inch thick. As a young lad in the 1930s, Wilfred Patenaude of Marten Creek Ranch never forgot that room. One very warm fall day Wilf accompanied his father Albert on a trip from the family ranch to Horsefly, a distance of about fourteen miles. They travelled in Albert's 1930 Chevrolet sedan, the springs of which were rather weak. Albert was never known to be a good driver and was inclined to run off the narrow road. He drove a car the way he drove a team of horses, letting it choose its path while he surveyed the countryside. After a good half hour of swaying around over the rough, winding, Black Creek road, Wilf's stomach was none too settled as the car pulled up in front of Meiss's hotel. In the warm atmosphere of the post office, where the noonday sun shone brilliantly through the stained-glass windows, the pungent odour of Matilda's red geraniums was just enough to send Wilf scurrying for the outhouse.

Just past the lobby and post office of the City Hotel was Matilda Meiss's private parlour. In this area, which was reserved almost exclusively for visiting women, tea was served along with the standard hotel cake — white, with thick, white icing. While the room contained many of the usual parlour furnishings, such as overstuffed chairs, a large Axminster rug, and an ornate wood heater, it also contained some most unusual and unique objects. Upon entering the room for the first time visitors were both startled and fascinated by the presence of a beautifully stuffed bald eagle, standing on the branch of a tree. With its menacing stance and piercing eyes, it appeared to be almost real. In another corner was an Edison gramophone, and a collection of cylinders in a nearby drawer Over the years, the Meisses had received hundreds of postcards and Christmas cards from friends and guests at the hotel, and Matilda saved every one of them. Displayed on wire racks and hung along the parlour walls, this impressive collection was long remembered by residents and children of the area.

As the young girls of the community grew up, Matilda Meiss hired them to help her with the housework and spring cleaning. Among these girls were Agnes Gruhs and Hazel Walters, and for them, at least on one occasion, spring cleaning proved to be a terrifying experience.

Early one spring Alex Meiss had adopted an orphaned bear cub. Considered cute at first, the fast-growing animal was, on occasion, allowed to roam through the hotel. Agnes and Hazel were petrified of it, and when it came romping into the rooms where they were working, they screamed and climbed up on the furniture, where they stayed until Alex came to their rescue. As the bear grew larger and more aggressive, it had to be shot. Unafraid of humans, it would soon have fallen prey to hunters had it been turned loose.

Alex Meiss was tall and well-built. His smiling brown eyes, "handlebar" mustache, and hearty laugh gained him many friends, especially among children. Alex and Matilda did not have a family of their own, and, perhaps for that reason, Alex was always adopting some waif or orphan boy to live and earn his keep at the hotel. These boys, some of whom remained for a number of years, received the benefits of Matilda's social training. Despite his physical handicap, Alex participated in almost every activity, even riding horseback. In 1910, he brought one of the first cars, a McLaughlin touring car, into the country. Later, when Alex had the mail route, he owned a Model T Ford truck. To accommodate his wooden leg, a hooking mechanism was installed onto the front windshield of the vehicle. On one occasion, when Alex had trouble getting his truck to start, he had his friend, Romeo McEachern, turn the crank. Alex's good foot had been on the brake until suddenly, when the engine started up, the truck shot forward,

After 1912, the Meiss Hotel included its first addition with the gabled windows, built in 1910, and, on the right, the newest phase,

knocking McEachern down and running right over him. Before it could be stopped, the truck had travelled across the yard and climbed to the top of a woodpile. Fortunately, the high wheel base protected McEachern, who was only shaken up by the experience.

As Alex Meiss grew older, his taste for hard liquor increased. Those who knew Alex remember often meeting him along the road, an open bottle of rum on the seat and a bologna sausage under his arm. He would flourish his knife, slice a hunk off the sausage, spear it on the end of the blade, and offer it to whomever he met. Alex Meiss had the mail-delivery contract from 1916 until his death in 1928, while Matilda was postmistress from 1921 to 1923. It was during this time that the name "Harper's Camp" was changed to "Horsefly."

Alex died of stomach cancer in November 1928, and Matilda carried on with the operation of the City Hotel until her death in 1942. They are both buried in the Roman Catholic cemetery in Horsefly.

Lot 348, Cariboo, on which stood the rambling old City Hotel, was bought in 1944 by Stan and Ruby Barrett, who lived there for only a few months before a fire gutted the building in May 1945.

THE HORSEFLY HOTEL, 1897–1915
Lot 341, G.1., Cariboo

A second hotel was built in Harper's Camp in 1897 by Harry Lincoln Walters. The Walters family had a long history of roadhouse keeping, dating back to the early 1860s, when Harry's father, Thomas, and his uncles, John and Richard, established several of the stopping houses along the Cariboo Road. Born at the 83 Mile House in 1866, Harry returned to Ontario with his family in 1870. Then, as a young man, Harry and his brother Thomas returned to the Cariboo in 1894. They found work at Harper's Camp in J.B. Hobson's Horsefly Hydraulic Mine. When a post office opened at the mine in 1895, Harry Walters carried the mail on horseback along the 108 Mile trail for delivery to the BC Express Company stagecoach. There were times when Harry's packhorse carried not only the mail but also the gold bullion from Hobson's mine, a fact which, fortunately, most people did not realize. Harry was married in 1895 to Alva Youngker, who, in 1893, with her mother and stepfather, W. P. Hall of Wyoming, was a member of one of the first families to settle at Harper's Camp. While in the process of acquiring property and building a home, Harry and Alva lived at China Cabin, just south of Harper's Camp, where, on 16 July 1896, their first child, Minnie Hazel, was born. The land Harry pre-empted had been part of Harper's mining lease and was located south of Meiss's hotel, between Harper's Lake and the highway.

The Walters' home, which often sheltered transients, was a two-storey log building measuring about thirty feet by thirty-five feet and was of saddle-and-notch construction. It had a shake-covered roof, which ran north and south, and an attic, in which two dormer windows faced west. The front entrance of the house, facing the road, opened onto a full-length porch. Within the year (1897), and in view of the increasing population of Harper's Camp, Harry Walters built a road-house on the northeast side of his home. While similar in size to the first house, it differed in that it was built with squared timbers and dove-tailed corners. Also in contrast to the house, the roof ran east and west and there were three dormer windows in the attic. In the narrow space between the two buildings, a covered stairway led up to a landing, where doors opened into the upstairs bedrooms. The hotel had two front doors, one of which opened into the saloon, the other of which opened into the hotel lobby, post office, and government telegraph office. Harry Walters was the first postmaster in Harper's Camp, and he held that position from 1897 to 1905.

During the first years of heavy mining activity at Harper's Camp, the dining room of the Horsefly Hotel served meals to twenty men at a sitting. Alva Walters did most of the cooking, but Chinese cooks were also hired from time to time. Special occasions called for special dinners: at Christmas it was plum duff, and at Thanksgiving it was roast grouse. On one occasion, Alva baked thirty birds.

Harry (left) and Hazel Walters stand with Pat Sharkey in front of their hotel in 1912. (COURTESY BCARS)

On New Year's Eve, much of the community gathered in the large open space between the saloon and the dining room, where schottisches, waltzes, quadrilles, and polkas were danced all night to the accompaniment of local musicians. Due to the shortage of women, it was not unusual to see men dancing together.

As the first salaried schoolteacher in Harper's Camp in 1910, Annie Moore boarded at the Walters Hotel and taught in the "bunkhouse" school (a building formerly used by mine workers) on the Walters property. While attending a dance in the hotel one night, Annie, who later married Albert Patenaude, could hear a baby crying. On tracing the sound, she found the poor little mite where it had been put to sleep in a nearby bedroom, its thumb bent back in a buttonhole.

During the frontier days of Horsefly's history, most of the money was made in the hotel saloons, where a shot of whisky was twenty-five cents and a bottle was $1.50. Harry Walters had his own unique method of dealing with intolerable drunks. When triggered, a trapdoor in the saloon floor sent undesirables down into the cellar, where they remained until they were sober enough to find their way out. One night, when Harry got tired of listening to a very large, very drunk Russian, he manoeuvred the man over to the door and sprang the trap. Luckily, no one understood the loud cursing and lamentations that rose from the cellar. Gambling, too, was rampant in the saloon. Some of the locals, like Tommy Peterson and Ole' Swede, were astute poker players, and they took a lot of money off the miners. As the Walters children grew up, the saloon, with its drunks and rough language, was off limits to them; but once they found they could con the miners into giving them a few cents for candy, it was hard to keep them out.

During the winter, the upstairs bedrooms of the hotel could get quite cold. With only the stovepipes of the several downstairs heaters and stoves to provide heat upstairs, as Glen Walters later remarked, "You sometimes had to shiver yourself up into a sweat to get warm."3

When local residents Agnes Gruhs and Joe Williams decided to get married on New Year's Day 1913, the ceremony was to take place in the Walters Hotel, performed by a minister from Clinton. A celebration, to which all the inhabitants of the village had been invited, was to follow. For this special occasion, Agnes's mother had spent months making a beautifully decorated, three-tiered wedding cake. On the appointed day, as the crowd of well-wishers assembled at the hotel and waited for the minister, people entertained themselves by dancing to the excellent violin music provided by the groom. Occupied with dancing, no-one

EXPRESS, FREIGHT

—AND—

PASSENGER LINE

STAGES.

AFTER THE FIRST DAY OF MAY, 1864, THE
Coaches of this Line will run as follows:

UP TRIP:
LEAVES YALE ON

MONDAYS & FRIDAYS, AT 3 A. M.,

PASSING OVER THE

SUSPENSION BRIDGE

—AND—

THROUGH THE CANYONS

By daylight, and reaching

Soda Creek

in time to connect with the stern-wheel steamer

'ENTERPRISE'

on Thursdays and Mondays, at daylight, reaching

Quesnelle City

on the same day.

DOWN TRIP:

Leaves SODA CREEK on the arrival of the "ENTER-
PRISE," on TUESDAYS and THURSDAYS, reaching
YALE on THURSDAYS and SATURDAYS in time
to connect with the steamers for NEW WESTMINSTER.

Yale, April 30, 1864.   F. J. BARNARD.

Both the mail and Fraser River Steamboat schedules relied on the "BX" arriving on time. (COURTESY British Columbia NEWSPAPER MAY 4, 1864)

Harry Walters delivered mail to 108 Mile where the Barnard Express stage-coaches or "BX" would carry mail south to Yale. Mail contracts demanded a rigid schedule and any road delays were overcome by sleepless nights. Horses were changed every ten to fifteen miles. (COURTESY VANCOUVER PUBLIC LIBRARY)

noticed when the wedding cake, which had been on display, suddenly disappeared. It had been stolen by pranksters, but, fortunately, it was retrieved undamaged. Due to bad road conditions, the minister never did arrive, but the celebrations continued all night. It was two weeks later, on 14 January 1914, when Agnes and Joe were finally married in the living room of Louis Crosina's 153 Mile House.

With the decline of mining and the establishment of ranches and farms in the area, business at the Walters Hotel diminished. By this time, the eight children of the Walters family were occupying several of the hotel bedrooms. The saloon closed when Harry came to realize that his only customers were those who could not get credit at Meiss's hotel.

During the First World War, in 1915, the Horsefly Hotel and the Walters home burned to the ground. A new log house, built across the road a year later by Ben Gruhs and his son Ben Jr, still stands today, occupied by Gilbert Walters, a grandson of Henry Lincoln Walters.[12]

Notes to Chapter 2

1. H. H. Bancroft, *Bancroft's Works. History of British Columbia,1793–1897*, Vol. 32 (San Francisco: The History Company Publishers 1887) 486, 487.

2. Alex P. McInnes, *Chronicles of the Cariboo* (Lillooet, BC: Lillooet Publishers Limited 1938) 20–23.

3. British Columbia Department of Lands and Forests, Map, Pre-emptor Series No. 3G, Quesnel Sheet, 1915, 1921, 1949.

4. *Cariboo Sentinel*, 17 June 1865, 1.

5. Ibid.

6. GR985, record 132, vol. 1, Cariboo, 21 November 1862, William Moore, 160 acres BCARS.

7. *BC Mining Journal*, 28 September 1895, 4.

8. Part A, Annual Report of the BC Ministry of Mines, 1887, 258.

9. Ibid., 1893, 1040.

10. Ibid., 1887, 485.

11. See *Trails to Gold*, 61.

12. Much of the information found in the sections on Meiss's City Hotel and Walters' Horsefly Hotel was compiled from transcribed tapes kindly lent by the Horsefly Historical Society.

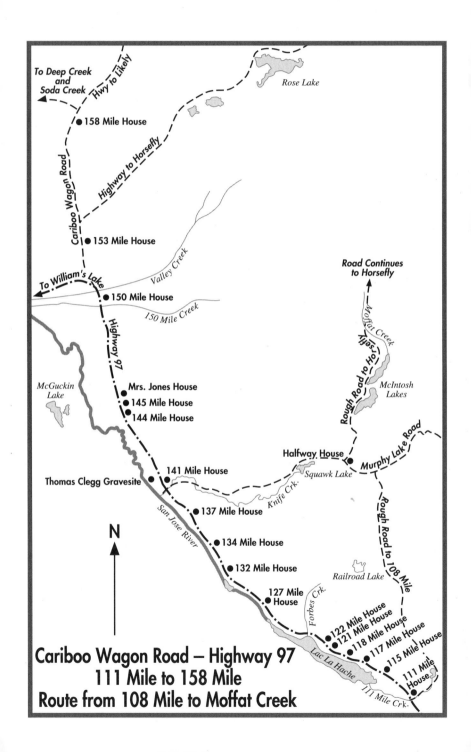

To Deep Creek
and
Soda Creek

Rose Lake

Hwy to Likely

158 Mile House

Highway to Horsefly

Cariboo Wagon Road

153 Mile House

Valley Creek

Road Continues
to Horsefly

To William's Lake

150 Mile House

150 Mile Creek

Highway 97

Moffat Creek

Rough Road to Horsefly

McIntosh
Lakes

McGuckin
Lake

Mrs. Jones House
145 Mile House
144 Mile House

Thomas Clegg Gravesite

141 Mile House

Halfway House

Squawk Lake

Murphy Lake Road

Knife Crk.

San Jose River

137 Mile House

N

134 Mile House

132 Mile House

Railroad Lake

Rough Road to 108 Mile

127 Mile
House

Forbes Crk.

122 Mile House
121 Mile House
118 Mile House
117 Mile House
115 Mile House
111 Mile
House

Lac La Hache

111 Mile Crk.

**Cariboo Wagon Road – Highway 97
111 Mile to 158 Mile
Route from 108 Mile to Moffat Creek**

CHAPTER THREE

111 Mile House to the 150 Mile House

THE 111 MILE HOUSE, 1862–95
Lots 190 and 191, G.1., Cariboo

Built during the summer of 1861, the first documented reference to the 111 Mile House is found in Bishop Hills' diary of July 1862. This diary was written as he and his party travelled along the brigade trail between the 100 milepost and Williams Lake en route to the gold-fields of the Cariboo:

Friday, July 11, 1862
The mosquitoes were bad the first part of the way but we soon got away from them and had a delightful ride through an open country of lakes and fine grassy slopes and plains. About 10 miles on we came to a farm lately taken up called "the Grange." The man and his wife are Canadians. We had some excellent milk and cake. Their name as far as I could gather was Coghan.[1]

While Hills did not have the name quite right, that fall, as James Thomson of Edwardsburgh, Ontario, proceeded south from the 127 Mile House, he mentioned the correct name of the first proprietors of the 111 Mile House.

September 25, 1862
Got to Cochrane's 16 miles. Stopped all night. Cold snow storm.[2]

"Cochrane's" was also mentioned in Sergeant McMurphy's diary during the building of the Cariboo Road in November 1862 and in May 1863.

Perhaps the most descriptive account of the 111 Mile House and its first proprietors is found in the account of Harry Jones, the Welsh miner, during his journey of July 1863:

After an early breakfast I struck out with long strides for Cariboo ... I was travelling on a Sunday, and if any bad luck was coming to me, I was afraid it would occur on this day. I reached the 111 Mile House early in the evening without mishap. This was a neatly built place, both inside and out ... From within a hundred yards of the House I could see no smoke from the stove pipe. The door was shut, and no one appeared to be stirring about. The two cows in the yard were the only signs of life. I decided these were religious people, for the place looked like a home in Wales on a Sunday. It was a few minutes before I could summon up the courage to knock, for I was afraid they would not approve of my travelling on a Sunday. But when the door opened I was met with smiles, for the proprietor and his wife were very nice people. There was no reference to Sunday. They assisted me with my pack, and after a good supper I went to bed with a light heart.[3]

Mentioned in a list of accommodations in Victoria's *Colonist* in 1863, by the spring of 1865 the 111 Mile House had been sold to the Blair brothers, David and John. Convinced that the building of Captain Mitchell's trail to Quesnel Lake would make the 111 milepost a strategic location, the brothers increased their land holdings and built a large, two-storey hotel on the site. An advertisement for the new facilities appeared in the *Cariboo Sentinel*:

111 MILE HOUSE.
Blair Bros., Proprietors.
This hotel is large and well fitted up for the comfort of travellers; the Table is supplied with the best of everything that can be had, and the cooking is not inferior to the best hotel in the lower country;
Bedrooms for families;
Stabling, Hay, and Oats.
The Stage stops at the 111 Mile House over night on its way down country.[4]

This rare photo of 111 Mile Ranch.showing structures built by David and John Blair, the second owners.was first published in H. J. Boam's and A. G. Brown's British Columbia in 1912. All these buildings are gone now, save one log cabin beside 111 Mile Creek.

Among the first to include "family bedrooms" in their facilities (a development brought about by the appearance of four-horse stagecoaches in 1864), Blair's hotel was situated on the north side of the 111 Mile Creek. An impressively large, frame-built, two-storey facility, it had a single gable window above a full-length front porch, which faced the wagon road. After only one year of operation, the Blair brothers sold out in the spring of 1866 to retired Hudon's Bay Company trader William Manson. Manson, who had married Adelaide Ogden, grand-daughter of the renowned Peter Skene Ogden, chose to settle at the 111 Mile House to be near his wife's relatives, the McKinlays. The Mansons, who had a family of half-grown children, were not affected by the lack of school facilities near their new home. As a graduate of Edinburgh University, Manson was able to teach not only his own children, but several of their cousins as well.

Although the first Lac La Hache school opened in 1875, by the late 1880s it had closed for lack of pupils, but the teacher, William Abel of Ontario, remained in the area. A farmer at heart, he bought the 111 Mile Ranch and, with the assistance of his family, operated the roadhouse and Barnard's horse-change station. At this time, the 111 Mile House was a regular stage stop on the Cariboo Road, and passengers on the northern run arrived at 6:00 a.m. for breakfast.

A Crown grant for land at the 111 milepost was issued to William Abel in March 1892, when these became lots 190 and 191, G.1,

Lillooet, containing 320 acres. Shortly after this, the Abels sold out and moved to Vancouver. For a short time, a family by the name of McLure ran the ranch and roadhouse. In 1909, when the old house had fallen into disrepair and the surrounding fields lay dormant, the property was sold to Walker and Slatter of Liverpool, England, and was managed by J. B. Caldwell. Prior to the First World War, the ranch, containing some 3,000 acres, became a part of Captain Geoffrey L. Watson's Highland Ranch. When Watson was killed in action, most of his property in the Cariboo was sold to Lord Edgerton. Just what became of the fine old stopping house at the 111 milepost is not known, but in all probability, it burned down, as have most wooden buildings. Today, only one small, ancient log building remains, situated on the upper side of the creek, and within sight of Highway 97.

THE 115 MILE HOUSE, 1862–1953
Lot 4, G.1., Lillooet

During many annual treks through New Caledonia in the late 1840s as a member of a Hudson's Bay Company brigade, Archibald McKinlay often camped at the southwestern end of Lac La Hache, a large body of water between Fort Alexandria and Fort Kamloops. To him, this was an area well-suited for habitation. With its rolling grasslands, where deer grazed like cattle, its many lakes filled with fish and fowl, and its comparatively mild winters, it was akin to paradise.

Archibald McKinlay started the 115 Mile ranch and roadhouse at Lac La Hache in 1862. Julia McKinlay became a respected pioneer of the Lac La Hache area. (COURTESY BCARS)

Born in Scotland in 1811, Archie was a lad of nineteen years when he first arrived at York Factory on Hudson Bay with George Simpson, governor of the Hudson's Bay Company. Described as a tall, sandy-haired, fair-complexioned Highlander of about 200 pounds, Archibald McKinlay soon came to be known as a sociable, clever, and lively fellow — a favourite of Chief Trader Peter Skene Ogden. Foremost among his abilities was his talent for diplomacy, which, on more than one occasion, averted a showdown with Native trappers. Shortly before his 1840 appointment as factor of Fort Walla Walla on the Columbia River, Archie married Sarah Julia Ogden, daughter of Peter Skene Ogden.

In 1856, following twenty-five years of service (during which time he was in charge at Fort St James, Fort Alexandria, and Fort Walla Walla, respectively), Archibald McKinlay retired and went into business as part owner of the firm Allan and McKinlay, merchants of Oregon City. While success attended the enterprise for several years, Archie suffered great financial loss in 1862 when the trading post was destroyed as a result of flooding along the Willamette River. It was then that the McKinlays decided to leave Oregon and to take up land in the Cariboo region of British Columbia.

That summer Archie left his family and travelled north to the spot beside Lac La Hache which he knew so well. By mid-July he had staked out a pre-emption of 160 acres of land, upon which he constructed several ranch buildings, including a good-sized log cabin, before returning south for the winter.

The following spring saw the McKinlay family travelling north on horseback from Oregon City, camping out along the way. Included in the entourage were Archie; his wife Sarah Julia; their three young sons, James, Archie Jr, and Allen; their two daughters, Sarah and Catherine Anne; the children's grandmother, Julia Ogden, and their uncle, Charles Ogden; and an associate, Peter Kittsen. Journeying by way of Walla Walla, Penticton, and Fort Kamloops, they reached Lac La Hache in early May. While Sarah Julia and her daughters moved into the big cabin built the year before, Archie and his sons constructed several additional buildings, including a store and a substantial two-storey log dwelling. This became the 115 Mile House, where the McKinlay family remained for the next seventy-nine years, catering to the many travellers on the Cariboo Road.

The need for improvement in the lives of Native peoples in the Cariboo region had been brought to the attention of the colonial government by Gold Commissioner Philip H. Nind in the early 1860s.

A decade later, realizing that Archie McKinlay had been a resident of the Cariboo for many years, the government appointed him as Indian commissioner. An announcement to this effect appeared in the *Colonist* of 1876: "A. McKinlay, of Lac La Hache has been appointed Indian Commissioner for the region by the Provincial Government. As a pioneer of BC Mr. McKinlay has had the advantage of extensive acquaintance with the habits and wants of Indians."[5] In this capacity, Archibald McKinlay was, for many years, a wise and hard-working advocate for Native peoples in the Cariboo.

By 1864, when the first of Barnard's four-horse stagecoaches ran as far north as Soda Creek, McKinlay's 115 Mile House had gained an outstanding reputation for good meals and clean beds. On the ranch, where a herd of cattle was increasing, Archie and his sons butchered their own beef, providing meat for the roadhouse and for their store beside the Cariboo Road. During construction of the Collins Overland Telegraph Line through the Cariboo in 1865 and 1866, the McKinlays supplied bags of pemmican to the work parties. Composed of dried beef and wild berries, with a layer of melted fat poured over it, pemmican could be stored for long periods of time.

There were very few White women resident in the Cariboo before the 1870s. And George Sargison, who travelled the area in December 1871 to take over the management of Barnard's Express & Stage Line in Barkerville, obviously had an eye for the ladies, especially young Sarah McKinlay. In his diary, he mentioned the names of all the women he came across between Clinton and the 127 Mile House: "I saw Mrs. Isaac Saul [70 Mile], Mrs. Mard Nelson [100 Mile], Mrs. Thomas Roper [108 Mile], Mrs. Gannon [117 Mile], Mrs. McKinlay and her daughter Sarah — a fine girl of marriageable age! [115 Mile] and Mrs. Wright [127 Mile]."[6]

Once the 115 Mile Ranch had been fully developed, Archie McKinlay and his brother-in-law, Isaac Ogden, turned to training fine horses to run on the Lac La Hache racetrack, which was situated on part of the McKinlay ranch. During the many events held at the meets, when keen competition was provided by riders from Alkali Lake, Clinton, Ashcroft, Kamloops, and Merritt, the McKinlay and Ogden horses were the most frequent winners. The horseracing, a part of the annual Native games and potlatch held at Lac La Hache each summer, featured foot races, wrestling, and games of La Halle. Arthur Haddock, a stagecoach driver, recalled the huge crowds that gathered for the games in the early 1890s:

Following the races, and for many years, a dance, which usually lasted all week, took place in the 115 Mile House. In later years they were held in a community hall built across the road from the roadhouse. The crowd broke into three groups, so that at any one time there was always a group sleeping, another eating, and a third one dancing. The celebration would have lasted even longer, if the 45 gallon keg of "Scotland's Finest" had held out.[7]

In preparation for his retirement in the late 1870s, Archibald McKinlay applied to have his land at the 115 Mile Ranch surveyed in order to apply for a Crown grant. It was then that a ghastly fact came to light: the original pre-emption of 1862 had never been registered. At the time of staking, when both Archibald McKinlay and his neighbour, William Anderson, attempted to register their pre-emptions, the nearest government land agency was at Lillooet — a journey of several days. (At this time, government agent Philip Nind was no longer at Williams Lake, and the agency at Quesnelle Forks was in the process of re-organization.) Hearing that Judge Begbie was at Bridge Creek (100 milepost), where the assizes were being held, McKinlay and Anderson rode down with their applications and gave them to him. Although Begbie had endorsed them, they were never recorded. To make matters worse, McKinlay had never applied for a certificate of improvement, the next stage of the pre-emption process and a point at which the initial discrepancy might have been discovered. As it was, it took some time to unravel the problem before a Crown grant was issued to Archibald McKinlay on 17 October 1878. Comprised of approximately 700 acres, these lands became Lot 4, G.1., Lillooet.

During the early 1890s, Archibald and Sarah Julia retired from their ranch to spend their remaining years with their married daughter, Sarah Ferguson, at Savona, British Columbia. At this time, the 115 Mile Ranch was operated by Archie's sons, Archie Jr and Duncan (the latter having been born at Lac La Hache in 1864). In charge of the roadhouse was Archie Jr's wife, Mary McKinlay (nee Ogden).

By the late 1880s, when traffic increased dramatically on the Cariboo Road, the 115 Mile House was enlarged and renovated. In a floor plan submitted by Molly Forbes of Lac La Hache, the enlargement, which included a big barroom and ladies' sitting room on the main floor, with bedrooms above, filled the area between the original cabin and the two-storey roadhouse built in 1863.

Molly Forbes, who married Gilbert Forbes of the 122 Mile House, is known today for her written histories of the early residents of the Lac La Hache area. Born Molly Barton in Clinton in 1900, Molly was the schoolteacher at Lac La Hache in the 1920s. While boarding at the 115 Mile House, she came to know the McKinlay family and the roadhouse very well. On weekends, Molly was often left in charge of the little post office, and on Sundays she played the organ for the church service, which was held in the dining room of the road-house. One of the many stories written by Molly Forbes over the years tells of the stagecoach drivers' concerns for the safety of their passengers, as well as of the time the 115 Mile House almost burned down.

On this particular trip, the driver of the stage was Curly Flenner, and one of the passengers was Mike McCarthy, of the 137 Mile House. Mike was a gregarious Irishman, well-liked, and always good company — when he wasn't drinking. As he travelled north on the stage, from roadhouse to roadhouse, Mike had, as usual, tanked up at every stop and was starting to make a nuisance of himself. At the 83 Mile House, where proprietor Dave Stoddard was a discriminating barkeep, Mike was denied a drink. But that didn't stop him from acquiring a flask to cache in his overcoat pocket. The stage drivers objected strongly to transporting drunks, as they not only annoyed the other passengers but had been known to sue the stagecoach company when they fell out of the coach.

The 115 Mile House was the dinner stop on this particular cold winter's day, and, as the coach swung up to the door, the passengers were welcomed into the men's sitting room, where they warmed themselves before a roaring fire in the big drum heater. Mike was in good humour as he staggered off the stage; his little flask, he said, had kept him from freezing to death. But as he went to remove his big overcoat, he backed right into the heater, bringing the almost red-hot stovepipe crashing down, filling the room with smoke and spewing live coals all over the dry wooden floor. Had it not been winter, with lots of snow to throw on the fire, the roadhouse might have been lost that day. Of course Mike took no blame — the heater got in his way!

Following the death of Duncan McKinlay in 1939, McKinlay's ranch and roadhouse was sold in 1941 to George (Bordy) Felker. Twelve years later, when a fire destroyed the 115 Mile House on 24 February 1953, it destroyed an important Cariboo landmark— not only for travellers but also for the local community, which had many fond memories of events that had taken place in the nearly century-old roadhouse.

THE 117 MILE HOUSE
Lot 5, G.1., Lillooet

William Anderson, formerly of Lake Simcoe, Ontario, had been the purser on the *SS Colonel Moody*, a steamship that plied the waters of the lower Fraser River in 1859. In 1862, when the ship was sold to Captain John T. Wright Jr, Anderson lost his job; and, by the end of July, he was on his way north to pursue a very different occupation. As Sergeant John McMurphy of the Royal Engineers mentioned in his diary: "Mr. Anderson late Purser of the *Moody* passed up today for Cariboo, intends to start a House on the road side."[8]

The site chosen by Anderson was beside Lac La Hache, just two miles north of the McKinlay ranch, where he built a wayhouse beside the Cariboo Road. That fall, Anderson applied to pre-empt 160 acres of land, running from east to west along Lac La Hache. Among Anderson's first guests at his "Lac La Hache House," as he called it, were a group of Overlanders, including Richard H. Alexander, who had reached Quesnelle Mouth on 13 October 1862. Over a month late in reaching their destination down the Fraser River, the party had been given up for dead. At Quesnelle Mouth, the Overlanders found a note from Harry Handcock of the Redgrave party, advising them to leave immediately. The very next day they proceeded south on foot in an attempt to reach the Coast before winter.

In September 1864, the area's first post office opened at the 117 Mile House, and William Anderson was in charge. By 1867, he had sold his roadhouse farm to the Walters brothers, who also owned the 105 Mile House. When the Walters family left the Cariboo in 1870, they sold the 117 Mile House property to Patrick Gannon, a farmer who had several sons. Gannon was the postmaster at Lac La Hache in 1872, but, when financial and marital problems forced the Gannons out, the property became part of the assets of the Oppenheimer brothers, who obtained a Crown grant for Lot 5, G.1., Lillooet, in July 1882. During the 1920s, Burton Wright (son of John Wright of the 127 Mile House) lived with his wife and family at the 117 Mile House. In 1935, the property was sold to George (Bordy) Felker.

THE 118 MILE HOUSE
Lot 148, G.1., Cariboo

John Deddrick Felker (commonly known as Dick), the second son of Henry and Antonette Felker, settled at the 118 milepost on the Cariboo Road in 1884, at the time of his marriage. Some time after the death of his wife, Sophia O'Neil, Dick married Isobel Gauld in 1890. From this union seven children were born, five girls and two boys. The eldest of these was George (commonly known as Bordy), who took over the management of his parents' ranch while still in his late teens. Through his exceptional business ability and his practical experience, Bordy Felker became one of the Cariboo's most successful landowners. At the time of his death in 1956, his estate included more than 12,000 acres and over 1,000 head of cattle. Although there was never a road-house at the 118 milepost, this history has been included to illustrate how one man, with neither title nor inheritance, managed, through hard work and perseverance, to become one of the Cariboo's wealthiest and most respected citizens.

THE 121 MILE HOUSE

Operated by Annie Mortimer for the owner, Steven Tingley, during the early 1900s, the 121 Mile House was really more of a boarding house for the men who worked there, than a roadhouse. Following the sale of the 108 Mile Ranch to Captain Watson in 1900, Tingley moved his horses to the 121 Mile House, where he built one of the finest stables on the Cariboo Road. The 121 Mile House closed in 1912, when the property was purchased by Mr and Mrs George Forbes of the 122 Mile House.

THE 122 MILE HOUSE, 1865–1952
Lot 345, G.1., Cariboo

Having established the 83 Mile House in 1862 and the 93 Mile House in 1865, John and Thomas Walters (the Walters brothers) bought the 122 Mile House and ranch in the spring of 1867. As indicated on a map published in 1866 by the Western Union Telegraph Company, a roadhouse kept by a "Frenchman" was already in operation at the 122 milepost. The roadhouse, seen to be on the upper side of the Cariboo Road, and just south of a marked creek, stood there for the next ninety-odd years.

Constructed of enormous logs, cut on site, the two-storey roadhouse measured thirty by forty feet. Squared with a broadaxe and dove-tailed at the corners, each log stretched the full length of the building. Above these were pole rafters which supported the roof, upon which were hand cut cedar shakes. Certainly this site, close to a beautiful lake and with a free-flowing creek running through it, was a natural choice for early settlement. By 1870 the 122 Mile House had been sold to

Thomas Roper, brother of William Roper, who had established the 108 Mile House. Tom Roper and his wife, the former Nellie Newman Jones, were a very enterprising and hard-working pair. While Thomas bred fancy horses to compete in the races held at Barkerville, Williams Lake, and the Cornwall Ranch near Cache Creek, Nellie opened a boarding and day school. As an advertisement in the *Cariboo Sentinel* of November 1870 pointed out: "Boarding and Day School. Lac La Hache. At the late residence of Thomas Walters, Esq. For further particulars apply to the lady principal. School opens Nov. 1."[9] While Nellie's school did open, comments made in a later issue of the paper suggest that its enrolment was not large.

The Ropers left Lac La Hache in 1875 and headed for the Kamloops area, where they eventually settled on a ranch that had belonged to John Ussher, the provincial constable murdered by the McLean boys in 1879. For the next few years, the 122 Mile House was operated alternately by two brothers, Robert and James Starrett, who had the property Crown granted to them in 1878 as Lot 345, G.1., Cariboo. A year later it was sold to John D. Felker, who kept it until 1883, when he sold it to Thomas McDougall. Married in 1882, McDougall and his wife, the former Catherine McKinlay, had lived at Fort Alexandria for a few months before moving to the 122 Mile Ranch, where they operated the roadhouse until 1893. At that time, the need for a school forced the family to move to Clinton.

The next, and last, owners of the 122 Mile House were George Forbes, his wife Elizabeth, and their two young sons, who had arrived in Canada from Scotland in 1889. When William Allen, a land surveyor and owner of the 100 Mile House and ranch, was unable to handle both the ranch and his surveying business, he brought the Forbes family from overseas to manage the former for him. In 1893, when the 100 Mile Ranch was sold, George Forbes bought the 122 Mile House at Lac La Hache. The former owners, the McDougalls, had left a well-worked garden patch; and, with its fresh vegetables, milk, and meat, the Forbes roadhouse soon became known for serving fine meals.

In 1912, by which time George, Elizabeth, and their five children had outgrown their surroundings, George Forbes doubled the road-house facilities by adding a two-storey extension on to the north side of the building. This allowed for six extra bedrooms in the second storey, a larger dining room and kitchen, as well as two extra pantries on the main floor.

In 1919, when Ethel Slater arrived in the Cariboo by way of a motorized BC Express Company stage, she and her husband appreciated their overnight stay at the 122 Mile House: "After two days journey from the Chasm [59 Mile House] by car [BC Express Company], a trip complicated by pot holes, mudslides, and car sick passengers, we were rejuvenated by a pleasant night of blissful repose at the 122 Mile House and the kindness shown by the whole family living there."[10]

During the 1920s, the 122 Mile House was frequented by guests from every walk of life. The BX stage drivers and their passengers, politicians and premiers, the would-be gentry from the Chilcotin and their very English visitors, and even cranky old Judge Calder, (a provincial court judge who held court in various locations in the district between 100 Mile House and Williams Lake) would all travel far into the night to reach this home away from home. The fastidious were always sure of clean sheets and good room service, which included lots of hot water and clean towels for washing up in the jug and basin found on every bedroom washstand. Each guest received the best treatment the house could offer, and only the delicate and indisposed were shown special favours. Premier John Oliver learned this lesson when he and his entourage stopped by for dinner one day. Following a most adequate meal, the premier was about to help himself to a couple of inviting looking apples for his afternoon snack, when he was told by the dining-room staff that the rules of the house were "to eat all one desired, but to pocket nothing."[11] Despite the decline of roadhouses during the 1930s, the 122 Mile House was one of the last to close. For a short time, it catered to holiday guests from the Coast, but when this no longer paid, the roadhouse closed. In an article pointing out the changing scene in the Lac La Hache Valley of 1935, historian Louis LeBourdais wrote: "Today at the 122 Mile a gasoline pump has taken the place of the watering trough, and tennis and badminton courts have replaced the vacant space where in earlier days freighters and swampers played their barnyard golf."[12]

In 1952, when changes to Highway 97 made it necessary either to move or to destroy the old roadhouse, it was suggested that the building might be used as a museum in Williams Lake. Unfortunately, the necessary funds were never raised, and the 122 Mile House was eventually demolished.

Like many Cariboo settlers, Henry George Felker had not quenched his thirst for gold in California. Antonette Felker is wearing a gold nugget around her neck, garnered in the California 1849 Gold Rush.
(Courtesy Dolly Petrowitz)

127 MILE HOUSE, 1862–1983
Lot 216, G.1., Lillooet

Seeking social freedom and business opportunity in the United States, Henry George Felker left Hanover, Germany, in 1848. Accompanying him was his young wife Antonette, his mother Mary, and two brothers. Upon their arrival in New York early in 1849, they heard of the gold rush taking place in California. Although it was known to be a long and dangerous journey, the family became part of a large wagon train leaving for the west that spring. Leader of the expedition was the legendary Kit Carson, who escorted the party safely through several Native attacks and much adversity. It was November before the Felkers reached St Louis, Missouri, the jumping-off point for the West. Anticipating the imminent arrival of her first child, Antonette and her mother-in-law remained in St Louis, while Henry and his brothers continued on to California. Although Henry made several trips back and forth to visit his family, it was four years before Antonette; her mother-in-law; the three children, George Henry, John Deddrick; and a baby daughter, Johanna, reached California.

The Felker brothers did extremely well in the goldfields, but, as they were a long distance from the nearest bank, they had to keep their gold with them and hide it from the marauders who frequented the gold camps. Empty coal-oil cans were chosen as inconspicuous containers, but apparently even they were not safe. Alone in camp one day, Henry's mother, armed with a loaded shotgun, single-handedly saved the family fortune from two strangers who were about to make off with it. As the best of the gold ran out and the population dwindled, the Felker family came to another turning point.

By spring of 1858, thousands of prospectors were leaving California for the Fraser River — a long, hard journey north into British territory — and Henry Felker, the gold seeker, was among them. This time he went alone, leaving his family with his brothers, who had taken up permanent residence in California. A year later, when Henry returned, it was to move his family to Yale, British Columbia, where, in 1861, he pre-empted 160 acres on a small creek half a mile south of the gold-rush town. While Henry mined, his mother and Antonette operated a store.

By spring of 1862, with reports of rich gold finds in the Cariboo region, the Felker family, now with four children, moved north once more. They travelled more than 200 miles to just beyond Lac La Hache, where they set up a blue and white striped army tent close to a sizeable creek. Here they resided and kept a saloon until the building of a permanent log roadhouse on land which, for many years, was known as the Blue Tent Ranch. In a faded old photograph belonging to the William Wright family, the original Felker roadhouse appears to have been a substantial two-storey log "square," with dove-tailed corners and a fairly sharp shake roof. A full-length, flat-roofed porch over the front entrance doubled as a verandah on the upper storey, where a door had been built between two windows.

Henry Felker's original pre-emption at the 127 milepost, recorded in January 1863, described the first 160 acres as "situated one mile north of Lac La Hache," which later became Lot 216, G.1., Lillooet.[12] As they grew up, the several Felker children helped with the operation of the roadhouse and with the many ranch chores. Eight-year-old Johanna, the eldest daughter, was not to be outdone by her older brothers. Harry Guillod, a young Englishman who had returned from the goldfields in the fall of 1862, described in his diary an incident with the Felker family:

We had a decided piece of amusement here in watching the reduction of a refractory cow, which after a race in which all the family joined, was finally lassoed, after escaping out of the enclosure several times in a most determined manner. I was most amused at one little girl about nine years old who certainly displayed more "cow" courage than many young men fresh from London would have done, meeting the animal with undaunted spirit on its attempts to clear the hurdles.[13]

In addition to establishing a popular roadhouse at this site, by 1864 the Felkers were also operating a dairy, where milk, butter, and cheese were produced and then transported by Henry to the markets on Williams Creek. During one of these trips, in the early summer of 1864, that Henry Felker became involved in a quarrel with a man named Bible in a saloon in Richfield. Bible was stabbed and later died; and Henry Felker was arrested on a charge of attempted murder. A year later, in June 1865, when Felker came to trial in Judge Begbie's court, the jury deliberated for only ten minutes before bringing in a verdict of not guilty. Begbie was angered at the verdict and chastised Felker: "There could be no moral doubt of your guilt, and every man in the court and on the Creek knows it ... but, as you have been found by a verdict not guilty, you are discharged. I do not wish to see you before me again, therefore go, and sin no more."[14] In spite of his public disapproval, in his private report to the Colonial Secretary, Begbie, albeit with resignation, accepted the outcome of Felker's trial:

The jury was a good one I thought, many of them I know personally as very trustworthy men, and I left it to them as a perfectly plain case — however, there is an end to it; cows, butter and milk will be plentiful on the Creek, for these are the articles Felker deals in and supplies. He is an energetic man, and I think he will keep out of rows for the future.[15]

But Begbie was wrong, Felker would not be supplying "the Creek" with his dairy products — at least not for some time. While the murder trial itself had put an awful strain on the Felker family, the situation was intensified when, awaiting trial, Henry lost the 127 Mile Ranch to E. T. Dodge & Company (the freighting company which held his mortgage). Following these disastrous events, and true to his gambling nature, Henry Felker decided on a way out of his dilemma. Hearing of a recent gold strike in Montana, he and his wife and five children left the Cariboo and made the long trek south. Somewhere on the overland route between Boise City and Salt Lake, a fourth son, William Philip, was born to Antonette and Henry Felker. It was almost two years before the family returned to the Cariboo.

Following its foreclosure of the Felker property, E. T. Dodge & Company leased the roadhouse to William Henderson until the spring of 1867, at which time the ranch was purchased by William Wright, formerly of Hamilton, Ontario. Wright had visited the Cariboo gold-fields in 1862, and, on 12 January 1863, he had filed a pre-emption application in Lillooet for "160 acres of land at Lac La Hache between the pre-emptions of W. Anderson and H. Felker."[16] This very ambiguous description referred to land somewhere around the 122 milepost. Following his sojourn to the goldfields, Wright returned east, surfacing once more in early 1867, this time with a family. William, a widower with a twelve-year-old son named John, had married Catherine Pratt, a widow with a grown son named David.

On purchasing the 127 Mile Ranch and roadhouse Wright lost no time in advertising the facilities:

BLUE TENT or 127 MILE HOUSE.
The undersigned having purchased this desirable property,
is now prepared to accommodate the travelling public.
The table is supplied with the very best of viands.
The bedrooms and beds are as comfortable as could be desired.
The Bar contains nothing but the best brands of Liquor and Cigars.
A good stock of grain & hay always on hand.
May 3rd., 1867. William Wright.[17]

During the mid-1860s, when Charles M. Beak, the early cattleman at the 108 Mile House, began to develop a market for the sale of beef and dairy products in Barkerville, he had the cooperation of several ranchers in the Lac La Hache Valley. Among these were William Wright and his son John, David Pratt, John Salmon, and John Walters. He also employed a young Irishman named Michael McCarthy, even though the latter did not at this time own any land at Lac La Hache. Between the several beef and dairy herds maintained by these men at the 105 Mile, 108 Mile, the 127 Mile, and the 137 Mile ranches, Beak was able to supply his retail outlets at Barkerville.

Following the death of William Wright on 7 July 1870 in Victoria, his wife Catherine sold the Blue Tent Ranch to her stepson John Wright and to her son David Pratt, who formed a partnership under the title Wright & Pratt. This arrangement was dissolved by July 1871 due to a quarrel. As in many family businesses, especially those in which step-mothers and stepbrothers are concerned, there was a certain lack of trust. In this case, John Wright did not trust his father's second wife. Wright sold his half interest in the 127 Mile Ranch to Michael McCarthy and bought John Salmon's land at the 137 milepost.

In early 1873, David Pratt made a trip back east where he was married. He returned with his bride to the Blue Tent Ranch in June of the same year. Shortly after this, Pratt purchased the 100 Mile Ranch from Charles Beak, using his interest in the 127 Mile Ranch as part payment. When Pratt and his wife moved to take up residence at the 100 Mile Ranch, Beak sold his remaining share in the 127 Mile Ranch to Michael McCarthy. A year later, in Clinton, McCarthy was married to Anna (Johanna), daughter of Henry and Antonette Felker, on 20 August 1876.

With the death of David Pratt in 1880, a general settlement of accounts and property was agreed to by Pratt's heirs and Charles Beak, who had left the Cariboo for the Nicola country in 1878. At this time, Michael McCarthy and John Wright exchanged properties. Apparently, Anna McCarthy wished to live closer to her parents, the Felkers, who had by this time settled at the 144 Mile Ranch.

And so it was in September 1880, just following the McCarthy-Wright exchange, that Sarah Crease and her husband found the Wrights at the 127 Mile House. In her diary of 13 September, Sarah made an extremely cruel assessment of the facilities:

Stopped the night at the "Blue Tent," a wretched, dirty, dilapidated House — and poor miserable looking young wife, with dirty barefoot children. Swept out our wretched bedroom after our hostess had, as she said "fixed things up." Removed the blankets and used our own. Henry caught some trout for supper. Bread and butter good. No sugar in the House. Dairy only decent. Wright the husband young and active looking.[18]

Obviously, Sarah was not aware of the fact that the Wrights had only just moved in and were not responsible for the sad condition of the roadhouse. A few weeks later, on her way south, Sarah's remarks were much kinder, albeit still rather condescending:

Stopped the night at "Blue Tent," 127 Mile House. Found a great improvement in the appearance of things. Poor little Mrs. Wright had done her best to make herself, the children, and the place, clean and comfortable ... Had a good supper, and fire in the bedroom, which was quite respectable this time.[19]

Through many years of changing economic conditions, John Wright, his wife Alice, and their twelve children continued to operate the 127 Mile House and ranch. Only once, just before the turn of the century, did the 127 Mile House come up in a tax sale, when the property was held for a short time by James Reid and William Webster of Quesnel. At this time, the property was Crown granted. In 1904, when the original roadhouse burned to the ground, it took with it Wright's cash reserve of $3,000. A second house burned down during the First World War. The present residence is an example of one of the Cariboo's earliest mail-order houses. Purchased in 1914 from the T. Eaton Company of Winnipeg, the components were shipped by rail to Ashcroft and then transported by wagon to the 127 Mile Ranch, where they were assembled by James Sutherland.

When John Wright died in 1916, Alice Wright and her children continued on with the family business. By the late 1920s, the need for roadhouse accommodations in the Lac La Hache Valley had all but disappeared. Of the six girls in the family, it was Gertrude, the youngest, who remained at home to care for her mother and who later inherited the property. During the 1930s, Gertrude married William Dingwall, who had been foreman at the 127 Mile Ranch for many years. In May 1940 a sister of Gertrude's, May Downie, and her husband Thomas, bought the adjoining 130 Mile Ranch and joined forces with the Dingwalls to form the Wright Cattle Company. In 1983, after over 120 years of continual operation, the 127 Mile Ranch was sold to Wendall Monical of the 105 Mile Ranch.

THE 132 MILE RANCH
Lot 146, G.1., Lillooet

For many years, the area of what became the 132 Mile Ranch was used as pasture by early settlers; it was also used by the BC Express Company, which operated a horse ranch and stage depot between the 132 and 134 mileposts. In April 1889, when Anthony S. Ulrich pre-empted 320 acres of land at the 132 milepost, he built a two-storey addition onto an existing cabin. Ulrich and his wife, the former Louisa Antonette Felker, had several children, all of whom attended the North Lac La Hache School with the Forbes and Wright children. Although they kept the BX Stage horses in a large barn built by Ulrich in the 1890s, the family did not operate a roadhouse. A Crown grant on Lot 146, G.1., Lillooet, was issued to Anthony Ulrich in 1901. In 1916, when the Ulrich family sold their ranch to the Enterprise Cattle Company, they moved to Ashcroft and opened a store. With the failure of the Enterprise Cattle Company ten years later, land at the 132 milepost was sold again, this time to Harry Wright, who, in turn, traded it to his brother Ernest. Today, Wilfred Wright, son of Ernest and Enid Wright, resides at the 132 Mile Ranch.

THE 134 MILE HOUSE AND RANCH, 1862–1920S
Lots 1 and 2, G.3., Lillooet

One hundred and sixty acres of land "situated 6 miles north of Lac La Hache" was first pre-empted in October 1862 by Peter Eddy, an Englishman. Accompanied by his wife Elizabeth, Eddy had travelled north by way of Lillooet and Pavilion Mountain just as the Cariboo Road was being built. This may have been the same couple who appear in Harry Guillod's diary of 17 July 1862, in which he mentions meeting

> a middle aged lady ... who had come out [from England] with her husband to open a House of refreshment in Cariboo; they were going up with a pack train, but she had started on before, by herself, to reach the next House ... When we caught up with her she was trudging along leading her mule, showing a very fine pair of legs, red petticoat, etc., although minus a crinoline ... a hat and feather completed her costume.[20]

By the following summer, having established a roadhouse and the beginnings of a ranch, the Eddys pre-empted a further 320 acres of adjoining land. Among those who came by their ranch that year was Captain John Evans, who, with his party of twenty-six Welshmen, was camped nearby. In the diary of Harry Jones, we read of the "big log house owned by an Englishman named Eddy. He was an interesting and learned old gentleman and he and Captain talked for hours that evening."[21]

The "big log house" built by Peter Eddy was a fine example of a European log house. Having a single storey, a sharp overhanging roof, and an attic containing three gabled windows, the house stood on a knoll facing the Cariboo Road. Two chimneys, one at each end of the roof, were probably built of bricks which came from Pinchbeck's kilns at Williams Lake. Obviously, from the size of the building, the Eddys had expected the steady flow of traffic on the Cariboo Road to continue forever. But this was not to be.

Within the next three years, the decline of the Cariboo gold rush took its toll. By 1866, the Eddys were deep in debt, with their assets seized and sold under warrant by the high sheriff of the Cariboo, Peter O'Reilly. Actually, it was O'Reilly's deputy, Mr Gompertz at Williams Lake, who conducted the sale. That fall, Peter Eddy sued O'Reilly for allowing his goods to be sold at far less than their real value. At the trial, the jury ruled in favour of Eddy but was overruled by Judge Begbie because it could not be proven that Gompertz was acting on behalf of O'Reilly. Shortly after this, John Robson, editor of the *British Columbian*, printed a letter accusing Begbie of committing a "gross invasion" of the jury's function. By fall 1866, Peter and Elizabeth Eddy had moved to Barkerville, where they leased Jacob Mundorf's Miner's Bakery & Restaurant.

By May 1867, Francis J. Barnard, owner of Barnard's Express & Stage Line, had made application for land "previously pre-empted by Mr. Eddy" and there established a horse ranch and stage depot. While it was never again used by the general public, the 134 Mile House was mentioned in the diaries and accounts of those employed by the express service. In 1871, George Sargison, agent for Barnard's Express at Barkerville, mentioned eating bread and butter "in Morrison's cabin" at the 134 Mile Ranch; and in the early 1900s, Willis West, general manager of the BC Express Company, mentioned the 134 Mile House, where there was a telegraph key.[22] In 1905, while James Leighton was superintendent of the BC Express Company, the 134 Mile House was sold to David A. Stoddard of the 83 Mile House. Stoddard hired John Ross and his family to operate the ranch, which still functioned as a stage depot for mail carriers.

By 1916, the 134 Mile Ranch had become part of the assets of the Enterprise Cattle Company, a cooperative formed by John P. Murphy of the 141 Mile Ranch and Senator F.S. Barnard of Victoria. When John Murphy, the driving force behind the venture, died in 1918, the 134 Mile Ranch once again passed into private hands. Following many years of use by successive owners, Peter Eddy's large, two-storey log roadhouse at the 134 milepost burned to the ground in 1960.

THE 137 MILE HOUSE AND RANCH, 1866–1970S
Lot 218, G.1., Lillooet

John Salmon, who arrived in the Cariboo during the 1860s, was the first to pre-empt land "situated between the 137 and 138 mileposts on the Lillooet/Alexandria wagon road," for which he received a certificate of improvement in 1867.[23] A cabin located at this site in 1866 was not known to be a roadhouse.

By 1871, John Wright, who was still a partner in Charles Beak's cattle and dairy enterprise, had purchased the 137 Mile Ranch, where he lived and worked as a dairy farmer. He was still there in 1874, a year before his marriage to Alice, the seventeen-year-old daughter of William Rowebottom, a sapper in the Royal Engineers. Three children were born to John and Alice Wright at the 137 Mile Ranch prior to the land "swap" in 1880, when the McCarthys exchanged ranches with the Wrights.

Once settled at the 137 Mile Ranch, Michael McCarthy and his wife Anna had a family of nine children, and, consequently, had need of the substantial log house built beside the Cariboo Road in the 1870s. While the McCarthys were not known to have catered to stage-coach passengers, their house became a popular way station for teamsters on the wagon road. The McCarthys were a fun-loving family, much given to partying; in fact, it was due to their love of dancing that a community hall was built at Lac La Hache, where Mike became known as the most popular square dance caller in the Cariboo. Very popular also were the daughters of the family, who were described as good looking, beautiful dancers.

For over thirty years the McCarthy family farmed and served the public at the 137 Mile House. When Anna McCarthy died in childbirth in 1893, the daughters carried on as hostesses at the house, until, one by one, they left to be married. At this time, with his wife and most of his children gone, Mike McCarthy prepared the property for sale. Crown granted in November 1904, the surveyed land of the 137 Mile Ranch became Lot 218 of the Lillooet District. Some years later, with the departure of his youngest daughter Anne, Mike McCarthy, the gregarious Irishman, also left home to take a trip back to St John, New Brunswick, the place of his birth in 1849. Upon being unable to find even one familiar face in St John, he took the first train heading west and returned to the Cariboo.

Mike McCarthy died at his home in the winter of 1915 and, according to one source, was buried standing up. As the grave diggers worked through the frozen ground to make a hole long enough and deep enough to hold the coffin in the usual position, they encountered a very large boulder lying horizontally along the line of the hole; in fact, it occupied most of the required space. Rather than attempt another hole in such extreme temperatures, they placed the coffin vertically in the one they had already dug.

Following the death of Mike McCarthy, the lands of the 137 Mile Ranch became part of the assets of the Enterprise Cattle Company. And, when this company failed, the property once again fell into private hands, serving as a residence to Clem Wright, Jack Wright, Bordy Felker, and Bill Downie. Leo Chenier, who purchased the ranch in 1972, owned it for only part of a year; but, during that time, he made two extensive additions to the old house. The next owners, Gerald and

Barbara Fisher, soon completed the renovations. The 137 Mile House of today contains three bathrooms, a luxury never dreamed of by the freight drivers of the 1880s.

THE 141 MILE HOUSE, 1861–1930S
Lots 8 and 9, G.4., Cariboo

Denis Murphy and his brother William, two young men from County Cork, Ireland, left home in the 1850s and headed for California, where the gold rush of 1849 was almost over. Upon word of new discoveries on the Fraser River in 1858, the Murphy brothers joined a party of prospectors and travelled overland to Bellingham, in Washington Territory. Here they built rowboats to transport them across the Strait of Georgia to British Columbia. While mining near Yale with his partner Frank J. Barnard, Denis Murphy pre-empted 160 acres of land at China Bar in November 1861.

As the gold discoveries progressed upriver into the Interior, so did Denis Murphy and his companions. But Murphy was not really a miner — to him, gold was only the means to secure a homestead where he could settle down with a girl he had met in California. So it was on 10 April 1862 that Denis Murphy, with three partners, pre-empted 640 acres of adjoining land, situated on the third creek (then known as Lower, or Little Deep Creek,) below Williams Lake.

One of the earliest references to Murphy's roadhouse and farm is found in a diary kept by James Thomson of Edwardsburgh, Upper Canada. Thomson, with two companions, was departing from the Cariboo on 24 September 1862. Starting at 9:00 a.m. from "Davidson's"

141 Mile House was built by Denis Murphy, 1870. (COURTESY BCARS)

Denis Murphy of 141 Mile House and Mrs. Denis Murphy, nee Ellen White.
(COURTESY BCARS)

(which became the 150 milepost), they "took dinner at Irishmans," and "got mutton for [the] frying pan" at Denis Murphy's roadhouse.[24] Fourteen miles further on, they reached the Blue Tent Ranch, where, tired out, they slept on the floor.

Sergeant John McMurphy of the Royal Engineers, while overseeing the work of building the Cariboo Road in April 1863, also mentions "Murphy's at Deep Creek," the name of present-day Knife Creek. In August of that year, "Murphy's House" became associated with the well documented murder of Thomas Clegg, a trusted employee of E. T. Dodge & Company of Lillooet.[25] Thomas Clegg was buried beside the road, close to where he fell; and for years after, the freighters piled rocks on the grave, until it became a cairn to the memory of the brave young man who died so violently. Although the cairn is almost gone, the site of Clegg's grave may still be seen, beside the original wagon road, halfway up the first hill south of the 141 Mile Ranch. On two occasions, when the route of Highway 97 was being changed, the British Columbia Department of Highways carefully avoided the demolition of this historic site, which today is more or less hidden.

Denis Murphy married his sweetheart, Ellen White, a farm girl from New York state, shortly after establishing his ranch in 1862; and by April 1865, he had become the proud father of two sons. With the commencement of Barnard's stagecoach service to Soda Creek in 1864, Murphy's House at the 141 milepost became a regular passenger stop, where meals were served at all hours. Murphy's House was first advertised in the *Cariboo Sentinel* of 14 October 1865, where "good food and good beds." were guaranteed. By 1870, with increased business on the road, the original log cabin had been replaced by a large, two-storey log house containing fourteen rooms. Across the front of the house a covered porch shaded the several downstairs rooms, while in the sharp roof, four gabled windows looked out on the road and the San Jose River valley. Later, during the early 1900s, the exterior of the house was covered with lumber siding and painted white. Following a survey of his property at the 141 milepost, a Crown grant was issued to Denis Murphy in November of 1870, when these lands became lots 8 and 9, G.4., Lillooet.

While neither Denis nor Ellen Murphy had themselves received advanced education, they were determined to see that their children were given every opportunity to do so. In 1866, with two sons to educate, Denis Murphy was instrumental in the acquisition of land near Williams Lake, on which the Oblate Fathers of the Roman Catholic Church had built schools for the children of the Cariboo. During their early years, the five Murphy children all attended school at St Joseph's Mission. Later, John, the second son, remained on the ranch to work with his father. However, Mary (the only girl); William, the eldest son (who became an ordained Oblate Father); Denis (who became the Honourable Mr Justice Murphy); and James (who also became a barrister)

John and Margaret Murphy outside their 141 Mile Road House, c. 1890s.
(COURTESY BCARS)

all went on to attend college and university in Eastern Canada. John Murphy, who eventually inherited the ranch, made many sacrifices, including delaying his marriage, to help his father finance the education of his sister and brothers. It was not until after his father's death in 1896 that John married Margaret Cameron, formerly of Cornwall, Ontario, on 30 June 1900. Three children were born, and they, too, were well-educated.

In the meantime, the tradition of roadhouse keeping at the 141 Mile Ranch continued on into the 1900s. In 1910, while Roddy Moffat of Alexandria was freighting on the road to Ashcroft, he became acquainted with Margaret Murphy (better known as "Mrs Johnny Murphy"), who hosted "stoppers". Roddy recalled Margaret as "a very large woman, and an avid gambler who used to skin the stoppers." An account of the 141 Mile "Enterprise" Ranch in 1912 described the buildings, which included "the house of two storeys and fourteen rooms, stables for 40 horses, cattle sheds, a granary, a dairy, an ice house, two bunkhouses for single men, and three small dwelling houses for married men."[26] Also mentioned were the 2,500 acres of land and the advanced methods of irrigation employed by John Murphy, who was the organizer of a small cooperative union involving several local ranchers. Such were the beginnings of the short-lived Enterprise Cattle Company, formed a few years before John Murphy's untimely death in 1918. In 1935, Louis LeBourdais of Quesnel described recent changes at the 141 Mile House: "The 141 recently purchased from Mr. and Mrs. Angus McLaughlan, by the Mayfield family of Oregon, has changed hands several times in the past twenty years."[27]

THE 144 MILE HOUSE, 1867–1964
Lot 28, G.1., Cariboo

Following an absence of nearly two years, the Felker family returned to the Cariboo early in 1867. Henry, the avid gold seeker, had done well in both Montana and Utah; but when the gold ran out, his family insisted on returning to British Columbia and the beautiful countryside of the Lac La Hache Valley. Reference to a pre-emption or purchase of land by the Felkers has not been found for this area; however, it appears that the family settled on open land, part of the late widow Jones's ranch at Mile 145 on the Cariboo Road.

On her arrival back in the Cariboo, Henry's wife Antonette swore she would never move again. By this time, there were six children — two of whom were almost grown. A seventh and last child, Emma, was yet to be born, but this time Antonette would give birth in comparative comfort, in her own home, attended, as she always was, by Henry's mother. Mary Felker, bold defender of the family fortune in California, remained with Henry and his family through thick and thin, until her death in December 1885.

The stopping house, built close to the wagon road by Henry and his sons George and John, was similar to their first home at the 127 milepost, only it was larger (fourteen rooms). In some ways it resembled Murphy's House, but had only three gabled windows in the upper storey. Also, like Murphy's House, the exterior of the Felker house was later covered with lumber siding and painted white.

Once the house was built and the family settled, Henry Felker was seldom home; he was usually either in California, where his two brothers lived, or off on another mining venture somewhere. He died at home on 3 June 1894 and was buried beside his mother in St Joseph's Mission Cemetery just south of Williams Lake.

As the younger Felker children grew up and attended the mission schools, George and John remained at home to work on the ranch. At the roadhouse, Antonette and her daughters cooked and cleaned, accommodating overnight teamsters and travellers on the road. By the 1890s, all the children but Will and the youngest girl, Emma, were gone from home; they had either married or taken up homesteads of their own in the neighbouring countryside.

William Philip Felker married Fanny Leach in 1899 but died in 1902. Ghost stories still abound near the ranch he built at 144 Mile. His grave is at St Joseph's Mission. (COURTESY DOLLY PETROWITZ)

Emma Allan Felker married Joe Bellmond and lived at Quesnel Forks
where they mined for a few years. She once owned the Clinton Hotel.
Her children are William Emile and Dora Antonette Bellmond.
Emma is buried at Port Alberni. (COURTESY DOLLY PETROWITZ)

William Philip Felker, born in a covered wagon on the trail between Boise City and Salt Lake in 1866, was still a bachelor living at home in the late 1890s when he fell ill and was found to have cancer. While recuperating from an operation in Victoria in the winter of 1898, Will met Fanny Leech, a musically talented, spoilt, and amazingly versatile young woman. The Felker family was also musical, and so Fanny and Will found some common ground. They were married on Boxing Day, 1899, and left town soon afterwards for the Cariboo and the 144 Mile House.

At home on the ranch, Fanny found it hard to like her mother-in-law, whom she found earthy and domineering. Will's mother also disapproved of Fanny's Bohemian ways. As hostilities between the two women worsened, Will and Fanny moved to a small house down the road. Here Fanny had two sons in quick succession, and Will grew ill once more. Following a second operation, Will returned to his mother's house, where he died in an upstairs bedroom in December 1902.[28] Naturally, Fanny was devastated, but the ordeal may have been even harder on Antonette, who passed away a year later in November of 1903. This left only George Felker, who lived and worked at the 144 Mile Ranch until his death in 1923. Many years later, George's son Harry, while occupying an upstairs bedroom in the roadhouse where his Uncle Will had died so long before, claimed to have seen two ghosts — not just once, but on numerous occasions. Sometimes it was Will, his tall, emaciated form wandering along the upstairs corridor; at other times it was Antonette, her warm breath brushing George's cheek as he lay in bed. As the years went by, the stories of the Felker ghosts became more numerous and more fantastic. Finally, despite the ghosts (or perhaps because of them), the Felkers sold their ranch in 1948 to Orville Fletcher, a local rancher. On 22 January 1964, while occupied by Fletcher's son-in-law, a fire that started in the chimney of the old roadhouse soon engulfed the whole building. The Felker ghosts and ninety-seven years of Cariboo history all went up in smoke.

MRS JONES'S HOUSE, TOM JONES'S RANCH
145 Mile House, Cariboo Road, 1861–67
Lot 44, G.1., Cariboo

Among the earliest of the roadhouses between Lac La Hache and Williams Lake was "Mrs. Jones's House," located on the upper side of a sizeable creek flowing into the San Jose River. This became the 145 milepost when the wagon road was built in 1863. Tom Jones, a Welshman, and his Irish wife had settled there sometime in 1861, and by the next year had established a roadhouse farm. The land on which the Joneses settled did not appear to have been purchased or pre-empted, so they were, technically speaking, squatters. Within a year, however, Tom Jones was dead. This information is found in the memoirs of another Welshman, Harry Jones, who passed up the Cariboo Road in 1863. Many years later, and with the assistance of Louis LeBourdais, Harry wrote of his long walk to the Cariboo and his encounter with Mrs Jones. To Harry, who spoke only a few words of English, it was a delight to find someone who understood him. Still very upset at the recent loss of her husband, Mrs Jones was unable to speak of it without weeping: "When I married Tom," she explained, "that made me half Welsh. Now that Tom is dead, I am all Welsh. He was very fond of reading his Welsh bible, and I used to read it too — although I could not understand it all."[29]

In spite of her great loss, Mrs Jones carried on with her roadhouse and ranch until her death in 1867. Buried close to her home overlooking the beautiful San Jose Valley, her grave was still in evidence in 1981. Following Mrs Jones's death, the land lay open for many years and was used as pasture by neighbouring ranchers. Among these were the Felkers, who had settled close by at the 144 milepost in 1867, the year of Mrs Jones's death. Many years later, in 1919, William Bellmond, whose mother was Emma Allen Felker, pre-empted and settled on Lot 44, the site of Mrs Jones's roadhouse. During the early 1950s, the Bellmonds sold the property to Orville Fletcher of the 144 Mile House. During an on-site inspection in June 1981, Mrs Bellmond mentioned that a white picket fence had been built around Mrs Jones's grave by members of the local community, who looked upon it as a historic landmark. On visiting the site a few months later, the grave was gone. Apparently Mr Fletcher had sold Lot 44, part of which was subdivided, and, in building an access road into the area, the bulldozers had gone right through the middle of Mrs Jones's grave.

THE 150 MILE HOUSE, 1862–1916
Davidson's Lake Valley Ranch and Roadhouse
Lots 11, 12, 13, and 14, G.1., Cariboo

Anticipating the sale of his Mission Creek farm and roadhouse at Williams Lake in 1861, Thomas Davidson began to acquire land and to develop a ranch near the head of Williams Lake. One of the earliest indications of this development is seen on Judge Begbie's map of November 1861, where a "camp" is marked at approximately the site of Davidson's "Lake Valley Ranch," as he named it. For the first year, Davidson lived in a tent, in which he also operated a store and a saloon. By 1863, he had accumulated nearly 2,000 acres in the vicinity, 175 of which were already under cultivation. To assist him in this enterprise, and to construct various buildings, Davidson hired a crew of sixteen men. Among these were five members of a group known as the "Cardinel Men" from Edwardsburgh, Upper Canada, known today as Cardinal, Ontario. These men, having tried mining and been unsuccessful, were seeking employment in order to finance their journey home. On leaving Quesnelle Forks on 17 July 1862, James Thomson and his four companions hiked south past Beaver Lake and Round Tent to Deep Creek, where they had dinner. From there they took the "new trail" which Davidson had blazed that summer and which led them to his Lake Valley Ranch. In a letter written a week later to his wife, Thomson explained:

> *Got here on Saturday night, staid [sic] over Sunday and on Monday morning took a job of building a clay oven for Mr. Davidson, proprietor of a Farm, Store & Tavern. He is newly settled here and is doing business in a large tent. Is now preparing to build a House and we will furnish the Lumber & Shingles.*[30]

Davidson's roadhouse, a very large, two-storey log building, sat close to Valley Creek on the rise of ground above today's Highway 97, at the northwest corner of the present community of 150 Mile House. By 18 September 1862, Thomson and his associates had completed their contract, earning between them a total of $588.22. On receiving their pay the Cardinel Men moved on.

In October 1863, when Lord Milton and Dr W. B. Cheadle remained for a few days at "Davidson's," the roadhouse was described as "a large square unfinished house billiard room, and lots of geese, ducks, and chickens. All kinds of vegetables. Mr. Davidson was very kind and hospitable."[31]

Although Milton and Cheadle were not generally impressed with the accommodations at most of the roadhouses they encountered, they declared the Lake Valley Ranch to be one of the best in British Columbia. Davidson was also said to have had some "good stock" on his ranch, brought in from Oregon by cattlemen Jerome Harper and the Jeffries brothers. Travelling by way of the Okanagan, the journey took several weeks, allowing for many stops along the way. One of these was Davidson's ranch, where the animals rested for a few days before being driven on to Harper's slaughter house on Williams Creek. Harper's partner in the firm of Harper & Tormey Wholesale Meat Distributors Company was Edward Tormey, a butcher from San Francisco. Tormey had mined in the Cariboo in the earliest days of the gold rush and, after amassing a fortune, established butcher shops in

The original buildings at 150 Mile House were built in 1862, followed by the store a year later. This house was destroyed by fire in 1916. [COURTESY BCARS]

Barkerville, Quesnelle Forks, and Quesnelle Mouth. While associated with
Harper, Tormey had often stayed at Davidson's ranch, and recognized
its potential value.

Certainly, by 1863, Thomas Davidson had achieved his ambition
— to create a much larger and even more successful roadhouse farm
than that which he had started in 1860 at Mission Creek (Williams
Lake.) By 1864, however, Davidson found himself in serious financial
trouble. For one thing, he hadn't counted on the economic slump that had
begun to show its effects in the latter part of 1863. Even more serious
were the repercussions of his association with G. B. Wright and the
Cariboo Road scandal that year. As his financial position worsened,
Davidson, who had borrowed money in the form of a mortgage from
Edward Tormey, fled the country in the spring of 1864. He had also
been in debt to Wright, who wrote to his lawyer Henry Crease, advising
him: "I have a bill of about $600 against T. W. Davidson, which has
accrued from freight on goods, etc., etc. Davidson has left the country,
and may not return."[32]

While the change in ownership at the 150 Mile Ranch had little
effect on its operations, the arrival of the Collins Overland Telegraph
Line in 1865 brought about enormous communication advances to the
Cariboo roadhouses, including the 150 Mile House, where the telegraph
key was located in a little room just off the store. With increasing
demands for cattle and livestock in the Cariboo, Edward Tormey and his
associates, Jerome Harper and Benjamin Von Volcanburgh, built up a
sizeable business at the 150 Mile House during the 1860s. However, in
June 1869, a fire completely destroyed the slaughterhouse and tannery
near Barkerville. The resulting financial setback may have been
responsible for the sale of the roadhouse. While retaining the land,
Tormey sold the facility in August 1869 to Samuel Adler and Thomas
Barry, former owners of the Gazelle Saloon in Barkerville. The fire
that levelled Barkerville on 16 September 1868 was said to have started
in a room above Barry and Adler's saloon. This calamity had put the
partners out of business until they bought the 150 Mile House, a most
auspicious move. Earlier in 1869, the economy of the country had
been rather dull, but, in October, word came of a new gold strike in the
Omineca, an area northwest of the Cariboo. By spring 1870, traffic
along the Cariboo Road had increased dramatically, and roadhouses
such as the 150 Mile House were enjoying renewed activity. In addition
to the usual attractions of drinking, gambling, and playing billiards,
Barry and Adler also offered performances by travelling variety shows,

such as that of Professor Endt of Victoria, a magician and "slight of hand" expert. While in Barkerville, Tom Barry had himself been a leading light in amateur musical circles.

As winter took hold in the Cariboo and mining came to a halt, most of the population moved south — some to the 150 Mile House. For most miners, winter was a time to relax. Living off their gold, they enjoyed themselves until spring and the beginning of another mining season. In the 150 Mile area, where the weather was comparatively mild and there was little snow, whole communities of miners, both Caucasian and Chinese, lived in little cabins along the creek, just south of the roadhouse. The miners were a gay bunch, and, as James Leighton wrote: "You could get up a poker game, horse race, or dog fight on short notice, and the sky was the limit on bets. There never was another place that took in the cash spent there — it was a gold mine!"[33]

In 1868, British Columbia passed a law prohibiting gambling in saloons. While barkeeps were forced to comply with the ruling, it did not stop the high-stakes poker games played in the back rooms of every roadhouse in the country. In the saloons, however, the law reduced brawls and put an end to the custom of playing cards to see who was going to buy the next round of drinks.

Although rather vague, the 150 Mile House had an association with the Cariboo camels. Introduced into the area as pack animals in 1862 by Frank Laumeister and his associates, the twenty-three Bactrian camels from California did not prove popular and were used for only a year. Able to pack 800-pound loads and travel long distances without water, the animals nonetheless had too many problems to last. Taken out of their natural surroundings the beasts were unhappy and, consequently, very bad tempered. Among their many bad habits they were given to spitting and biting. Harry Guillod, on his way to the goldfields in 1862, came across the camels at Cottonwood. In his diary he complained that they had "a neat habit of walking over your tent, and eating your shirts."[34]

Far worse than any of these problems was the camels' very offensive odour, which drove other animals quite mad. After facing a number of costly lawsuits, Laumeister and his partners gave up using the beasts. Rather than return them from whence they had come, however, they were turned out to fend for themselves in the countryside between Williams Lake and Cache Creek. The poor beasts fared well in summer but suffered badly during the cold winters, when many died. During their tenure as proprietors of the 150 Mile House, Adler and Barry had occasion to receive the carcass of one of the remaining camels. While some have gone so far as to suggest that camel meat was served in the dining room of the 150 Mile House, Dr Mark Wade, to whom the story is attributed, said no such thing — only that Adler and Barry, after butchering a camel, "offered it for sale, but ... no one would buy."[35]

While Adler and Barry operated the 150 Mile House for a period of two years, Edward Tormey, cattleman and butcher, had remained to operate the ranch until the early spring of 1871, when he left on a short trip to California. Only a month later, subscribers to the *Cariboo Sentinel* read of Tormey's death in San Francisco. Following this unexpected event, Martin Tormey, brother of the deceased, and Adler and Barry, owners of the roadhouse, arranged for the sale of the property to Aschel Sumner Bates, originally of Boston, Massachusetts.

Known to be one of the earliest of the American miners to reach the upper Fraser River in 1858, Bates soon switched from mining to cattle ranching at Savona in the Thompson River area. During the late 1860s, it paid Bates to invest in various business enterprises in the Cariboo, such as Peter Dunlevy's Exchange Hotel at Soda Creek and G. B. Wright's sternwheeler, the *SS Victoria*. By 1871, Bates owned several of the largest ranches in the Cariboo; he had ranches at Sugar Cane, Deep Creek, and the 150 Mile House, where he had 2,000 acres of land, several hundred head of cattle, a store, a roadhouse, and a blacksmith shop. With Bates's diversified interests, the operation of his holdings, including the roadhouse and stores, was leased to various persons. In 1875, the 150 Mile House was operated by a one-armed Welsh miner, James Griffin, who was also the postmaster.

There were periods between 1860 and 1890 when the Cariboo was without a bank, and the practice of sending cash through the mail to banks in the south was very common. Mail for the post offices between Yale and Barkerville travelled by stage and was kept in a locked box. At each post office, the box was opened by the postmaster, who dealt with the contents and then locked it up again. It so happened at this time that a registered letter from Thaddeus Harper of Barkerville, addressed to Cornelius O'Keefe of the Okanagan, and containing $1,800 in cash, went missing. The post office traced the letter to the 150 Mile House, where Jim Griffin was in charge. Fortunately, Harper had kept the serial numbers of the missing banknotes, and lists of these had been forwarded to every roadhouse in the district. Living in the area at the time was a young remittance man, Fred Harrison, a recent arrival from England. Every six months, when his allowance arrived,

Harrison would celebrate at the 150 Mile roadhouse, buying drinks for everyone and gambling his money away. He had just received an allotment when the $1,800 went missing. Soon after this, Harrison and James Griffin were amongst the players in a big poker game held one night in a back room of the roadhouse. The stolen banknotes were used in the game, and when Harrison wasn't looking, the thief put several of the marked notes into his pockets. Too drunk to notice, Harrison kept playing and lost all his money, including the marked notes. When these were discovered, Harrison was arrested, charged, and held in custody to await trial before Judge Begbie. At the trial Harrison claimed he knew nothing, which was true, but the evidence against him was too strong, and he was sentenced to five years in the New Westminster penitentiary. It was generally understood that his relatives pulled some strings and had him returned to England. The missing money was sent back to the post office, and, although nothing could be proved, there were many who suspected Griffin, the postmaster and proprietor of the 150 Mile House.

During the several years of his tenure at the 150 Mile House, Aschel S. Bates was mentioned in various newspaper reports for his progressive farming and ranching practices. In 1872, he harvested a large crop of wheat which was milled into flour in a steam mill he had built himself. This same mill was later converted into a steam sawmill, capable of cutting 10,000 board feet of lumber daily. In 1874, Bates married Caroline Lindhart, widow of J. W. Lindhart of Van Winkle. They were a very happy couple, but, within five years, Caroline Lindhardt Bates was again widowed when Aschel died of a heart attack on New Year's Day 1879. He was only fifty years old.

Just prior to his death, Bates sold the 150 Mile Ranch and roadhouse to Gavin Hamilton, retired Hudon's Bay Company factor of Fort St James.

Born in the Orkney Islands in 1835, Gavin Hamilton came of very excellent Scottish stock, being directly descended from the Ayrshire branch of the House of Hamilton. After thirty-five years of service to the company, Hamilton and his wife Margaret, a daughter of Peter Skene Ogden, retired and moved south to put their more than twelve children to school at St Joseph's Mission at Williams Lake. While visiting the school in the summer of 1878, Hamilton had met Bates, who offered to sell him the 150 Mile Ranch and roadhouse. This suited Hamilton, and a deal was made. The asking price of $35,000 included the flour and sawmill machinery.

Following the arrival of the Hamiltons, the roadhouse and post office continued to be operated by James Griffin, the one-armed Welshman involved in the robbery of $1,800 a few years earlier. Having established themselves at the 150 Mile House, a series of unfortunate and tragic circumstances befell the members of the Hamilton family. To begin with, only a few months later, the sawmill and storehouse burned to the ground, with an estimated loss of $9,000. The following spring (1880), a further financial loss of $13,000 was suffered when land was swept away by floods. In September, when Sarah Crease and her husband Judge Crease stayed over at the 150 Mile House, she wrote in her diary:

"Reached 150 Mile, formerly known as Bates's, of good repute is now kept by a kind good natured man from the Peace River country named Hamilton, late of the H.B.C. His wife is a half breed, nee Ogden, and they have a family of fifteen children ... Our host much disheartened by his recent losses of $25000. by fire and flood. Sawmill burnt and land swept away by overflow of creek. Gave us a large comfortable room."[36]

In spite of these setbacks, business at the roadhouse, as seen by another observer, appeared to be quite normal:

At the 150 Mile House, the Gavin Hamiltons and their family of fifteen children were in charge. There were thirteen boys and two small girls sitting at the dinner table with us — a party in itself, and a Chinese cook in attendance. Several freight teams were there for the night, and the place seemed alive with travellers. In the large bar room half breed cowboys dozed on tilted chairs lined along the walls of the room.[37]

Not long after this, an even worse tragedy befell the Hamiltons. They had an infant daughter, a delicate child of two, who had not been walking long. The child disappeared, never to be seen again, on the afternoon of 5 September 1881, while in the care of a servant girl. Margaret Hamilton, the mother, gave the alarm, and soon everyone in the neighbourhood was out searching. They drained wells, ditches, and creeks; they scoured the area for miles around but to no avail. For months the search continued. Reports of the tragedy appeared in the *Victoria Colonist*, which called for government assistance in the search, but still nothing was ever found of the little girl. Nine months later, in the summer of 1882, a Native woman out picking berries, nearly a mile away, found the dismembered remains of the child. Foul play was suspected, but no-one was ever arrested.

By 1883, while still recovering from the several heartbreaking occurrences of the previous seven years, and faced with a mountain of debt, Gavin Hamilton sold the 150 Mile House Ranch and roadhouse for $5,000 to Veith and Borland of Keithley Creek. Due to the neglect of the property during Hamilton's tenure, it took several years of steady work to return the roadhouse and ranch to its former state. In spite of this, the new owners could not have bought at a better time. With the resurgence of mining in the Cariboo in the 1890s, brought on by the arrival of the railway to Ashcroft, the Cariboo Road was never busier. At the roadhouse, an extensive renovation project included the refurbishing of the rooms and the application of numerous coats of white paint to the exterior. The *BC Mining Journal*, which began publication in 1895 and became known as the *Ashcroft Journal* in 1900 stated: "Veith and Borland are fitting up the old Hamilton House in good style."[38]

In 1898, when news of the Klondike gold strike brought yet another rash of travellers onto the Cariboo Road, the hotel at the 150 Mile was a hive of activity. Bent on reaching the Yukon by way of the Collins Overland Telegraph route, many parties of prospectors travelled north on horseback, seeking shelter at the roadhouses when night fell. One such group, the entourage attached to the expedition of Sir Arthur Curtis, an English lord, caught the particular attention of hotel manager Joseph P. Patenaude:

> We at the 150 were highly amused at the different groups passing through the country. One day there arrived a party dressed in regular "wild west" regalia, with wide brimmed hats, red bandannas, chaps, belts, hunting knives, and cowboy spurs. For all their equipment they did not seem experienced with handling their horses, which were of excellent stock. After remaining overnight, they took their leave the next morning.[39]

As it happened, Sir Arthur Curtis disappeared a short time later and was never seen again.

By the 1890s, the vast business interests of Veith and Borland began to break up. While Bob Borland bought the former Pinchbeck Ranch at Williams Lake from the Western Canada Ranching Company (a.k.a. the Gang Ranch) in 1899, George Veith, whose health was failing, went into semi-retirement at Keithley Creek. At this time the partnership was dissolved, and the 150 Mile Ranch and hotel was sold for

*According to the Daily Colonist, Veith and Borland sold
the 150 Mile House February 3 1899. (COURTESY BCARS)*

$90,000 to an English syndicate, the Cariboo Trading Company. In 1912, the company reported:

> *The property, under the direction of Mr. H. P. Cunliffe has been enlarged from 1,500 acres to 4,000 acres, with a cattle herd of 800 head, mostly shorthorn. Evaluated at $220,000, it had this year a turnover of $98,000. Two large buildings, the hotel and store, supply all the needs of the local district. There are extensive store houses and stables, one of which has space for 66 horses, and lofts to hold 80 tons of hay. A good annual crop of garden produce supplies the needs of the hotel and the store.*[40]

In August 1910, when Annie Moore left Vancouver to become the first salaried schoolteacher at Harper's Camp, a small community northeast of the 150 Mile House, she took the train to Ashcroft, where she boarded the BC Express Company stagecoach and headed for the 150 Mile House. Many years later, Annie, who, as has been mentioned, married Albert Patenaude in 1911, recalled her initial trip to the Cariboo: "The ticket agent at Vancouver told me that Harper's Camp

[Horsefly] was not far from Ashcroft. Actually, it was two days travel by stagecoach to the 150 Mile House, and part of another day's travel from there to Harper's Camp." When questioned about the stagecoach, her sparkling Irish eyes would light up as she recalled the experience.

> It was a thrill to watch the stage prepare to leave the roadhouse. Once the freight and mail was loaded, and the passengers seated in the coach, the horses were led out of the barns in pairs, by the hostler. The first team, called the "wheel" team, was backed into position out in front of the stage, one on either side of the pole. Then a second, or "swing" team was led out, and positioned ahead of the "wheel" team. Last came the "lead" team, the most spirited of the horses. These two had to be held down, "close to the bit," as it was said, to keep them from figiting, until the lines were threaded and hooked up, and the harness adjusted to the satisfaction of the driver. Once this was done, the driver climbed to his seat and gave a nod to the hostler, who let go of the lead horse, and quickly jumped aside — and they were off! Some teams terrified the passengers by standing up on their hind legs, and winneying before starting off. They were gone two miles down the road before they finally settled down to a steady pace.[41]

150 Mile House as seen at the turn of the century was a Cariboo landmark for over fifty years. (COURTESY BCARS)

This ritual was repeated at every roadhouse where the BC Express Company kept a stable. When the horses thundered out of the yard, everyone stopped to watch as startled chickens flew up, dogs barked, children clutched their mothers' skirts, and young men stood and admired the beautiful stagecoach horses.

The lack of central heating in the roadhouse meant the only warmth to reach the upstairs bedrooms in winter came from the stovepipes of the downstairs heaters which extended to the roof. Only in extreme cold did the stoves burn all night and it was common in the morning to wake with one's face stuck to the hoar frost on the quilt. These rigorous conditions were reason enough for early roadhouse keepers to offer each guest a before-breakfast "toddy."

Alvin Johnston, born and raised in Quesnel, took his first trip to the Coast in 1910. On his return in December of that year, he travelled north from Ashcroft on horseback. Arriving late one night at the 150 Mile House, he took the only available room — a small, chilly cubby hole at the back of the establishment. Numerous hot rums consumed just before retiring enabled Alvin to sleep for several hours, but by early morning he awoke shivering from the cold. Summoning up his courage, he got dressed and crept down to the lobby to find his coat. A few minutes before this, an early-morning traveller had arrived in the lobby, where he sat against the heater in an attempt to thaw himself out. As Alvin reached the bottom of the stairs, he came face to face with the poor frozen creature — the collar of his mackinaw pulled up to meet the cap, which was pulled down over his ears, his frozen fingers combing the icicles out of his moustache. Alvin stared at him for a moment, then asked, "My God, which room did you have?"[42]

Just as many other roadhouses had done before, and as still others did later, the 150 Mile House burned to the ground early on the morning of 13 February 1916. The fire, which started in the liquor cellar, spread quickly due to the lack of water. While there was no loss of life, guests had to flee without their possessions; that is, with the exception of Alex Meiss of Horsefly, who was able to save his most valued possession, his wooden leg. Alex, who had lost the limb many years before, had been asleep when the fire broke out. Carried to safety by the hotel manager, Mr Champion, Alex kicked and screamed all the way out, complaining that his wooden leg was still in the burning building. Fortunately, there was still time to save it. Following this disastrous fire, the Cariboo Trading Company continued to operate the store and ranch at the 150 Mile until 1928, but it did not rebuild the hotel.

Notes to Chapter 3

1. Bishop George Hills, Diary, 11 July 1862, Anglican Provincial Synod of British Columbia Archives, Vancouver.

2. James Thomson, *For Friends at Home: A Scottish Emigrant's Letters from Canada, California, and the Cariboo*, 1844–1864 (Montreal: McGill Queen's University Press 1974), 309.

3. Louis LeBourdais, "Harry Jones Story," addit. MSS 676, vol. 7, 15–16, BCARS.

4. *Cariboo Sentinel*, 6 June 1865, 1.

5. *Colonist* (Victoria), 15 November 1879, 2.

6. George Sargison, Diary, December 1871, E/C/Sa7, BCARS.

7. *Williams Lake Tribune*, 12 March 1953.

8. Sergeant J. McMurphy, RE, Diary, 29 July 1862, 12.

9. *Cariboo Sentinel*, 8 October 1870, 2.

10. *Williams Lake Tribune*, 29 September 1959, 2.

11. Molly Forbes, Lac La Hache, BC.

12. *Province* (Vancouver), 7 December 1935, 7.

13. Harry Guillod, Diary, 30 September 1862, E/B/G94A p. 51, BCARS.

14. *Cariboo Sentinel*, 24 June 1865, 1.

15. Birch Family Papers, ch. V11, Begbie to Birch, 24 June 1865, Colonial Correspondence, BCARS.

16. William Wright, P.R.148, p. 38, Cariboo Pre-Emptions, 1860–1869, BCARS.

17. *Cariboo Sentinel*, 13 May 1867, 3.

18. Sarah Crease, Diary, 13 September 1880, A/E/C86, p. 8, BCARS.

19. Ibid., 6 October 1880, 24.

20. Guillod, Diary, 17 July 1862, 16.

21. LeBourdais, "Harry Jones Story," 15.

22. *Province* (Vancouver), 7 December 1935, 7.

23. GR827, vol. 1, 210, 11 October 1867, BCARS.

24. Thomson, *For Friends at Home*, 296.

25. Irene Stangoe, *Cariboo-Chilcotin Pioneer People and Places* (Vancouver: Heritage House 1995), 88–90.

26. H. J. Boam and A. G. Brown, *British Columbia* (London: Sells Ltd. 1912).

27. *Province* (Vancouver), 1936.

28. Esther Darlington, "The Fabulous Fanny Faucault," unpublished manuscript.

29. LeBourdais "Harry Jones Story," 16.

30. Thomson, *For Friends at Home,* 301.

31. Dr W. B. Cheadle, Journal, 14 October 1863.

32. G. B. Wright to HPP Crease, letter, 16 April 1864, Colonial Correspondence, BCARS.

33. *Province* (Vancouver), Sunday Magazine, 20 April 1935, 33.

34. Guillod, Diary, 20 August 1862, 33.

35. Mark S. Wade. *The Cariboo Road,* (Victoira: The Haunted Bookshop), 81.

36. Crease, Diary, 13 September 1880, 8.

37. M.W. Boss, "A Tale of Northern BC to Cassiar," addit. MSS 771, BCARS.

38. *BC Mining Journal,* 15 November 1895, 3.

39. *Province* (Vancouver), 1936.

40. H. J. Boam and A. G. Brown, *British Columbia,* 396–400.

41. Willis West, "Staging And Stage Hold-ups In The Cariboo," *BC Historical Quarterly,* 12 (July 1948), 193, 194.

42. Alvin Johnston, "Birchbark To Steel," unpublished manuscript, 1959.

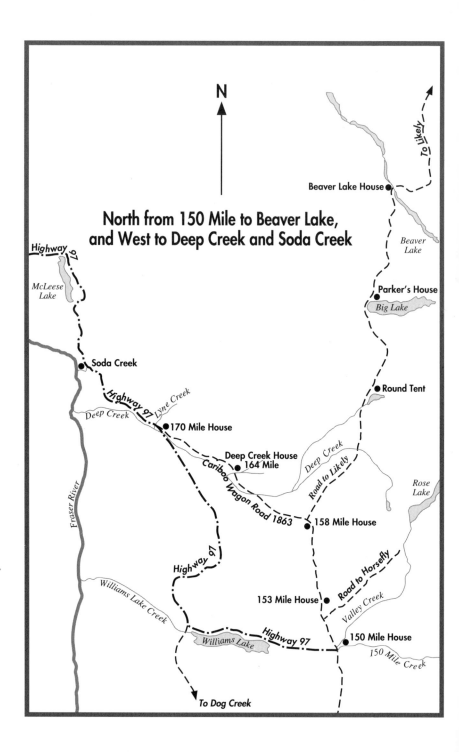

North from 150 Mile to Beaver Lake,
and West to Deep Creek and Soda Creek

CHAPTER FOUR

158 Mile House to the 170 Mile House

Despite lingering criticism over the building of the Cariboo Road by way of Deep Creek, the development of several ranches and road-houses along that route between 1863 and 1900 gave further evidence to its popularity.

THE 158 MILE HOUSE, 1862
Lots 166 and 167, G.1., Cariboo

Carpenter's House, 1863
The Mountain House, 1896

As the building of the Cariboo Road proceeded uphill from Davidson's Lake Valley Ranch in the summer of 1863, Sergeant John McMurphy of the Royal Engineers made camp at the 158 milepost: "Arrived at my camp which is 158 miles from Lillooet having measured 47 miles from the 111 Milepost."[1] That summer, Captain Carpenter, an employee of G. B. Wright, took up land at this site, where he established a ranch and a roadhouse known in 1865 as "Carpenter's House."[2] Consequently, the rise of ground in that area became known as "Carpenter's Mountain." Captain Carpenter was still farming at the 158 Mile Ranch in the 1870s.

158 Mile House, also known as the "Mountain House," was built in the 1880's by Stephen Tingley, owner of the BC Express Company. It is pictured here about eight years before it burned in 1943. (COURTESY BCARS)

In 1896, when Steven Tingley, owner of the BC Express Company, was nearing the end of his career, he purchased land at the 158 milepost, where he kept horses on what was known as the Mountain House Ranch. These acres, when surveyed, became lots 166 and 167, G.1., Cariboo. The following year, having lost the mail contract, Tingley retired and gave up many of his holdings, including the 158 Mile Ranch. At this time, the property was rented to Louis James Crosina, a young Italian immigrant who had worked at Tingley's main horse stables at the 134 Mile Ranch. Tingley had met Louis Crosina a few years earlier at Yale, where the latter was driving freight wagons up the Fraser Canyon. Appreciating his talent with horses, Tingley hired Louis to work on his ranch in the Cariboo. Considering the circumstances of his arrival in Canada, it was a miracle that Louis had lived to reach British Columbia.

Leaving his home in the Italian Tyrol in 1882, the fifteen-year-old Louis, with three older companions, set sail for British Columbia, where his uncle was working in Yale. The uncle, who had written to invite Louis to join him, had given his address as "British Colombia." When purchasing tickets for the journey, the misspelling of the word "Columbia," plus the fact that none of the Italians spoke English, resulted in their passage on a ship bound for Colombia, South America. Once the terrible mistake was realized, the captain of the ship put them off at Colon, a port on the Isthmus of Panama. Lacking the funds to continue their journey, the companions were forced to work as labourers in the Panama Canal project, which was under way at that time. In the hot, humid atmosphere of Panama, the work was extremely hard, and living conditions pitiful. As a result, the labourers were dying like flies from malaria and yellow fever. Within a month, two of Louis's companions were dead. Louis also contracted the dreadful diseases but somehow managed to survive long enough to secure a working passage on a ship bound for San Francisco. It was a whole year after his arrival in British Columbia before Louis was strong enough to do any physical work.

On reaching the Cariboo, Louis worked off and on at Tingley's 134 Mile Ranch and made improvements to his own pre-emption behind the 122 Mile Ranch. During this time, he met and courted the local school-teacher, Clara Noble, from St John, New Brunswick. With the prospect of renting the Mountain House Ranch in 1897, Louis and Clara were married and soon moved to their new home. During their stay of several years, two children were born to the Crosinas, William James and Alice Lillian, and Clara started a hobby that soon became a full-time business. Most of the men hired to work at the Mountain House were from the nearby Native reserve, and, while serving meals in the roadhouse, Clara Crosina learned to speak Shuswap. When the women came to visit, Clara complimented them on their baskets, embroidered buckskin gloves, moccasins, and jackets. It was then that she realized that most Native people preferred to be paid in groceries and tobacco rather than in money. Before she knew it, she had invested in a set of weigh scales and was operating a trading post at the 158 Mile Ranch.

By the turn of the century, the resurgence of mining activity in the Horsefly and Quesnel River areas had brought a dramatic increase in business to the 158 Mile House and store. Situated, as they were, at the top of an eight-mile hill, the facilities proved a welcome stop for teamsters with loaded freight wagons. In spite of travelling together in groups and pooling their horses, it still took two days to get to the top of that hill. With the great number of horses on the road, Louis Crosina spent many long hours in his blacksmith shop, repairing the ironwork on the wagons and mending harnesses.

When the Mountain House Ranch was sold in 1902 to stage driver William Parker, Louis and Clara Crosina left to establish a ranch of their own at a point halfway between the 150 Mile House and the Mountain House.

Bill Parker, who lived at Big Lake, owned his own stageline in 1895 and used the 158 Mile Ranch as pasture for his horses. Following his death in September 1927, the 158 Mile Ranch was again sold, this time to Louis Crosina. Louis's son, Willie Crosina, rented the ranch for some years and eventually inherited the property. On a winter evening in 1943, an overheated stovepipe was the cause of a fire that started in the upper storey of the old roadhouse. Flames soon engulfed the tinder-dry logs and destroyed the whole building; while no-one was hurt, few effects were saved.

THE 153 MILE HOUSE AND STORE, 1902
Lots 195 and 196, G.1., Cariboo

Prior to his departure from the Mountain House Ranch in 1902, Louis Crosina pre-empted 640 acres of land three miles up Carpenter Mountain, where he and his wife Clara established the 153 Mile Ranch. This became lots 195 and 196, G.1., Cariboo, Crown granted in 1912. At the new ranch, Louis had a number of men who had worked for him at the Mountain House ranch, to assist in the construction of the first buildings. Within the year, they had built a two-storey log store, with living quarters in the upper storey, a blacksmith shop, and a small barn. Five years later, and with two more children, the Crosinas had outgrown their quarters above the store and had begun building a more permanent residence. Situated beside the Cariboo Road, about seventy-five yards north of the original buildings, the large, two-storey squared-log house had a sharp-angled shake roof, through which protruded two metal chimneys made from hydraulic mining pipe. The 153 Mile House operated continuously for over thirty-five years. As an integral part of a family enterprise that included ranching, blacksmithing, and operating a general store, this roadhouse ranch was one of the area's focal points for many years.

When the Crosina's moved into their new home in the early months of 1906, the interior was far from finished, especially on the second floor, where the ceilings were still open and there were no partitions between the bedrooms. Just at that time, word came of the imminent arrival of a group of government men, who were expected to remain overnight at the new roadhouse. Realizing the primitive state of the house, Clara immediately surveyed her stock of store supplies and found a large roll of heavy, canvas-backed oilcloth, the type widely used at that time to cover rough-built kitchen tables. As necessity is the mother of invention, the oilcloth was used to provide a measure of privacy and warmth for those first guests. Disguised under many coats of calcumine, the oilcloth remained for the next forty years.

The front entrance of the roadhouse faced southwest (onto the Cariboo Road), and it was not long before a full-length porch was built to protect the parlour from the powerful rays of the afternoon sun. Included on the main floor of the original twenty-five foot by twenty-five foot "square" was a parlour, kitchen, dining room, and one bedroom. In the upper storey, accessed by a set of rather steep and narrow stairs in the middle of the house, was the children's room and a number of small bedrooms. By the 1920s, a second house of the same size, but with a lower-pitched roof, was added onto the back of the original. This allowed for a larger kitchen, a pantry, and two small bedrooms on the main floor. In the upstairs of the addition was a large bedroom (known as "the bull pasture," where single cots accommodated the teamsters and their swampers) and four small but well-appointed bedrooms (reserved for more discriminating guests). A doorway between the back bedrooms and the front area was kept closed in slack times to conserve heat. In later times, when central heating was installed, a single cement block chimney replaced the original metal pipes. As can be imagined, an enormous supply of firewood was required to heat the house. In the Cariboo, where frigid temperatures sometimes prevail for seven months of the year, it was not uncommon to go through fourteen cords of wood in twelve months.

The 153 Mile Ranch House, a roadhouse for 35 years. Taken in 1981 by the author, this photo shows the addition at the back, and the full covered porch.

At the "53," the work of running the roadhouse, the store, and bringing up four lively children soon became too much for Clara, who hired young women from neighbouring ranches to help in the kitchen. Two of these were Mrs Henry Windt of Alexandria and Mrs Jimmy Wiggins of Miocene. The cost of overnight accommodation at Crosina's was fifty cents per meal and fifty cents per bed; and, as each teamster usually had a swamper, the roadhouse was assured of at least three dollars per visit. Down at the barn, the cost of stabling a horse overnight was also fifty cents, but grain was extra.

As a young boy, Willie Crosina, the only son, was known to be a terrible brat, probably spoiled by the visiting teamsters. In 1910, when Roddy Moffat of Alexandria was freighting, he watched as an associate, Norman Much, taught young Willie a bit of a lesson. After having had his hat knocked off several times by Willie's snowballs, Norman grabbed the child and rubbed his face in a fresh cow pie. "Now you little bastard," he said, "go tell your old man what I did!"[3] Of course he knew young Willie wouldn't dare tell his Dad, because he'd only get another licking! All he could do was wash himself off at the pump.

As they grew up, the Crosina children took on their own responsibilities in the roadhouse and on the ranch. While the girls cleaned and cooked, Willie did the outside chores. (Eventually, each of the Crosina children was sent away to school in Victoria for a few years, where they resided with an elderly aunt.) The Crosinas were very proud of the fact that there was never a bedbug found in their roadhouse. Each Saturday morning, all the beds were stripped, the mattresses washed down with disinfectant, and the floors scrubbed with lye soap. Out in the laundry cabin, the sheets were boiled in copper cauldrons and hung out to dry in the sun.

While most of the success of the Crosina family enterprise could be attributed to good meals and hospitality, a great deal of popularity was gained by the blacksmithing services provided by Louis Crosina, a skilled and innovative craftsman. For example, Louis was making his own brand of steel cable long before it was manufactured commercially. Closely involved with the teamsters and their horses on the road, Louis designed and made many sets of little brass bells that hung from the hames, above the horses heads. The Crosina children were said to have helped to achieve just the right tone for each bell. These delightful decorations became a fad, with some teams having as many as thirteen bells hanging from the harness. Closer to home, Louis's blacksmithing talents saved his eldest daughter, Lilly, from having to put up with

Willie Crosina, born in 1898, stands at 153 Mile Ranch prior to 1914, when a second store was built across from the roadhouse. The original ranch building in the distance was built in 1902. (COURTESY E. J. PATENAUDE FAMILY)

permanently bowed legs. As a small child, Lilly had rickets, and, from the time she first walked, she wore little metal braces forged by Louis. As Lilly continued to grow, Louis forged larger braces, until, as a teenager, she was finally able to discard them.

By 1912, business at Crosina's store, the first building on the ranch, had completely outgrown the premises, and a new store was built in 1914 across the road from the stopping house. Built of enormous logs, fourteen to twenty inches in diameter, it took several men with horses as well as block and tackle to hoist them into place. Soon it became possible to purchase everything from postage stamps to farm machinery from Crosina's 153 Mile Store. As cars replaced horses on the road, a Home Gas pump was installed outside, and even Model T parts and rubber tires were kept in stock.

Clara Crosina, the congenial proprietor of the store, enjoyed dealing with her customers (the ranchers, trappers, and miners of the region), sharing in their lives through friendly gossip over the counter. The Native people also had a special friend in Clara, as she sold their birchbark baskets, tanned leather jackets, and beadwork. As she grew older, Lilly Crosina also developed a special talent for store work, and, when the younger daughters, Clara and Dolly, married and moved away, Lilly remained and eventually bought both the store and ranch from her parents. With Clara Crosina's death in 1936, Louis moved to

The 153 Mile Store was built in 1914 and is now a museum operated by Peggy Patenaude. Clara Crosina, on left, and daughter Lilly pose in the 1930s. (COURTESY BCARS)

Abbotsford to live with his married daughter, Dolly, leaving Lilly to carry on with the operation of both facilities until 1939, when the roadhouse closed due to a labour shortage during the Second World War. Following this, Lilly, who never married, hired Bryson Patenaude to run the ranch while she operated the store. Continuing in her mother's tradition, Lilly also had a close affinity with the local Native people, speaking their language and handling their work in the store. A hard worker, Lilly devoted her life to the service of her customers, sometimes going to great lengths to oblige them. As a result, her clientele spread far and wide. Lilly was also a guiding influence in the life of Bryson's son, Joe, to whom she eventually sold the ranch.

The Crosina Museum, 153 Mile House Ranch

When Lilly Crosina died of a sudden heart attack in 1963, Joe Patenaude and his wife Peggy closed the store, supposedly forever. During the 1970s, when Peggy began to sort through the wealth of artifacts in the store and attic, she came to realize the potential value of these items. The result was a museum — a typical Cariboo general store as it existed between 1900 and 1963, with all its original artifacts. Operated as a private concern, and open only by appointment, the 153 Mile Store is visited by hundreds of school children and history buffs during the summer months. The Joe (E. J.) Patenaude family, who continue to operate the 153 Mile Ranch, have restored all the original buildings, and still reside in the old roadhouse built in 1906.

DEEP CREEK HOUSE, 1863
Lots 3, 4, and 5, G.3, Lillooet, 1870

Soda Creek Indian Reserve, No. 2, 1882

Land at Deep Creek, approximately ten miles northwest of Williams Lake, was first pre-empted in July 1861 by Charles Fisher, William Pinchbeck, and Moses Dancerault. Following the issuance of certificates of improvement in May 1862, Dancerault bought out his partners, Fisher and Pinchbeck, and acquired a total of 1,400 acres in the Deep Creek area. Dancerault had also been T.W. Davidson's partner in acquiring land at Williams Lake in 1860, and was party to two trails to Deep Creek, built by Davidson in 1861 and 1862, respectively. The trail ran through the Deep Creek property, where it connected with trails leading to both the Quesnel and Fraser Rivers, making it a very strategic junction. Here Dancerault built a log cabin, where he kept a store and catered to a few overnight travellers.

Two of the earliest references to Deep Creek farm are noted on Judge Begbie's map of 1861 and on G. B. Wright's map of the same year, where it appears as "Fisher's."[3] A later reference to "Deep Creek House," as the cabin was so grandiosely referred to, is found in the diary of C. W. Buckley, a British sea captain on his way to the goldfields in the summer of 1862: "Took trail to Deep Creek — trail opened up by Davidson to where a Frenchman keeps a ranch and sells fresh beef, bread and milk."[4] The Frenchman Buckley refers to was probably Dancerault. That same year, Dancerault sold the Deep Creek property to Franklin Way, formerly of Spuzzum; but by the time a formal conveyance of the property had been executed, G. B. Wright, the road contractor, had also become part owner. An article printed in the *Victoria Colonist* in May 1863 describes the activity at Deep Creek farm:

> At Frank Way's place at Deep Creek twenty hands are employed ploughing, harrowing, fencing, etc., and where it is intended to put in 150 acres of grain and a quantity of vegetables. Mr. Way intends to put up a large hotel this summer and to have the stage running between this house and the steamer landing at Soda Creek. When the road is complete it will be possible to travel from Yale to Soda Creek in less than four days.[5]

In his 1863 diary, Sergeant John McMurphy, who was supervising the road-building project that summer, also mentioned the roadhouse at Deep Creek: "The 164 Post is opposite Frank Way's House. There is a great amount of traffic coming this way in wagons and pack trains."[6]

Passing through the country that summer was young Harry Jones and his companion, William Davies, both members of Captain John Evans's group of twenty-six Welsh miners. While on their way to Lightning Creek, they sought shelter for the night at Deep Creek House. Bedded down in their blankets before the roaring fireplace, they looked forward to a good night's rest, but this was not to be. In the same room with them was proprietor Frank Way and his friends, who played cards, drank, swore, and made merry all night, with no thought for the men who were attempting to sleep. When, on several occasions, Davies pleaded with them to be quiet, Frank Way responded: "If you don't like the ways of Way, you can go your merry way."[7] A photograph of Deep Creek House, taken in 1867 or 1868 by pioneer photographer Frederick Dally, shows it to be a substantial, two-storey log structure, built in a "T" shape. To the left of the roadhouse is Dancerault's original log cabin with its brick chimney.

With the completion of the Cariboo Road past Deep Creek in the summer of 1863, business at the roadhouse was undoubtedly brisk, despite Frank Way's reputation as a crude practical joker and incurable loudmouth. Two visitors to the area late in 1863 were Dr W. B. Cheadle and his companion, Lord Milton, who were returning from the gold-fields. Having remained overnight at Deep Creek House, they travelled on to Davidson's 150 Mile House, where they spent nearly a week waiting for the stage. While there, Frank Way arrived from Deep Creek, seeking surgical assistance, for "having [been] in a drunken row with an Irishman [he] had his lower lip almost bitten off, and a finger to the bone. I stitched it up for him, making a very neat job, but foolishly refused any fee."[8]

Despite the economic downturn in 1864, the building of the Cariboo Road brought about many improvements for travellers. Where in 1863 Francis J. Barnard had operated two-horse stagecoaches between Lillooet and Soda Creek, by the following spring, he had introduced a four-horse coach that could transport thirteen passengers along with freight and mail. Commencing from Yale, at Clinton these coaches connected with stages from Lillooet and, at Soda Creek, they connected with the SS Enterprise, bound for Quesnelle Mouth. The schedule of two trips a week never varied. By using relays of horses every ten to thirteen miles, the journey from Yale to Soda Creek could be made in about forty-eight hours. Above Quesnelle Mouth, a saddle train connected with the stages until the fall of 1864 and the completion of the road to Cottonwood. At this time, the Cariboo Stage Company, operated by Humphrey, Poole, and Johnston, began operating between Quesnelle Mouth and Cottonwood. It was fall of 1865 before stage-coaches ran the whole distance to Barkerville.

During the early years of the gold rush the existence of prostitutes (women of every race) at the roadhouses was ever present . With direct stage service available, White women began to travel to, and settle in, the Cariboo; at first these were only married women with their husbands. Before long, groups of a dozen or more passengers would arrive at the roadhouses, requiring meals and overnight lodging. These people were not at all like the first miners, who had been content to sleep in their blankets on a dirt floor. These new travellers included businessmen, entrepreneurs, and settlers with families. Their arrival placed new demands on the roadhouse keepers, forcing them to provide more sophisticated accommodations, such as private bedrooms, separate parlours for women, and sitting rooms.

Deep Creek House was never known for its hospitality, and accommodations received mixed reviews. In 1865, when Magistrate Henry Ball stayed overnight, he paid a bill of $7.50 and left this note in his diary: "Excellent House, but dirty rooms."[9] With more than 100 roadhouses operating from time to time on the trails and roads to the Cariboo, it was not long before each had gained a reputation of one kind or another. As early as 1862, an article appeared in the *Victoria Colonist* which brought to the attention of the public the number of stopping places that did not measure up.

The Fust Man To Complain.

Three or four of the wayside inns between Lillooet and the Forks of Quesnelle River are well kept, and a "square" meal may be found always on their tables. The remainder of the houses on this route are maintained in a disgracefully filthy condition and the food served up is generally of the meanest description. Complaints by travellers to landlords of being compelled to pay from $1.25 to $1.50 a meal are frequent, but when questioned are met with "Cap, if you don't like the way we do things, you'd better go on to the next House." [Which of course was usually another ten or more miles away.] A few days ago, several miners on their way down to Victoria stopped at one of these Houses and called for supper. The landlord, whose face and hands were remarkably dirty, busied himself in setting a scanty meal on a rude table, first placing on it a food stained, greasy tablecloth. As the

*The pioneer upper Fraser River sternwheeler Enterprise at Soda Creek in 1868,
with the Exchange Hotel and Colonial Hotel in the background. (COURTESY BCARS)*

men sat down and noticed the filthy cloth, one of them called the
landlord over to complain. "What's the matter with it?" asked the
landlord. "Why, its black as ink," was the reply. "Say look here
Cap," said the proprietor, "You should be thankful you are eating
off that tablecloth. Six or seven hundred other men have eaten off
it, and you're the fust to complain.[10]

As Wright's *SS Enterprise* carried most of the traffic back and
forth to Quesnelle Mouth, and with Deep Creek House receiving the
benefit of the resulting business for the next two years, there were soon
public complaints that this constituted an unfair monopoly. Thus, the
government was pressured to complete the wagon road to Quesnelle
Mouth. Actually, the government had opened tenders for a contract on
this stretch of road in 1863, but no-one had put in a bid. Later, when
Allen "Peg-leg" Smith signed a contract to complete the road by the
end of 1864, Wright and Way saw the end of a profitable era. Within the
year, stagecoaches were running from the 150 Mile House to Quesnelle
Mouth in less than a day. Except for going to Barnard's Horse-Change
at Deep Creek farm, there was really no need to stop there.

When he received a contract to build the wagon road from
Quesnelle Mouth to Cottonwood in 1864, G. B. Wright was financially
strapped, and was forced to mortgage off all his major assets, including
his interests in the Deep Creek roadhouse and farm. With a worsening
economy, and without Wright's financial support, Frank Way was soon

deep in debt. In July 1865, the bank foreclosed on his property and Frank fled the country. A report in the *British Columbia Tribune* of September 1866 traces his whereabouts: "Franklin Way and Billy Armstrong, both well known in BC have made a lucky strike of gold in Montana. The company of five, in which Way and Armstrong were involved, took out 1,600 ozs. of gold out of a claim on McLennan's Gulch in a very short time."

Following Frank Way's departure, Deep Creek farm and roadhouse were taken over by the Bank of British Columbia and leased to Aschel S. Bates of Bates & Company of Soda Creek. In May 1866, the facilities were advertised in the *Cariboo Sentinel*:

> DEEP CREEK HOUSE.
> Deep Creek House is open for the accommodation
> of the travelling public.
> The bedrooms are spacious and airy and the beds cannot be
> surpassed for cleanliness and comfort
> by many in the lower country.
> The table is always supplied with the best victuals.
> Stabling for horses, hay, oats and barley constantly on hand.
> Bates & Co.[12]

This arrangement continued until 1870 when Bates assumed full possession of Deep Creek farm. Although the roadhouse did not bring in much money, it was subsidized by the crops grown on the farm.

Following the death of A. S. Bates in January 1879, Deep Creek farm became part of the Deep Creek Indian Reserve. In September 1880, when Sarah Crease passed through the area, she wrote in her diary that Deep Creek farm was "formerly the supply house for Cariboo and the Forks of Quesnelle. The large houses [are] now all in ruins and washed away in the floods."[13]

LYNE'S 170 MILE HOUSE, 1895–1935
Lots 1931 and 1930, G.1., Cariboo

Yet another roadhouse farm along G. B. Wright's road, between the 150 Mile House and Soda Creek, was established in 1889, when a great demand for blacksmiths gave Billy (William) Lyne Jr and his brother John a chance to become independent businessmen. The two brothers had grown up on a large ranch at Williams Lake, where their father, William Lyne, had been William Pinchbeck's partner for many years.

Like most pioneers of the country, both Lyne and Pinchbeck had

Native wives. William Lyne's wife, Lucy, lived with him for only a short time following the birth of two sons, Billy and John. After spending several years at boarding school in Cache Creek during the 1870s, the boys returned to Williams Lake. Here, they worked on the ranch, became expert blacksmiths, and, thanks to William Pinchbeck, were introduced to sawmilling.

As a young man of nineteen, Billy Lyne married Angelique Dussault of Dog Creek, a clever, attractive Metis woman who was employed as the nursemaid for Peter Dunlevy's children in Soda Creek. Following their marriage, Billy and Angelique lived on Pinchbeck's upper ranch at Williams Lake, where Angelique ran the store for Pinchbeck's sister, Annie Anders, and Billy worked on the ranch. Bypassed by the Cariboo Road in 1863, Williams Lake had, by the 1880s, become somewhat of a backwater. To become independent, young men such as the Lyne brothers had to go elsewhere.

In the early spring of 1887, Billy, Angelique, and one-year-old daughter Vivian left Williams Lake for Quesnel, where, for two years, Billy worked as a blacksmith in partnership with Robert Middleton. Business was good, and the little family lived well. Despite this, Billy and Angelique realized that town living was not for them, and they looked for a chance to return to rural life.

In the spring of 1889, Billy moved his family and blacksmithing business to Nine Mile Creek, south of Soda Creek, where the wagon road passed through a tract of arable land. With feed and water available, Nine Mile Creek had become a stopover point for the slow-moving freight wagons. Billy's ability as a blacksmith was much appreciated by the teamsters, and, as his reputation spread, he had to call in his brother John to assist him. The two men often toiled for eighteen hours at a stretch, shrinking wagon wheels, shoeing the horses, and mending harnesses. Before long, Billy and John formed a partnership under the title of Lyne Brothers. At first, there was no time to build even a black-smith shop on the new ranch, and the work was carried out in tents. Angelique and her two small daughters, Vivian and Edith, also lived in a tent until Christmas of 1890, when they moved into a log cabin near Nine Mile Creek.

Angelique's account books record Billy's service to passing freighters as well as the meals she served in that first cabin:

Nine Mile Creek, 1890
June 2, Peter Eagan, freighter.

To 4 meals and 9 shoes @25cts . . . .$4.25.
391 lbs. grain @ 2 1/2cts . . . .$9.77 ¹/₂
190 lbs. hay @ 2 1/2cts $2.85
17 horses hay @ 25cts $4.25
3 men board . . . .$3.00 ¹⁴

By summer of 1890, Billy and Angelique had decided to remain at this site, and a pre-emption of 160 acres was recorded in July; but it was another year before they were able to start building. The first to go up was a barn that accommodated fifteen horses; the second a bunkhouse for freighters; and the third was the sorely needed blacksmith shop. Fortunately, Billy's pre-emption included a large stand of straight, clear-grained fir, which provided all the logs required for building. In later years, when Billy started sawmilling, these trees became a valuable source of income. Finally, in 1893, the roadhouse, a two-and-a-half-storey squared-log building, was started. Evelyn, the last child in the family, was born in the new house in 1896; but it was another ten years before it was completed.

At first the Lynes had had no intention of starting a roadhouse. Granted, Angelique had cooked meals for passing freighters for several years, but neither she nor Billy had anticipated the growing demands and opportunities of the early 1900s. The original twenty-six by thirty-two foot house contained a kitchen, two sitting rooms, a dining area, and one bedroom on the main floor. Upstairs were several unfinished bedrooms, where wallpaper pasted on lengths of cheesecloth served as partitions. Before long, due to the increased number of meals served in 1896, a whole new kitchen was built across the back of the house, extending out for twelve feet. With its shed roof, this addition gave the building an unbalanced appearance, known as a "salt-box house." (The building of "salt-box houses", where lean-to kitchens had been added on, is said to have originated in the colony of Connecticut, during the 1600s. They were named after the shape of salt boxes used by the pioneers.) A portable sawmill, which came from the Pinchbeck farm, was used to cut the wide floorboards.

Although it was a few years before Billy Lyne turned to full-time sawmilling, an 1891 account book shows the sale of some lumber for that year:

27 July 1891
P.C. Dunlevy, Soda Creek.
*   To 293 ft. lumber and scantling* $5.84

August 29, 1891.
   Vieth & Borland, 150 Mile House.
     To 580 ft. lumber @ 1 ¹/₂cts. . . . .$8.70[15]

Both Billy and John Lyne were experienced carpenters and, as the need arose, produced many pieces of furniture for the roadhouse.

A photograph of the Lyne roadhouse, taken in 1912, shows a stoutly-built, two-storey log building (with attic) facing west, beside the original wagon road. A covered verandah, built in later years, stretched across the front of the house, above which the generous overhang of the steep shake roof covered the tops of three second-storey windows. Flanking the wide front door were two double-sash windows. Built of solid fir, the door was typical of those manufactured and transported from Eastern Canada. In the upper section, a large, fogged, pink glass window was surrounded by carved wood scrolling. In the centre, and immediately under the glass window, a spring-triggered doorbell sent a sharp, but not unpleasant, signal to those within. Above the door, a transom of the same pink glass opened on a catch, sending cool breezes through the house on hot summer days. In the front hallway, a handsome, carved wooden staircase led up to a generous landing, and on the wall beside the front door were dowelled wooden coat pegs, which supported an abundance of children's clothing. Over the years, Angelique, a woman of deep compassion and generous heart, brought up not only her own five children but several grandchildren.

In the ladies' sitting room, to the right of the front door, were several pieces of furniture made by Billy Lyne, including a chaise lounge couch at the far end of the room. The couch became a favourite place for children to play, with the wallpaper behind it in constant need of repair from the rough and tumble of little feet. Facing the hills to the southeast, the three double-sash windows of the sitting room caught the afternoon sun, which shone in on several pots of begonias, oxalis, impatiens, and geraniums growing along the wide window sills close to Angelique's treadle sewing machine. (With her dressmaking abilities, the several girls of the family, and Angelique herself, were always well-dressed.) In another corner was a large pump organ, manufactured in 1901, brought up by freight wagons from Ashcroft. Although Angelique did not play, several of the children were able to accompany Uncle Pete Dussault on his fiddle at family gatherings. In later years, when Father McIntyre of Williams Lake held mass at the roadhouse, the promise of music brought even Billy Lyne into their midst. Above the sewing machine was a howler type telephone. One of the first in the Cariboo, this convenience allowed Angelique and her friend Clara Crosina, at the 153 Mile House, to keep each other informed of the guests expected for lunch or dinner. On 15 April 1912, news of the sinking of the SS *Titanic* was received over the phone.

When a new kitchen was built in 1897, eight feet of the north end of the house was made into a pantry, where much of the fresh food was prepared and kept. Lining the walls were cupboards and bins, where sacks of flour, salt, and porridge were stored. On a large table near the window, many fancy desserts were concocted. Delicate doughs rolled out on handmade pastry boards were turned into delicious fruit pies, while tempting cakes and puddings were made from fresh farm eggs and home-made butter. At first, Angelique did all her own cooking, but, as business increased, extra help was hired. Some of these cooks were Chinese, and one in particular, a very good cook who was always anxious to please, caused Angelique considerable embarrassment. Once, when there were special guests for dinner, the cook appeared at the dining room door with a delicious-looking roast chicken. The guests looked pleased, until he triumphantly announced that it was a chicken that had died. As it happened, there was really nothing wrong with the bird, except that it had suffered a broken leg; but, from that point on, it was too late to explain, and the chicken remained untouched. One final incident ended this particular cook's employment. As Angelique entered the kitchen one morning where the cook was glazing pies, she was horrified to see him fill his mouth with milk and spray it all over them.

As they grew up, Angelique's daughters and, later, her grand-daughters, all helped in the kitchen and were known for their culinary skills. During the late 1920s, Georgina Lyne, the last child left at home, cooked and helped with the ranch work. As a little girl she remembered the great freight wagons pulling up at the barns across the road, where, on some nights, as many as fifty horses were stabled. Two regular freighters on the road at this time were Curly Flenner and his wife, both of whom drove six-horse teams in the early 1900s. The arrival of the freight teams brought an air of excitement and expectation to the roadhouse, for with them came the delivery of long-awaited supplies and news of the outside world.

For many years, all the cooking was done on a large Gurney stove that sat on the kitchen floor. The enormous firebox used mountains of wood to heat the oven, where as many as twelve loaves of bread could be baked at a time. During the busy years of the roadhouse, and before any plumbing was installed, the copper reservoir, attached to one side of the stove, provided most of the hot water for dishwashing. The faithful old stove continued to serve in Angelique's kitchen until one sad day in the 1930s. During one of his trips to Williams Lake, Billy Lyne, in an extravagant mood, made a deal with hardware merchant Gosman for a new kitchen range. A few days later, when the stove was delivered, Angelique, who knew nothing of the transaction, was shocked and crestfallen. She loved her old stove, even though the top sagged and the oven door refused to shut tight. In spite of Angelique's protests, the old stove was replaced with the brand-new McClary. Billy only got ten dollars for the old relic, and it was a long time before he stopped hearing about the shortcomings of the new stove.

In the large dining area, a table made by Billy Lyne from a single fir slab seated fourteen people. Everyone ate at that table: ranch workers, stage passengers, the family, and neighbours who came to call. Angelique, being of mixed blood, had experienced the pain caused by racial prejudice; she firmly believed in equality and would not allow any behaviour to the contrary. Once, when some wealthy American women arrived at the roadhouse, they brought with them their Black maids. At dinner, when the women informed Angelique that their maids would eat in the kitchen, she refused, and these fancy Southern ladies had to endure dining with their maids.

Listed in daybooks dating from the early 1900s to the late 1920s are further records of the many business transactions on the Billy Lyne Ranch:

12 January 1901
B.C. Express Co.
   To 4 horses shod, steel heeled . . . .$ 4.50
Paid by cheque, March 5, 1901.

5 June 1911
Long Bros.
   To 9 meals, 3 beds . . . .$ 5.25
   17 horses stabled . . . .$ 8.50
   1 wagon tongue $10.00
repair on wagon . . . .$ 2.50
   . . . . .$26.25

11 October 1911
Fruit man.

```
To 6 horses, hay, noon . . . . . . . . . . . . . . . .$ 2.50
1 meal . . . . . . . . . . . . . . . . . . . . . . . . .$  .50
Bought of fruit man, 2 boxes apples  . . . . . . . .$ 6.00
Dentist. To 1 horse stabled, 2 nights  . . . . . . . .$ 1.00
    "      To 4 meals . . . . . . . . . . . . . . . . . . . .$ 2.00
To services of dentist.
1 tooth, gold crowned . . . . . . . . . . . . . . . .$10.00 16
```

The dentist, an American Black, arrived at the ranch with a horse and trap, in which, during the summer months, he travelled up and down the Cariboo Road. Most of his money was made from the sale of false teeth, "China Clippers," as they were known, which were fitted to the customers' needs but which were almost always very uncomfortable.

The Lyne roadhouse differed from most roadhouses in that it was a "dry house"; that is, no liquor was sold (but those who wished, could drink in the bunkhouse or the barn). In place of a saloon was the men's sitting room, where, after a hearty meal, freighters swapped stories and were entertained with the sentimental songs of Caruso, played on a cylinder gramophone.

As Billy and John Lyne's talents in carpentry became better known, they took local contracts to build barns and houses. One of such contracts was for Henry Moffat's second roadhouse, which was built in 1904. Billy also made and sold coffins.

Although Billy was talented and accomplished, he was also given to wanderlust and erratic behaviour. At the onset of the Klondike gold rush in 1898, he went off, leaving Angelique to shoulder the responsibility of the roadhouse, the farm, and the care of five growing children. Fortunately, Angelique had many loyal friends and relatives who rallied around to help: the Pickards, the Collins boys, and the Evans family, all of whom lived close by. Angelique commanded a lot of respect. With her considerable height (5 feet, 10 inches), her forthright manner, her lustrous, long brown hair, which she wore in a bun, and her perceptive brown eyes, not much got past her. Born 14 April 1867 at Dog Creek, the daughter of a former Hudson's Bay Company voyageur, Joseph Dussault, and his Metis wife, Helene, Angelique had to work hard for her education at St Joseph's Mission School at Williams Lake. Her special interest in medicine might have led to a career in nursing but, in those days of limited opportunities for women (especially women of mixed blood), Angelique had no chance. All through her life and into her seventies she studied medicine from books, putting her knowledge to work in the community as a midwife. Occasionally she assisted local doctors in operations. With a thorough knowledge of bone structure, Angelique was also able to set disjointed limbs; and, on one occasion, she did this for herself. While Angelique was driving a buggy near Morgan Creek, her horse suddenly spooked, throwing her to the ground and dislocating her shoulder. Before any swelling could occur, Angelique instructed her daughter Edith to "pop" the shoulder back into place. Edith was almost ill, but Angelique took it all quite calmly.

Billy Lyne did not make his fortune in the Klondike, but on his return to Nine Mile Creek he found many new opportunities awaiting him. The building of the Grand Trunk Pacific Railway to Fort George was attracting thousands of settlers to the north. Once again the Cariboo Road teemed with activity, and the roadhouses and camping spots along the way were filled. At Lyne's roadhouse, Angelique and her staff were kept busy providing dozens of meals and beds. In fact, it was so busy that a cashier had to be installed in the front hallway of the roadhouse to make sure everyone paid.

Following the retirement of the *SS Victoria*, the upper Fraser River was without a steamer for ten years, but, in 1896, with prospects of a business boom in the north, Senator James Reid built the *SS Charlotte* at Quesnel. Within a few years, several more sternwheelers were plying the river, and, with the resulting population explosion at Soda Creek (the southern terminus for the riverboats), there was an unlimited market for lumber. Taking advantage of the opportunity, Billy Lyne logged his farm at Nine Mile Creek and, with his own steam sawmill, produced boards and timber to sell in the local market. In 1909, when the BC Express Company entered the riverboat trade with the building of the *SS BX*, timbers for its hull were cut on Billy Lyne's sawmill. By 1912, Billy, fully occupied in the sawmill business, was cutting 12,000 feet of lumber per day and employing a dozen or more men.

To accommodate Billy's sawmill crew, and the freighters on the Cariboo Road, another large two-storey house was built, adjoining the north side of Lyne's roadhouse. Almost as large as the original, the addition was built of lumber from Billy's mill. At this time, the interior of the original house was renovated, with solid lumber partitions being built between the rooms, and the upstairs bedrooms being completed. As a finishing touch, the outside of the house was covered with planed drop siding and painted white to create a smart, modern appearance. In summer, a heavy growth of hops cascaded over the porch and almost to the roof, sheltering the buildings from the hot afternoon sun.

It was in 1914, just following the building of this addition, that Billy and Angelique had a serious disagreement, ending with Billy moving into the new house, where he lived alone for the rest of his life. The quarrel, partly over Billy's extravagances, was really over his drinking habits. It wasn't that he drank continuously, for most of the time he was a hard worker and a good provider; but when he got to drinking, his behaviour was intolerable. While drunk he would go off on long trips, taking large amounts of cash with him. His extravagance knew no bounds. Once, on a trip to Vancouver, he took with him $2,000 from the office safe. Three weeks later, without having communicated with his family, Billy phoned for more money to enable him to get back home.

In earlier times, Billy always had a team of expensive, high-spirited horses, which he usually drove too fast. On one occasion, while taking Angelique and the children to town in the cutter, he turned a corner of the road too quickly and dumped them all out into a snowbank. It was quite a while before he realized he had lost his passengers, but by that time they had found their own way home. When cars became fashionable, Billy had one of the first in the country, along with Bill Collins, Alex Meiss, and riverboat captain Donald Foster of Soda Creek. One day, Captain Foster just happened to have an unopened bottle of rum on the seat of his Grey Dort. Also in the car was Foster's fierce bulldog. When Foster announced that he would give the bottle to whomever could get it past the bulldog, Alex Meiss, with his peg-leg, won easily. While the wooden leg held the dog at bay, Alex reached in and grabbed the bottle; but his peg-leg bore the scars forever.

Preparations to install water into Lyne's roadhouse first began in 1915. Up the creek, now known as Lyne Creek, piping was installed to carry the water down to the house, but that was as far as it got. In October that year, a contingent of young Cariboo men left home to serve in the First World War, and David, the only son of Billy and Angelique Lyne, was among them. Almost every eligible male in the area signed up, creating a severe labour shortage, and for years the water pipes and equipment lay waiting to be connected. Finally, in the early 1950s, when Jim Rankin, Angelique's great grandson, was a teenager, he helped to install a bathroom behind his granny's bedroom.

While the sluggish economy and the common use of cars and trucks almost eliminated business at the roadhouses, the building of the Pacific Great Eastern Railway to Quesnel in 1920 brought temporary relief. During construction, gangs of railway workers lived in camps up and down the line, and roadhouse farms sold meat and vegetables to the camp cooks. The building of the railway also gave Billy Lyne a few contracts to supply bridge timbers and ties.

A decade later, Billy, now in his seventies, turned the ranch over to his son, David. Having given up drinking entirely, he spent a lot of time at Williams Lake with Sam Marwick, renewing his blacksmithing skills. The change in management was not sudden, for David Lyne had been slowly buying the ranch from his father since his return from the war. Through the years, Angelique continued to live at home, caring for her mother, Helene Dussault. Bedridden and almost blind before she died, Helene was almost 100 years old.

Billy Lyne died at home on a very cold day in December 1949; he was eighty-three years old. Angelique, who lived to be ninety, died on 26 February 1957. Following the sudden death of David Lyne on 2 June 1960, the ranch was sold to Charles and Verna Groundwater. During their tenure, they donated the land for the Lyne family graveyard. Maintained by the descendants, it contains all the original members of the William Lyne Jr family as well as a number of other relatives. When the Groundwaters sold the ranch to George Lumley in the 1970s, the original buildings were replaced with a modern ranchhouse.

ROUND TENT, 1861

The earliest reference to a stopping place known as Round Tent may be found on Judge Begbie's map of November 1861, which refers to "Round Tent Lakes," situated on the trail south of Big Lake and north of Deep Creek. Almost the identical reference is found on Lieutenant H. S. Palmer's map of 1863, where "Round Tent Lakes" connects with a trail to the west at Mud Lake. In a reference found in a travel brochure entitled *Three Years in Cariboo*, published in 1862 and written by ex-packer Joe Lindley, Round Tent is estimated to be twelve miles north of Deep Creek.[17] The only known application for land at this site was registered on 24 January 1863, when a pre-emption for 160 acres of land "situated at Round Tent" was recorded in the name of Charles Guntrot; but it was never completed.[18]

In 1862, when the largest wave of population to the Cariboo gold rush passed through the country, Round Tent was mentioned in a number of diaries. Captain Buckley, who travelled on horseback, bemoaned the lack of feed there; and James Thomson of Edwardsburgh, Upper Canada, "passed Round Tent" twice that summer. Presumably, then, as early as 1861 Round Tent was a campground beside the trail to the Quesnel River, where some enterprising person (perhaps Charles Guntrot himself) had erected a round canvas tent and conducted either a saloon, a gambling place, or a store (or perhaps all three).

BIG LAKE RANCH AND ROADHOUSE, 1896
Lot 461, G.1., Cariboo

Land at Big Lake, a sizeable body of water located twenty-four miles northeast of the 150 Mile House, was first settled by A. Anderson, William Nicholl, and George Agard, who pre-empted 480 acres there in June 1862. The lack of further development at this site indicates that the pre-emption was made on the assumption that the wagon road to the goldfields would pass this way. When the road was built via Soda Creek and Quesnelle Mouth instead, the property was abandoned.

Thirty-four years later, in October 1896, William Parker, a quiet, well-mannered young man from Wisconsin, applied for 343 acres of land situated "on the north shore of Big Lake, near the road to the 150 Mile House."[19] Having established his own stage line and obtained the mail contract, Parker and his associates built a large stopping house, barns, and cowsheds on the north end of the lake. An article in the *BC Mining Journal* of 4 July 1895 stated: "Mr. Parker was for many years a trusted employee of the BC Express Co., and drove from Quesnelle to the 83 Mile House and back, for several years, and is now in the employ of the government, as a special policeman."[20] His appointment as special policeman was to ensure the safe delivery of gold bullion, via Parker's Stage Line, from Hobson's mine on the Quesnel River to Ashcroft.

The Big Lake stopping house, a large, squared-log building operated by Parker's housekeeper, Mrs McNutt, was a lively place during the early 1900s. With a post office located in the roadhouse, and a constant flow of overnight guests travelling on Parker's Stage Line, Mrs McNutt was a busy woman. A 1990 advertisement in the *Ashcroft Journal* read:

Parker's Stage Line.
Leaving Ashcroft every Monday for Clinton, 150 Mile, Quesnelle Forks, Cariboo Mine, and Horsefly. Stage will connect with steamer "Charlotte" at Soda Creek for Quesnelle, Barkerville and other northern points.[21]

While most ranches in the area raised only cattle, William Parker also kept flocks of sheep, which were butchered and sold to the mines. As

William Parker's House at Big Lake. The roadhouse was built in 1895 and burned in 1954. (COURTESY BCARS)

he grew older he became very hard of hearing, finally resorting to carrying scraps of paper on which people wrote messages. While he was never ill a day in his life, Bill Parker died in his sleep on 16 September 1927 due to high blood pressure.

The Big Lake Ranch and lodge was purchased in 1939 by Paddy Harrison (nee Patricia F. Wynn Johnson) and her husband "Pack" of Alkali Lake. When Pack died a year later, Paddy carried on until her marriage to Harold Cripps, an employee of the Wynn Johnsons at Alkali. During this time, a Mrs Clegg ran the Big Lake Lodge. In 1954, shortly after the Big Lake Ranch was sold, the old house burned down.

Notes to Chapter 4

1. Sergeant John McMurphy, RE, Diary, 23 June 1863, E/B/M221, BCARS, 35.

2. Route of Western Union Telegraph Line, Yale to Quesnelle Mouth, BC, drawn by J.C. White from notes by J. McClure, June 1866, 17B8, map collection, Bancroft Library, Berkeley, California.

3. Sketch from Lillooet to Quesnel River drawn by Gustavus B. Wright. S/615pBC/W947, 1862, BCARS.

4. Captain C. W. Buckley, Diary, 9 July 1862, E/B/B85, BCARS.

5. *Colonist* (Victoria), 18 May 1863, 3.

6. McMurphy, Diary, 25 May 1863.

7.   Louis LeBourdais, "Harry Jones Story," addit. MSS 676, vol. 7, pp. 15–16, BCARS.

8.   Dr W. B. Cheadle, Journal, 13 November 1863, E/B/C42.1, parts 3 and 4, BCARS.

9.   Henry M. Ball, Diary, 22 May 1865, addit. MSS 681, BCARS.

10. *Colonist* (Victoria), 6 October 1862, 3.

11. *British Columbia Tribune*, 10 September 1866, 3.

12. *Cariboo Sentinel*, 5 May 1866, 3.

13. Sarah Crease, Diary, 15 September 1880, A/E/C86, BCARS, 9.

14. William Lyne Jr, account books, blacksmith, 1890, addit. MSS 714, BCARS.

15. Ibid., 1891.

16. William Lyne Jr, blacksmith, 1891 and 1911, addit. MSS 417, BCARS.

17. Joe Lindley, "Three Years in Cariboo," Nwp/971.35c/L740 BCARS, 7.

18. GR 112, Cariboo Pre-Emptions, 1860–69, BCARS. "Charles Guntrot, January 24, 1863, 160 acres, situated at Round Tent."

19. GR 112, Cariboo Pre-Emptions, BCARS. William Parker, 16 October 1896, Big Lake, BC.

20. *BC Mining Journal* 4 July 1895.

21. *Ashcroft Journal*, 19 May 1900.

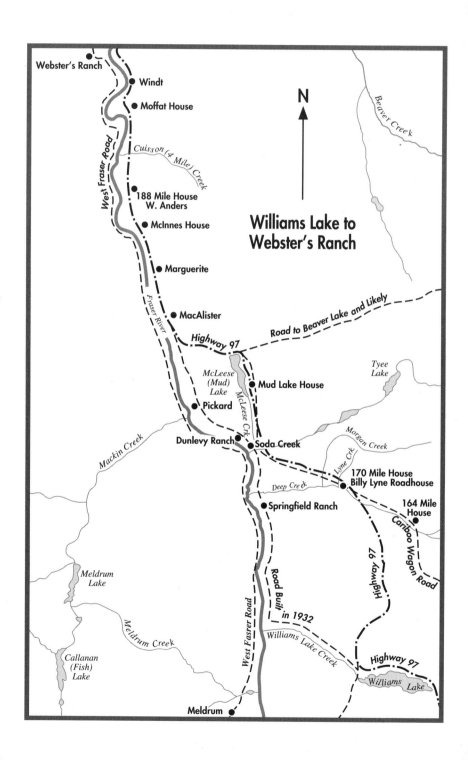

Webster's Ranch

Windt

Moffat House

Cuisson (4 Mile) Creek

188 Mile House
W. Anders

McInnes House

Marguerite

MacAlister

West Fraser Road

Fraser River

N

Williams Lake to
Webster's Ranch

Beaver Creek

Road to Beaver Lake and Likely

Highway 97

McLeese (Mud) Lake

Mud Lake House

Tyee Lake

Pickard

McLeese Crk.

Dunlevy Ranch

Soda Creek

Morgan Creek

Lyne Crk.

170 Mile House
Billy Lyne Roadhouse

164 Mile House

Springfield Ranch

Deep Creek

Mackin Creek

Meldrum Lake

Meldrum Creek

Callanan (Fish) Lake

West Fraser Road

Road Built
in 1932

Williams Lake Creek

Highway 97

Highway 97

Cariboo Wagon Road

Meldrum

Williams Lake

CHAPTER FIVE

The River Trail, Williams Lake to Webster's Ranch

By the year 1862, many hundreds of prospectors had tried their luck in the Cariboo goldfields. Most were unsuccessful, and, when funds ran out, they had to leave or find alternate means of survival. Some found employment as labourers in established mines, while others turned to the land and became farmers. North of Williams Lake lay thousands of acres of arable land along the tiered benches of the Fraser River. There were two types of land pre-emptors — the speculators, who sold their land for profit as soon as regulations permitted, and the settlers, who took up permanent residence, clearing the fields and raising crops for sale to the mines.

During the summer of 1862, a year before the Cariboo Road reached Alexandria, Bishop George Hills and his party travelled north, en route to the goldfields. Leaving Williams Lake by way of the Mission Creek Roadhouse, they took the river trail:

> *Wednesday, 16 July 1862. Rain early. Left our Camping Ground at 9. Took the River Road by Alexandria. The Road lay up a steep ascent onto a Bench over which we travelled for about 8 miles. There was a great deal of Forest, grass, and small trees without much underwood ... Passing a creek, we came to the Fraser, and rode 4 miles over fine open country to Deep Creek.* [1]

SPRINGFIELD RANCH, 1862
Lots 3, 4, 5, 6, and 7, G.4., Cariboo

In 1862, a large tract of arable land a mile south of Deep Creek was occupied by five returning miners. These were speculators who went by the name of Edward Packe & Company and who, very shortly, sold their pre-emptions to Frederick Townsend of Quesnelle Mouth. For a time, Townsend rented the land to the Beck brothers, two young Englishmen who kept up their English traditions on a certain field on the ranch still known as "the cricket field." By 1865, Townsend had sold the property, which now contained about a thousand acres, to John Colin Calbraith, one of G. B. Wright's partners in the road-building project of 1863. Calbraith took on a partner, John Frances Hawkes of Springfield, Ohio, and, between them, they produced many acres of hay and grain. By 1866, "The Springs," as their home was known, had become a popular stop for travellers. A frequent visitor was Judge Begbie, who made a point of staying at the ranch during his annual assize circuits. On one occasion, Begbie presented Hawkes with a gift of two white lilac plants from his garden in Victoria; it is said that they are still flourishing.

During the early 1870s, when John Calbraith left the Cariboo, he sold his interests in the ranch to his partner Hawkes, who renamed it "Springfield," after his home town in Ohio. As an entrepreneur, Hawkes was involved in several local enterprises, including the Protection Flour Mills on Soda Creek. Prior to his departure from the Cariboo in 1890, John Hawkes sold Springfield Ranch to Herman Nichols, who continued to reside in the old house built by Calbraith until March 1897, when it was destroyed by fire.

The Calbraith & Hawke's farm, south of Soda Creek, is pictured in the 1860s before it became known as Springfield Ranch. (COURTESY BCARS)

By 1900, William Adams, the new owner of Springfield Ranch, built a modern residence. Adams, a successful miner on Lightning Creek (and, later, an MLA for the Cariboo in the provincial elections of 1893) had a daughter, Katherine, who married John Hargreaves, a remittance man. When Adams retired, he sold the ranch to the young couple. The Hargreaves, who operated an efficient ranch, were also known for their lavish entertaining. Their most famous house guest was Prime Minister Mackenzie King, who visited there during the 1930s. When Hargreaves's dog barked at the distinguished visitor, King was told not to worry, for the dog only attacked Conservatives.

During John Hargreaves's tenure, Springfield Ranch grew to include over 2,000 acres of land. Upon his death in 1950, his son, Rae Hargreaves, continued the operation until 1963, when it was sold to C. W. Hoffman Jr of Oregon.

SODA CREEK, 1863–1930s

Even as G. B. Wright negotiated the terms of his road contract in 1862, he and his associates, the Douglas Navigation Company, were arranging construction of a steam-driven sternwheel riverboat to carry passengers and freight from the upper Fraser River terminus of the Cariboo Road to Quesnelle Mouth, sixty miles upstream. News of these plans, reported in March of that year, were met with great interest by merchants and entrepreneurs in Victoria, California, and New Westminster.

The steamer was built at Four Mile Creek, but not until after its launch in May 1863 was the site for a southern terminus chosen. The most favoured site was a small bench of land at the mouth of Soda

John F. Hawkes of Deep Creek and Springfield Ranch. 1870s. (COURTESY BCARS)

Creek, south of Fort Alexandria: "A feasible place for the approach of mule trains."[2] With a government reserve placed on the site early in 1863, it was still uncertain whether a steamer could safely navigate the rapids just north of Soda Creek. Following the launch of the *SS Enterprise* on 9 May 1863, Captain Doane found a channel through the dreaded rapids and piloted the boat safely down to Soda Creek. An excited and jubilant G. B. Wright wrote to Colonel Moody a few days later:

My Dear Colonel,

We have accomplished what we undertook, the building of a steamer on the upper Fraser and made successfully, a trip from Fort Alexandria to the Mouth of Quesnelle, and down the river to Soda Creek ... the little boat performs to our perfect satisfaction, the river much better than anticipated ... We shall make two trips a week ... We have reduced the price of freight from 5cts. to 2 1/2cts.[3]

Wright and his associates were assured all the business the boat could handle. Within two years, *SS Enterprise* had earned three times the $75,000 spent building it. With Soda Creek as the southern terminus, passengers leaving the evening boat from Quesnelle Mouth had just enough time to reach the roadhouse at Deep Creek, in which Wright held half interest.

As Wright's road approached the area of the steamer landing at Soda Creek, a branch road was built up the steep hill from the river. Sergeant McMurphy's diary of 16 July 1863 records the fast-moving events:

Showery, a camp of seventy six Chinamen has gone down into Soda Creek and will work back towards the junction of the trail and wagon road ... There is a great deal of traffic coming this way in wagons and pack trains ... At the steamer landing found Mr. McLeese of New Westminster, building a house for himself to carry on the Whiskey Trade.[4]

Robert McLeese, a native of Carrdreagh, County Antrim, Ireland, arrived in eastern Canada in 1858, and travelled west to New Westminster in 1861 to work as a carpenter and building contractor. In 1862, he became chief engineer of the New Westminster Fire Department. Upon reading of Wright's road and his sternwheeler on the upper Fraser River, McLeese and his partner, Joseph T. Senay, recognized potential business opportunities. That summer at Soda Creek, they obtained a building site close to the steamer landing and pre-empted some nearby farm land.

THE COLONIAL HOTEL, 1863
Lot 6, Townsite of Soda Creek

From an 1868 photograph of McLeese & Senay's Colonial Hotel at Soda Creek, taken by Frederick Dally, the building appears to be a tidy, well-designed structure consisting of two, thirty-foot sections of squared logs dove-tailed together in the centre. The northern half was a two-storey hotel, with a shake roof running east and west. The single-storey southern section, with the roof running north and south, housed the saloon and store. The two main entrances faced the river, and, over these, a full-length roof which doubled as a balcony. Upon this was displayed a large sign, with "COLONIAL HOTEL" painted in very large letters.

A rather nondescript advertisement of the Colonial Hotel appeared in the *Cariboo Sentinel* of 7 May 1866:

> *COLONIAL HOTEL, SODA CREEK.*
> *The public are invited to call at this House.*
> *There is good meals, good beds, stabling for horses.*
> *Barley, Oats and Hay.*
> *McLeese & Senay, proprietors.*[5]

THE DUNLEVY ROADHOUSE AND FARM, SODA CREEK, 1862
Lots 1 and 2, G.4, Cariboo

Following their successful mining ventures at Little Horsefly Creek in 1859, Peter Dunlevy and his partners invested their fortunes in several profitable roadhouse farms at Beaver Lake, Mud Lake, and

Frederick Dally's 1868 photograph of the Colonial Hotel built by Robert McLeese, 1863. (COURTESY BCARS)

Williams Lake. When news of the building of G. B. Wright's steamer on the upper Fraser River broke in early 1862, Peter Dunlevy, with great foresight, pre-empted and bought a large tract of land about two miles north of Soda Creek. Here he established one of the most valuable farms in the upper Cariboo and opened a roadhouse beside the Hudon's Bay Company brigade trail, which ran through the property. Even prior to the rise of Soda Creek, this roadhouse farm was a busy place. Sergeant John McMurphy, writing in his diary of the exciting developments at Soda Creek, also mentions Dunlevy's farm:

> *From Soda Creek up it will all be farmed in a short time, in fact already above the steamer landing is a farm of 640 acres ... The only drawback along the Fraser will be the scarcity of water. The party preempting two miles above Soda Creek will have to bring their water from a creek, by ditching, which will be expensive ... The steamer is doing very well making two trips a week, and getting a good amount of freight.[6]*

The Sergeant was correct in predicting the need to irrigate the rich soil of the river benches above Soda Creek. By 1869, with over 200 acres under cultivation, Dunlevy was having to carry water by flume from Mud Lake, (McLeese) three miles away. The expense incurred was justified in the heavy crops of grain and three crops of alfalfa harvested

At his Soda Creek house, Robert McLeese stands on the far left, with Jean McLeese, his only child, second from the right. (COURTESY BCARS)

each season. Once the wagon road was built and Soda Creek became established as the southern terminus of the steamer, Dunlevy and his partners opened a hotel, saloon, and store close to the landing.

THE EXCHANGE HOTEL, SODA CREEK, 1863
Lot 7, Townsite of Soda Creek

While there had been only one hotel at Soda Creek in July 1863, by August a second facility appeared right beside it. So close together were these two buildings that, to the unknowing eye, they appeared as one. This was the Exchange Hotel, saloon, and store, built by George Hendricks for Peter Dunlevy and his partners. Largest of the two hotels, the Exchange was built of log timbers, measuring about eighty by forty feet. Of a simple but practical design, it had, in comparison to McLeese's Hotel, an austere and uninviting appearance due to the fact that none of its windows faced the street. Of rectangular shape and composed of two full storeys, the logs were dove-tailed in the middle and on the corners. Between the logs were wide bands of lime and mortar, which were used to hold in the moss chinking. Two rock chimneys, one on the north wall of the hotel, and another in the store, appear to have provided the only sources of heat. A single shake roof, without much overhang, ran north and south.

In conjunction with the saloon, housed in the southern section of the building, Dunlevy's store was of particular interest to miners on their way to the goldfields. As one of the first free traders in the country, and as an experienced miner, Dunlevy sold a wide variety of mining tools and equipment. Local Native trappers and their families also frequented Dunlevy's store, trading their furs and leather goods for flour, tea, sugar, and tobacco.

One of the first of many groups of miners to visit Dunlevy's store was Captain John Evans and his company of twenty-six Welsh miners, who reached Soda Creek in the summer of 1863. Harry Jones, one of the youngest of the group, was not with them, having been sent back to Lillooet on a special errand. When Harry reached Soda Creek a short time later, he found that Captain Evans had arranged with Peter Dunlevy to see that he got a square meal and a ticket on the steamer to Quesnelle Mouth: "He took me into the hotel for supper," wrote Harry in his diary, "then later, at 9.00 p.m. he piloted me down to the boat where I was put in the care of the purser."[7]

During the first two years of operation, and before the wagon road reached Quesnelle Mouth, the two hotels at Soda Creek did a fantastic

The Exchange Hotel at Soda Creek was built by Mr G. Hendricks in 1863 and purchased by Dunlevy that same year. (COURTESY BCARS)

amount of business. With the arrival of at least two pack-trains a day, the twice-weekly stagecoach, and the comings and goings of dozens of miners, the hotels, along with their saloons and stores, were never closed. After 1864, when there was a downturn in the economy, the hotels became more competitive. To encourage business, each hotel acquired some franchise or service unavailable at the other. At the Exchange Hotel, the proprietors, as agents of Barnard's Express & Stage Line, contracted to build a large barn and livery stable behind the hotel. While the first post office, housed in the Colonial Hotel had opened in 1864, within the year the service had been moved to the Exchange Hotel, with Joseph Senay as postmaster.

During the early years, while Peter Dunlevy operated the Soda Creek farm and managed the store at the Exchange Hotel, his partners (Thomas Menefee, Ira Crow, and Thomas Moffitt) operated the hotel and saloon. Jim Sellers, the other partner, remained at Beaver Lake, where he operated the roadhouse there until 1865. Unlike many partnerships, the Dunlevy consortium continued long after its members made their initial fortunes in 1859. Thomas Menefee, who suffered great financial loss when Wright's road bypassed Williams Lake, was, at the time of his death, a half owner of Dunlevy's Soda Creek farm and the Exchange Hotel. A considerable force to be reckoned with was Thomas Moffitt, proprietor of the saloon. Never considered to be much of a miner, Moffitt more than proved his worth at the gaming tables. His uncanny memory, coupled with his dextrous fingers, fooled even the sharpest eye. Ira Crow, described as "the typical lean and lanky all around Californian,"[8] was perhaps the most competent miner of the group , and when he wasn't mining, was also involved in the operation of the Exchange Hotel. Crow was proprietor early in 1868, when the partners entered into an agreement with Aschel S. Bates. At this time, the hotel underwent extensive renovations. Once these were completed, Bates and Crow placed a lengthy advertisement in the *Cariboo Sentinel* detailing the good, clean, and airy bed chambers; the well-stocked bar; the luxuries of the table; and the first-class hostlers which tended the stables. However, despite its length, this advertisement failed to point out a most important feature of the newly renovated premises. Consequently, a shorter notice appeared soon after:

> *"We take pleasure in calling the public's attention to improvements in hotel accommodation. The latest addition in this respect is the Exchange Hotel at Soda Creek. The rooms have been fitted up with special reference to the comforts of ladies and families travelling to and from this district, and all the little appliances for comfort, equal to an Victorian hotel may be enjoyed.*[9]

These "considerations for ladies and families" were now becoming standard facilities in all roadhouses and hotels along the Cariboo Road.

In describing the excellent meals served at the Exchange Hotel, the advertisement of March 1868 did not exaggerate — at least not during the summer months, when fresh vegetables and fruit were available. Grown on Dunlevy's farm, these luxuries did much to add to the popularity of the hotel. In July 1868, while on business at Barkerville, Dunlevy left a gift of fresh garden peas for the editor of the *Cariboo Sentinel*. From his own early experiences, he knew what it was like to live where almost all food had to be imported. The resulting public acknowledgement, published in the 13 July 1868 issue of the *Cariboo Sentinel*, offers a sample of the menu at the Exchange Hotel:

> *We must say we envy the guests of mine host of the Exchange Hotel who are now daily treated to roast lamb and fresh garden peas, together with all the other delicacies of the season.*[10]

By 1869, the Exchange Hotel was once again managed by Dunlevy & Company. Bates, who was arranging to purchase the Deep Creek farm, dissolved his partnership with Crow, who left Soda Creek soon after for the Omineca gold rush, where he managed one of Dunlevy's trading posts.

Over their many years of operation, frequent social events were held at the two hotels in Soda Creek, especially during the long winters, when things could get very dull. A New Year's Eve ball held at the Exchange Hotel on 31 December 1872 was attended by about fifty men and twenty women, and it continued for the better part of two days and nights, with only one fight reported. But the changing scene at Soda Creek was not confined to the Exchange Hotel. At McLeese's Colonial Hotel, many events, both joyful and sad, were also occurring.

During the summer of 1868, Joseph Triffle Senay had married the former Annie Wall of Victoria, and, following a short honeymoon, the newlyweds returned to make their home at Soda Creek, where Senay was postmaster and part owner of the Colonial Hotel. Barely a year later, on 19 June 1869, Oscar Tallman's canoe ferry capsized while crossing the river at Quesnelle, and all the occupants, including the Senays, a Mr Livingstone, and Tallman, were pitched into the icy water. Just downstream, at the mouth of the Quesnel River, Gus Wright, at work with two labourers, was preparing for the launching of his second sternwheeler, the *SS Victoria*.10 On witnessing the accident, Wright quickly set out upon the river in a small rowboat and managed to rescue Joseph Senay and Mr Livingstone, but Annie Senay and Oscar Tallman were drowned.[11]

This tragedy seriously depressed Joseph Senay, who left the Cariboo soon after, dissolving his partnership in the hotel and resigning as postmaster of Soda Creek. While Bob McLeese was appointed post-master in Senay's place, there appeared to be little remuneration for the position: "These appointments, we believe are honorary, or at most the allowance is minimal, as the gentlemen appointed being engaged in trade, the advantages derived from the location of the post office in his respective establishment must be considerable."[12]

Peter Curran Dunlevy, Cariboo Miner and Entrepreneur, 1859–1904.
Jane Elizabeth Huston, second wife of Peter C. Dunlevy. (COURTESY BCARS)

There may, indeed, have been "considerable advantage" to having the post office in the Colonial Hotel, especially in 1869, when the merchants, bogged down in the financial slump of the mid-1860s, experienced a sudden upswing brought on by the discovery of gold in the Omineca, located northwest of Fort George. As word spread of the new strike, hundreds of prospectors and opportunists arrived at Soda Creek, where G. B. Wright and his associates were operating two steamers. The increased activity more than doubled business at the hotels and stores. The farmers of the area, from Quesnelle Mouth to Williams Lake, took advantage of new markets in the Omineca, where they opened stores and hotels wherever the miners congregated. At Soda Creek, where John Adams had built a mill in 1867, locally produced flour was shipped to the Omineca; and, from Williams Lake, Pinchbeck's distilled whisky made its way to the goldfields. Transportation to the Omineca was mostly by way of river barge, although some entrepreneurs, such as William Pinchbeck, had a boat built especially for transporting goods to his hotel and store at Manson Creek. So great was the exodus of labouring men to the Omineca that, in the spring of 1871, farmers feared their crops would not get planted.

By 1872, with the end of the short-lived Omineca gold rush, things settled down again, and Robert McLeese was appointed as Justice of the Peace in Soda Creek. The following year, while his brother John ran the hotel, Bob made a trip to Renfrew, Ontario, to marry Mary Sinclair, a girl he had known when he first arrived in Canada. A daughter,

Old jail at Soda Creek. Built by William Lyne Jr 1900. Still standing in 1996.

Jean, was born the following year, but Mary Sinclair McLeese died in 1876, while giving birth to a second child.

As did most White men of the 1860s, Peter Dunlevy married a Native woman — "a Dene beauty from Fort Alexandria"[13] — and soon had a family of several children. These youngsters were half grown in 1873, when Dunlevy married a White woman, Jennie Huston of Victoria, who lived with him at Soda Creek not on the farm, where his first family lived, but in a house built close to the Exchange Hotel. (During the fur trade era, and even up until 1900, it was common for White men to discard their Native wives in favour of a White woman. It is said that in these instances the first wives usually accepted the situation with equanimity.)[14]

It was here that Sarah Crease and her husband visited the Dunlevys while on their trip to Barkerville in the fall of 1880. In her diary she wrote:

> Went down very steep, winding sandy road into Soda Creek, light rain. Arrived safely at 6.00 p.m. at Dunlevy's house. Mrs. D. received us in her nice little parlour with nursemaid and two children. Dined at the public table — slept on board the steamer. Stage came in at midnight bringing lawyers Davey and Harrison. Got up steam and left at 4.00 a.m.[15]

On her way south in October, Sarah Crease wrote again of Soda Creek, the Dunlevys, and the Exchange Hotel:

> Arrived Soda Creek at 6.00 p.m. Mr. and Mrs. Dunlevy received us at their private house and Mrs. Dunlevy gave us some music on her fine piano, (a Steiner, from New York) — would play well with more practice ... Retired early to our own room in the wayside House — a wretchedly dark and dirty place — Bedroom very small and open at the top to other rooms. Double bed with very short clothes. Towel, a kitchen runner! Chairs in sitting room, three out of four without seats! Our host and hostess were, however, personally kind and attentive. Their two small children and their nurse were always present at the table.[16]

While Henry Crease was Dunlevy's lawyer, and the Creases had obviously been invited to call on the Dunlevys while in Soda Creek, it is still surprising that Sarah made no mention of Robert McLeese, who, at that time, was gaining stature in political circles within the Cariboo. In 1882, McLeese became the member of the legislative assembly

This photo of Soda Creek shows the steamboat landing site in the 1930s.
(COURTESY BCARS)

(MLA) for the Cariboo, a position which he held until 1888. Retired from politics, but still operating the Colonial Hotel, Robert McLeese died at his home at Soda Creek on 29 March 1898. At this time, his estate, including the hotel and the farm in the Mud Lake Valley, fell to his daughter Jean. Owing to her mother's death while she was still very young, Jean McLeese had been sent away to school in Victoria and, except for annual visits, had remained away until her father's death.

Peter Dunlevy, a man in his mid-sixties in the 1890s, was also beginning to slow down, living the life of a country gentleman on his farm at Soda Creek. Through the years he had continued his keen interest in mining and mining exploration in British Columbia. Heavily involved in the operation of a stamp mill at the Island Mountain Quartz Mine in the mid-1880s, Dunlevy experienced one of his very few failed ventures. "He spent a fortune there trying to extract gold from a rebellious ore, and failed, only because at that time there was no known process for doing this commercially."[17]

Peter Dunlevy died at his home on 15 October 1904, a few days short of his seventy-first birthday. He was survived by his wife Jennie and five children. This did not include the several children from his Native family.

Jennie, who later married Dr Mostyn Hoops, maintained a controlling interest in the farm and hotel at Soda Creek until 1920, when the farm was sold to Thomas Douglas, an Alberta cattleman, and the hotel property was sold to William G. Crowston. During the 1920s, when William Crowston owned most of the land in Soda Creek, many of the old buildings were torn down, including the two original hotels. The Dunlevy residence, which had served as a roadhouse on the farm in the early days, remained standing until 1990. The owners at this time, the Kaufman family, wished to dispose of the old building but were hesitant to do so, realizing its historical significance. However, after several failed attempts to find it a new home, the building was torn down.

THE PICKARD RANCH AND ROADHOUSE, 1898
Lot 5100, G.1., Cariboo

Seven miles north of Soda Creek was the Pickard farm, a property first pre-empted by John Mackin and later owned by James Conroy of the Okanagan Mission. George Pickard, a man of French and Welsh extraction from St John, New Brunswick, had made his way across Canada to the West Coast in the late 1870s. An uncle of George's, Fabien Picard, a Hudson's Bay Company voyageur, had been at Quesnelle Mouth in the 1860s, and George followed in his footsteps, arriving there around 1880. By 1885, George Pickard had married Caroline (Carrie) Agnes Elmore. From the time they were small children, Carrie and her older sister, Cecilia, daughters of Marvin P. Elmore of Quesnelle Mouth, had attended St Joseph's Mission School in Williams Lake. Carrie was only sixteen when she married George Pickard, a man more than twice her age. For a while, the Pickards farmed at Quesnelle on land that is today known as LeBourdais Park; from there they went into partnership with Robert Middleton, becoming part owners of a ranch on the west side of the Fraser River, about twenty-five miles south of Quesnelle. The partnership was a stormy one, lasting only a few years. Following a serious quarrel, the alliance was dissolved, and George Pickard and his family left the ranch. With the money from his share of the Middleton Ranch, Pickard purchased 160 acres of land on the east bank of the Fraser River, seven miles north of Soda Creek.

At first, the Pickards, with their family of seven children, lived in a small log house on the property, but by 1900 they had moved into a new, two-storey log house built beside the original wagon road, which passed through the north end of the ranch. The house, of saddle-and-notch construction, (round logs) contained eight rooms, including five bedrooms. The kitchen range and the living-room heater provided warmth to the whole house, including the upstairs bedrooms. Six other children were born in the roadhouse, making a total of thirteen, and all lived to adulthood. Carrie was forty-four and George was seventy-three when their last child, Roy, was born in 1916.

Situated in a most pleasant climate where it was possible to grow almost anything, even fruit trees, Pickard's ranch, with a large vegetable garden, a few head of beef cattle, a milk cow, chickens, and a number of sheep, provided many of the basic needs of this very large family. Carrie and her daughters made good use of the sheep, selling wool and making quilts and mattresses for the family beds. In addition to her other work, Carrie Pickard cooked meals for the freight-wagon drivers and, occasionally, for individuals. With her large family occupying most of the house, only one bedroom was kept aside for paying guests, and the freighters slept on straw mattresses in a nearby bunkhouse.

George Pickard was also a hard worker, and, in addition to developing the land, he took whatever outside work was available. For a period of ten years, between 1886 and 1896, when the river was without a steamboat, Pickard took contracts to raft lumber and shingles from the Reid and Johnston sawmill at Quesnel, downstream to Soda Creek. The loads averaged about 1,000 feet of material, and, at times, could be a dangerous undertaking.

A photograph of the Pickard roadhouse, taken in the 1920s, shows a typical Cariboo farmyard; the two-storey log house with overhanging front porch, the fenced vegetable garden, the family wash on the line, and the several milk cows reclining in the shade of the barn. As the

The house, built in 1900, is still standing at George Pickard's ranch and roadhouse eight miles north of Soda Creek. (COURTESY BCARS)

children grew up, they were able to take over many of the farm chores and the housework. While horses were still being used on the road, the eldest son, Ralph, operated a successful blacksmith shop; and Tom, who was born on the Middleton farm, was a freighter by the time he was fourteen. At that time, it took thirty-five days to make a return trip from Ashcroft to Barkerville.[18]

Following the death of George Pickard in 1923, Carrie left the ranch in the care of her sons, Roy and Marvin, and her daughter, Bertha, while she went to live with Ralph in Alberta. Marvin Pickard eventually bought the farm and lived there until 1958, when he sold out to rancher Huston Dunaway. For the last few years of her life, Carrie Pickard lived with her daughter, Vera Morrison, at Quesnel. She died on 13 January 1952 at the age of eighty-three.

Until very recently, the old roadhouse of 1900 was still occupied by Jack Lozier and his family. With the building of a new home on the property, the old roadhouse now stands empty, its future uncertain.

MARGUERITE AND MACALISTER

From their camp near Mud Lake, (now called McLeese Lake) on 17 July 1862, Bishop Hills and his companion, the Reverend C. Knipe, rode through eight miles of dense woods before the trail rose to open benchland overlooking the Fraser River. This area was to become known as Macalister. It was in the summer of 1911 when James Macalister first settled on the land named in his honour.

The region known as Marguerite, about three miles further north, had been named much earlier, after a beloved Native woman who ran a ranch there in the 1860s.

FORT ALEXANDRIA AND ALEXANDRIA

It was well known that the Hudson's Bay Company had cultivated many acres of grain on its lands surrounding Fort Alexandria (1821–1867), and had operated a grist mill at Four Mile Creek, just north of the fort. Here flour and cereals were produced for its own use, and for shipment to the northern posts of New Caledonia. With the abandonment of these lands in the late 1860s, many of the company's employees remained to live in the existing buildings and to farm the land. One of these was Baptiste Paquette, a French voyageur who made application to pre-empt 160 acres of land seventeen miles north of Soda Creek and within a mile of Fort Alexandria. Pacquette's land had been the site of the North West Company trading post at

Alexandria, which was established in 1814 by Lieutenant John Stuart. It was known that Pacquette kept a stopping house in the building believed to be a remnant of the original post. By 1873 this land had changed hands again.

MCINNES HOUSE, ALEXANDRIA, 1873
Lots 444 and 445, G.1., Cariboo

Residing in Nanaimo in 1860, Alexander Douglas McInnes, a Glasgow Scot, had, by 1863 arrived at Williams Creek, where he purchased an interest in the Cameron claim. There McInnes met Anna Elizabeth (Lizzie) Roddie, an Irish woman who had arrived in the goldfields the year before to work for her sister, Mrs Richard Cameron. Lizzie, a comely lass, did not lack for suitors, and among these were Alexander "Mac" McInnes and another miner, Joseph Carruthers. Her affair with Carruthers took a serious turn when she accepted his proposal of marriage and, along with it, a share in a rich claim. When Lizzie changed her mind and married Alexander McInnes, Carruthers sued his former fiance for the return of the claim. In a court case before Judge Begbie, the recently married Lizzie denied that the gift had anything to do with her engagement to Carruthers. Judge Begbie, however, did not agree, and ruled that she was to return the mining share, as he was sure Carruthers would not have otherwise offered her such a gift.[19]

For a few years, McInnes and Lizzie kept a boarding house for the miners of the Cameron claim. During this time three children (John in 1866, Alexander Patrick in 1868, and Mary in 1869) were born in the hospital at Marysville, a community near Cameronton. By 1870, the McInneses had moved from Barkerville to Lightning Creek, where they managed a hotel at Van Winkle. A second daughter, Anne, was born there in 1873. An advertisement in the *Cariboo Sentinel* of 11 October 1873 indicated another, and final, move for the McInnes family:

New Wayside House near Alexandria.
The undersigned will open a wayside House near Fort Alexandria
at the place formerly known as "Paquette's," on November 1st.
Good stabling, Hay and Oats, and accommodation for travellers.
A.D. McInnes.[20]

With traffic passing up the Cariboo Road to Lightning Creek, where new discoveries had caused a sudden rush of staking, the McInnes family roadhouse did well during the 1870s. Situated on a high bench above the river, the house was built on a pleasant flat, close to an accommodating creek flowing down from the hillside behind. In a declaration made by A. D. McInnes in 1880, when the Hudson's Bay Company finally released all claims on land at Alexandria, the McInnes roadhouse was described as a "two storey log house of seven rooms." Also mentioned were "stabling for 40 horses, a granary, a blacksmith shop, a warehouse, and a chicken house [as well as] 140 acres under cultivation [and] two miles of fencing."[21] In 1902 when a Crown grant was issued, these lands became lots 444 and 445, G.1., Cariboo.

Above the original, single-log "square" of the North West Company post of 1814, a second storey had been added; and all around it were several other additions, each with a shake roof set at a different angle. During the 1920s, when Alvin Johnston of Quesnel began to travel the Cariboo Road, he came to know the McInnes road-house well. He described it thus: "Had you seen the place at dusk, it would have reminded you of an old mother hen, trying to cover up an oversized brood of little chicks."[22]

With "Old Mac" McInnes as the jovial host, McInnes House was a popular place with both travellers and locals. Appearing like a character out of Dickens, McInnes, with his mutton-chop whiskers, long sideburns, and tam o' shanter, ran the stopping place like an old country inn. Drinks were served at tables set around the main dining room, but, at night, the bottles were kept locked up in a cupboard under the bar. McInnes was known for his eloquence and loved to entertain his guests with stories of his years at Barkerville. A favourite of his was the story of Judge Cox, the resident magistrate in Barkerville in the early 1860s.

Cox, an Irishman, got along with everyone and, like many of his countrypeople, had kissed the Blarney Stone. While lodging at the McInnes boarding house in Cameronton, he and McInnes were always thinking up practical jokes to play on each other. During the gold-rush years, the miners hunted and ate many of the caribou that were living in the hills around Barkerville. One day, early in the winter of Judge Cox's first year, one of the miners of the Cameron claim shot a fine bull caribou and, after removing the entrails, left it out on the hillside while he returned to camp for help to pack it out. Upon hearing of this event, Cox immediately expressed a desire to hunt caribou. But the majestic beasts were scarce by this time; in fact, Cox might never have got a shot at a caribou had it not been for the following hoax.

In order to please the Judge, and also to play a joke on him, it was decided to forego looking for another animal and, instead, to stand the frozen caribou on its legs at one end of an open hillside, close to a

The McInnes roadhouse at Marguerite. The original "square" of the building had been a North West Comany fur depot in 1814. (COURTESY BCARS)

bushy pine tree. Behind the tree, the miner who had shot it would hold on to a stout rope attached to the carcass. It was planned to lead Judge Cox to within sight of the caribou and, when he fired his gun, to have the miner behind the tree pull on the rope. Everything went as planned, until Cox fired his gun. Unfortunately, his aim was so poor that, instead of hitting the caribou, the bullet whistled past the ear of the miner behind the tree, narrowly missing him. When the caribou went down, Judge Cox was ecstatic, believing he had killed the animal; but the miner behind the bush was not so pleased. Traumatized at being almost killed, he couldn't keep quiet. When the truth came out, Judge Cox had a hard time living it down.

Besides being able to tell a good yarn, McInnes, a true Scot, also played the bagpipes. On occasion, he would walk up and down in front of the roadhouse and, depending on his mood, play either a mournful dirge or a gay highland tune. The sound of the pipes drifting down from McInnes House, high above the river, fairly terrified the Native people living on the reserve below.

The steady rise in population in the Alexandria area in the late 1870s led to the opening of a district post office at McInnes House on 31 March 1877, with A. D. McInnes as postmaster and Justice of the Peace. Housed in a room off the kitchen, the postal service brought increased traffic and trade, especially with regard to the dispensing of alcoholic beverages. As did most roadhouses on the Cariboo Road,

McInnes's sold liquor both by the glass and by the bottle. In November 1905, when McInnes was thought to have supplied liquor to a Native, jealous neighbours circulated a petition to have his licence removed. However, when it went to court, the matter was thrown out due to insufficient evidence.

While they were growing up, the five McInnes children were away a lot, attending school at St Joseph's Mission at Williams Lake, after which the girls remained at home until they were married. The two sons, John and "Sandy," established a ranch of their own at Beatty Creek in Beaver Valley, northeast of Williams Lake.

A. Elizabeth McInnes passed away on 26 April 1892 at the age of fifty-three and was buried in the cemetery at St Joseph's Mission. Alexander D. McInnes retired from his duties in 1904 but continued to live at home until his death on 8 April 1911. Mary, the eldest and only daughter living at home, inherited the McInnes Ranch and roadhouse. Mary had married George Rowed in 1900, and, together, they carried on with the family business. A son, Ivan, was born in 1902.

In 1905, the Roweds acquired a property at Marguerite, where they built a two-storey hotel on a hill overlooking the Fraser River. With George's death in January 1907, their plans to operate the hotel were shattered. For many years the unfinished building was used as a community gathering place and dance hall. In the meantime, Mary and her son confined their interests to the McInnes House, where Mary looked after the post office and kept boarders and overnight guests.

One of Mary Rowed's boarders was Walter H. Gurney, the first schoolteacher at Alexandria (1922) and, later, principal of the Kamloops High School. In 1971, Walter wrote an account about his two years at Alexandria, describing quite vividly both McInnes House and his hostess, Mary Rowed:

The House itself was a rambling log structure with the typical overhanging roof to protect passengers from the weather as they alighted from the stages. A back porch, pantry, kitchen, dining room and large living room comprised the main areas. Several add-on's made extra bedrooms, and there were other extra beds in the second storey at the head of a narrow stairway. Mrs. Rowed was indeed the hospitable hostess, and her home was the social centre of the neighbourhood. It did not take me long, however, to realize that Mrs. Rowed's style of housekeeping left a lot to be desired. Although accepted by the locals through long association, this condition was an awful shock to newcomers and transients. The farm yard chickens and pigs wandered in and out of the House at will; the chickens roosting behind the kitchen stove at night, while pigs slept at random on the kitchen floor. During one of my meals with Mrs. Rowed we got through the main course without incident. Then came dessert, when the Indian servant girl was sent to the pantry for canned fruit. Suddenly there was a terrifying screech, "Mrs., there's a mouse drowned in the peaches!" Mrs. Rowed's response was quick, "Well, throw out the mouse, and bring in the peaches!" Not long after that I took up housekeeping on my own in a cabin by the schoolhouse.[23]

Another story, told by a salesman who remained overnight at Mary's establishment, described how, on retiring early to his room in the upper storey, he heard Mary, who was also retiring, call out to the servant girl, "Don't forget to turn the chickens before you go to bed." Thinking that a chicken was probably cooking in the oven, the salesman thought no more of it, until early the next morning as he passed through the back porch on his way to the barn. There, roosting around an open barrel of flour, were several chickens, their heads turned in.[24]

The old house was also known to be badly infested with bedbugs; the ceilings of the upstairs bedrooms were both smeared with blood and smoke-damaged (where candles had been used to kill the bugs). The foreman of a road crew scheduled to sleep overnight at McInnes House was heard to say to his men, "Huh, if you think you had a rough day, just wait 'til tonight!"[25]

Following the death of Mary McInnes Rowed in April 1937, her brother Sandy gave up his ranch at Beatty Creek and moved back to Alexandria. Like his father, Sandy was a very sociable person; artistic and able to write a good story. Growing up before the turn of the century, the McInnes children had known personally the first pioneers of the country (their own parents and relatives), as well as many of the famous miners, such as Peter Dunlevy and his partners, who lived at Soda Creek, not far from McInnes House. In 1938, Sandy wrote a short history of Dunlevy and his discovery of gold in the Horsefly country; this story was published by the Murrays of Lillooet. Had he chosen to do so, Sandy could have written many other stories of the early days of the Cariboo. Instead, he spent his time travelling and visiting his friends and neighbours, sometimes for weeks on end, all over the country. Of course he also took along all the local gossip. One of his favourite haunts was Beaver Lake, where he visited with the Hamilton family. It was said that Christine Hamilton and her several daughters dreaded the arrival of Sandy McInnes, who not only spread gossip but spent his time drinking gin and eating garlic — a deadly combination, and quite repulsive when he decided to whisper some secret into one's ear. Alexander Patrick "Sandy" McInnes passed away in the Quesnel hospital in June 1946.

By the late 1940s, McInnes House had fallen into a sad state of disrepair. During the next decade, the Cariboo Historical Society made a brave attempt to have McInnes House restored. As a remnant of an original North West Company fur-trading post, it was certainly worth saving. However, as time went by and nothing came of the effort, the old house disintegrated to such a degree that it had to be torn down. For some time a historic sites sign, erected by the provincial government, stood beside the highway at the site of McInnes House. But now, even that is gone.

ANDERS' 188 MILE HOUSE, 1896
Lot 371, G.1., Cariboo

William Johnson Anders and his wife Annie first arrived at Williams Lake from Sheffield, England, in 1884. Annie's brother, William Pinchbeck, who had been in Canada for many years, travelled to England that summer to be married. Prior to his return, he persuaded his sister and her husband to accompany him to his ranch in the Cariboo. For nine years the Anderses lived and worked on the Pinchbeck Ranch — Annie as housekeeper at the upper roadhouse and William as bookkeeper and storekeeper. William Anders was a man of many talents. As a youth he had been a champion walker and athlete, and as a shoemaker he was once commissioned to make a pair of boots for King Edward VII.

Following the death of William Pinchbeck in 1893, when the ranch was seized by creditors, Annie and William left Williams Lake to start a roadhouse farm of their own. Suitable land was found just south of Four Mile Creek, in the Alexandria District. Here Anders pre-empted 320 acres on 12 February 1895, through which ran the Cariboo Road. An adjoining 160 acres, purchased from Tommy Barrows, had a small house on it, where the Anderses lived while their roadhouse was being built. Many more acres, the Freeman field and Thomas Moffitt's "upper field" were added later. In 1902, when these lands were Crown granted, they became Lot 371, G.1., Cariboo.

It was the spring of 1896 before the Anderses moved into the two-storey, frame-built roadhouse, which was constructed by John Mackin, a master builder. Situated on a grassy knoll close to the Cariboo Road, the 188 Mile House soon became a regular stopping place for freighters and BX stagecoaches. The house itself was of a salt-box design; that is, the back side of the roof was longer than the front, giving the building an unbalanced appearance. Facing the road, the front door opened in on a long, open hallway, the walls of which were covered with a yellow and brown floral-patterned oilcloth. An ornately carved and carpeted staircase on the south wall led up to the second storey, where there were four guest bedrooms and a large room that was reserved for single men and freighters. The well-appointed guest bedrooms, each with a differently coloured home-made quilt, were decorated with matching rag mats and curtains. One of these was known as the "Pauline Johnson" room, as the renowned poet had slept there while on tour in 1904. Just off the front hallway on the main floor was the ladies' parlour, a fashionable but sombre room where the walls were decorated with photographs of family gravestones in England. Across the hall was the office and barroom, a much more cheerful room, where drinks were served and where travellers sat around the cosy heater to await the stagecoach. This room also contained the telegraph key, where Louis LeBourdais, the popular historian, journalist, and, later, MLA for the Cariboo, started his career.

W. J. Anders Roadhouse, Mile 188 at Alexandria was built in 1895.
(Courtesy QDMA)

Soon after it was built, Native people from the nearby reserve began to appear at the roadhouse, wanting to trade their furs for groceries and hardware. This prompted the Anderses to establish a store (also built by John Mackin) just north of the roadhouse. Annie, a shrewd businesswoman, tended the store, and, of the many items sold to the Natives, her home-made boiled candies were the most popular.

While William and Annie Anders did not have a family of their own, William Broughton, Annie's great nephew, arrived from Yorkshire, England, in 1903 to work at the 188 Mile House. A year later, Billy's fiance, Ada Littlewood, joined him. With her came many other settlers, most of them from the north of England. These were relatives of families already settled in the Alexandria and Kersley area. Their arrival in the community was the reason for the first Australian picnic, an annual event held at the Australian Ranch, and one which continued for many years. (See Chapter 6, The Australian Ranch, 1863.).

A year after their marriage, a son, William Jr, was born to the Broughtons, but before little Billy was a year old, his father died. For some years, Ada and her son remained at the 188 Mile farm, where she ran the roadhouse and Annie Anders operated the store.

Through the years, William Anders gained a reputation as a crack shot, and, when the locals heard how he had killed several grouse with one blast of his gun, they began to refer to him as "Buckshot Anders." Never having heard the appellation before, it was a great shock to William Anders when, one day, a salesman came to the door enquiring for "Mr Buckshot."

In 1913, Ada Broughton married Frank Aiken, a provincial policeman. For some years, the little family lived in Lillooet and then Clinton. With the deaths of William and Annie Anders in the 1920s, the Aikens, with their sons Bill, Edward, and Leslie, returned to the 188 Mile House and farm. By this time the need for wayside houses had passed, but the old building continued to be used as a family home.

In 1941, Edward Aiken, who had remained to operate the farm, married Louise (Lal) Marie Vasseur, and together they worked and raised a family in the old house. With the passing of Frank Aiken in October 1955, Edward and his wife moved into a modern house (built across the road) and the roadhouse was left empty. For some years it was rented off and on by transients. Following Lal's death in July 1991, the farm was sold. Still standing beside Highway 97, the 188 Mile House is now virtually beyond repair. Annie Anders's store is still in use. Moved from its original site beside the roadhouse, it has become home to a flock of chickens out behind Lal Aiken's modern home.

William Johnson Anders and his bride, Mary Hannah (Annie) Pinahbeck,
worked on her brothers ranch for some years before building their own ranch.
(COURTESY QDMA)

MOFFAT HOUSE, LANSDOWNE FARM, ALEXANDRIA, 1883
Lot 316, G.1., Cariboo

During the 1870s, a spirit of adventure was the driving force behind a young man from Ontario. Henry (Harry) Moffat, a third-generation Canadian, was born in 1853 at Pembroke, Ontario. Leaving home in the early 1870s, Harry went to work on a Canadian Pacific Railway survey crew, heading west across the Prairies. By 1875, he was working along the Yellowhead to Tete Jaune Cache route.

Arriving in the Cariboo in the fall of 1876, Harry found work on the Peter Dunlevy ranch near Soda Creek, where he freighted goods for Dunlevy's store. Supplies at that time were transported in heavy wagons pulled by oxen all the way from Yale — a long, slow journey. In his determination to speed up the freighting business, Harry sent back to Ontario for two "bains" (light wagons) suitable for hauling perishable goods. Instead of oxen, horses were hitched to the wagons, sometimes sixteen at a time if the loads were heavy. The combination of the light wagons and the horses proved to be very much faster than the ox-carts, and this method of transportation soon became known as "Moffat's Fast Freight."

Harry's ability to handle horses soon landed him a job driving stage between Ashcroft and Barkerville for Steve Tingley of the BC Express Company. Life as a stage driver was not easy, especially in winter, when heavy snow blocked the roads between Quesnel and Barkerville. There were times when Harry had to leave his team at Stanley, buckle on his snowshoes, and carry the mail and express on his back for ten miles.

It was during one of these runs when Harry had his first serious accident. On leaving Cottonwood House for Quesnel, the team of six horses was suddenly spooked and ran down the steep Eleven Mile Hill. Concerned for the safety of his passengers, Harry jumped from the driver's seat down on to the back of the lead horse. Pulling up on the lines, he managed to slide over to one side, and, after several agonizing minutes of trying to keep his feet off the ground, the weight of his body pulled the horse's head down and brought the team to a halt. As a result, Harry's feet were badly trampled, his knees permanently injured, and his whole body bruised; but it would have been much more serious had the stage overturned.

During his many trips up and down the Cariboo Road, Harry noticed the rich soil of the Alexandria area, thirty miles south of Quesnelle, where there was still quite a bit of open land. Selecting a spot where a clear spring ran year round, Harry settled there in 1883, naming it "Lansdowne Farm" after the Governor-General of Canada. By

The Moffat House original log building was built in 1883 when the road ran through Moffat's best field. With the road moved in 1896, the original house was reconstructed behind the new roadhouse.

November 1885, 320 acres of land had been pre-empted at this site. For some years, Harry Moffat was in partnership with another stagecoach driver, Robert L. Shaw, who had pre-empted adjoining land to the north, but this alliance was dissolved in 1898. In the 1860s, this same Bob Shaw, more familiarly known as "Gassy Shaw," had also been in partnership with James M. Bohanon.

Soon after settling in Alexandria, Harry built a two-storey, squared-log house beside the wagon road, which ran through the property. Measuring twenty feet square, the building faced southwest. On the main floor was a sitting room, kitchen, dining room, and pantry, while in the upper storey were four small bedrooms with dormer windows. These were accessed by a steep set of stairs built in the centre of the house.

By this time, Harry had more or less given up driving stage and was in business for himself, freighting hay and feed to Barkerville. While he was gone, Chinese labourers worked on the farm and kept his house. One of these was Sidoo, and, of the many Chinese to work at Moffat's ranch, he remained the longest, assisting in all facets of ranch work and housekeeping.

To keep track of his business transactions, Harry Moffat began to keep a daybook. Commencing in January 1889, the leather-bound ledger contained not only accounts of daily expenditures and monies received, but also visitors, family happenings, and the neighbours. As

Corners of the original log building at Moffat House. Individual logs were marked for rebuilding.

the years went by, the practice continued (to this day, the current Moffat family keeps a journal). Harry's first daybook also indicated that he was operating a roadhouse:[26]

January 14, 1889
"Dunlevy by staying overnight and 4 horses . . .$ 6.00

March 11, 1889
A.D. McInnes, to 50 lbs butter @35 cents lb . . .$17.50
*   "   "   freight on box . . . .$ 2.00*
*   "   "   staying over . . . .$ 5.00 [27]*

The BC Express Company stage stopped at Moffat's House and sometimes left its horses.

Tuesday, January 27, 1889
B.C. Express Co. to keep of 2 horses,
400 lbs.oats . . . .$ 4.00
John Peebles and passengers on B.X. stage . . . .$ 3.00
Pinchbeck of Williams Lake . . . .$ 1.50

Wednesday, November 20, 1889
Left here today with team loaded for Barkerville, 4001 lbs.
December 17, 1889
William Adams 4 horses and 1 man overnight,
4 meals $17.00

December 21, 1889
To Sidoo Chineyman, sundries . . . .$ 23.00
*   "   "   cash $100.00*

It was spring of 1889 when Harry met Jeannie Roddie of Scotland, who was in the Cariboo for a short holiday with her aunt and uncle, the McInneses of Marguerite. The short stay turned into a lifetime when, on 25 August 1890, Harry and Jeannie were married. The notation in the daybook, written in Harry's large, sprawling hand, reads: "I Henry Moffat and Jeannie Roddie got united in matrimony at A. D. McInnes' at 11.00 a.m. by the Holy Father Martiat; had a good dinner and then drove home, arriving here at 7.00 p.m."

The honeymoon took place in November, when the young couple spent ten days at Quesnelle. In the meantime, Harry was on the road continuously, hauling hides to Ashcroft and grain to Barkerville. Jeannie, who was only seventeen, accompanied Harry on the shorter trips to

Quesnelle or Soda Creek, but when he went on longer trips she either visited her aunt, "Lizzie" McInnes, or stayed with their friends, Sam and Ellen Bohanon. Jeannie found winter to be a very lonely time. After Christmas, when the heavy snows came, there might not be any traffic for days, and no visitors to the roadhouse until the BX stage got through.

In the middle of January 1891, there was some most unusual excitement when an election took place, and Moffat House became the polling station:

Wednesday, January 14, 1891
To elections held at Moffat House . . . . $ 50.00

By February, the Cariboo Road was passable once more.:

10 February 1891
Lewis's team passed up, Boulanger driving [this was August Baker, who changed his name, because hardly anyone could spell or pronounce his French name].

By March 1891, with spring in the air, things were beginning to stir. Those fortunate enough to have wintered in southern climates were returning:

March 7, 1891
B.C. Express Co. Passengers going north: John Bowron, Gold Commissioner., Dr. Watt, John Stevenson, Mrs. Nason, Judge Heath.

March 31, 1891
Commenced plowing.

April 13, 1891
Visits from Mr. and Mrs. Pinchbeck on way to Barkerville and Mr. W. Stephenson and wife of Quesnelle Forks, staying overnight. Thunderstorms.

May 11, 1891
Harry left this morning for Barkerville. [This was the first of Jeannie's many entries.]

It wasn't long before Jeannie came to realize that Harry's varied occupations kept him away from home a lot. She expressed her frustration in the daybook. When Jeannie was happy with her husband, he was mentioned as "Harry," when she was mildly annoyed, he was "Moffat," but when she was thoroughly exasperated, he was "the Boss."

With the birth of their first child in June 1891, the joyful event was entered in the daybook:

June 16, 1891
Born this day at about 6.00 p.m. in the evening at Lansdowne farm, a fine son weighing about 10lbs. All well, thank God! [signed] Harry Moffat.

The baby, Alexander Bohanon Moffat, was named for his paternal grandfather and Samuel Hall Bohanon, a close friend and neighbour. A second son, Roddy Roy, was born a little more than a year later. These were the first of nine children born over the next fifteen years. As the Moffat family increased, religious differences threatened to tear the marriage apart; Jeannie was a strong Roman Catholic and Harry was a staunch Presbyterian. The parents decided that the boys would follow in their father's faith, while the girls would become Catholics. This pact was broken on at least one occasion, when Harry arrived home unexpectedly to find a priest baptizing one of his sons.[22]

By 1897, with several children in the household, Christmas had become an important event, with a big dinner, presents, and lots of visiting on Boxing Day:

The original Henry Moffat family at Lansdowne farm, c. 1903.
Back Row: Henry Hudson, Roddy Roy, Alex.
Third Row: May, Eveline, Agnes, Frances.
Second Row: Henry Moffat and Jeannie (Roddie) Moffat.
Foreground: Jack and Jim. (COURTESY QDMA)

December 26, 1897
Alex McInnes and the girls were up to see us, and we went to see
the Bohanons'.

For the adults, New Year's festivities were celebrated with equal enthusiasm:

January 2, 1894 [written by Jeannie Moffat]
Mr. Middleton, Mr. Craig, Mr. Olson, Mr. McLeod and John
McInnes all came here this morning and drank whisky and ate
cake so they could not see straight.

This was typical of the close alliance between neighbours in the Alexandria area. While they had their petty jealousies, there was always a strong bond of friendship. As time went by, and as several families were united through marriage, these bonds became even stronger.

Not long after the birth of their first daughter, Frances Jane, in March 1895, Harry Moffat began to plan some changes to Lansdowne farm — changes that would have a profound effect on Moffat House:

25 March 1895
I went over the river to see Mr. Adams [MLA for the Cariboo, 1892-97]
to consult with him about moving the wagon road through my ranch.

At this time, the wagon road ran right through some of Harry's best fields, and it was thought that, for a distance of about a mile and a half, the road could be relocated further to the east, on less productive land. In due time, Harry's request was granted, and Henry Giles was hired to clear the ground for the new roadway. The whole project, financed by the government, took over a year to complete. Finally, the daybook read:

June 21, 1896
The first teams and the stage started over the new road today.

Moffat House was now off the main road, and it was several years before any further changes took place. In the meantime, with the road relocated, Harry contracted a man to start clearing his fields:

June 18, 1895
A coloured man John Henry commenced grubbing ground today
at $2.00 an acre.

The winter of 1896 started early and proved to be one of the coldest on record. The *SS Charlotte*, the first steamer on the upper Fraser River since the *SS Victoria* ten years before, made its initial run in

October. Three weeks later, in temperatures of minus forty degrees, the steamer was caught in an ice flow north of Soda Creek and was forced to remain there all winter. With the river frozen over, Harry and Jeannie, with their five children, often visited the Webster family on the west bank of the Fraser River.

By the fall of 1897, Harry was ready to have the ranch surveyed. The surveyor, Sidney Williams, and his helper, Mr Stewart, did the job in two days; it cost Harry eighty-nine dollars. December came, and Harry was gone again, freighting hay and grain to Barkerville — a trip that often took ten days. Although it was the same every winter, Jeannie never got used to being left on the farm with just the children and a few oriental labourers. One of the worst winters was that of 1899, when the weather turned extremely cold:

> December 14, 1899
> The water barrel in the kitchen is frozen hard. I sat up all night to keep the fires on.

The very next morning proved almost disastrous, when little Aggie, only three years old, almost set fire to the house:

> December 15, 1899
> Aggie took a candle upstairs and set fire to the curtains. Ah Men and I put it out.

There was actually much more to this story than is indicated in Jeannie's reference. While busy in the kitchen that winter morning, Jeannie smelled smoke. Rushing upstairs to the children's room, she found the curtains ablaze. In her panic to get rid of them, she opened the window and threw them out, whereupon they landed on the porch roof and the wind again ignited them. Jumping out onto the roof, Jeannie smothered the flames with snow; but when she attempted to get back through the window, she found it had slammed shut. All she could do was jump nine feet to the ground, where, fortunately, she landed in a snow bank.

By the year 1900, the question of educating the children had to be faced. Alex, the eldest, was nine; Roddy was eight; and Henry Jr was seven. And the three younger children would soon be ready for school. After much deliberation, it was decided that the children would attend school in Quesnel, where Jeannie would look after them during the school year. On the purchase of a surveyed lot in Quesnel, on the corner of McLean Street and Barlow Avenue, Harry had Steven Hilborn build a house. It was Boxing Day when Harry moved his family in.

Moving to Quesnel started a new era in Jeannie's life — one that eased her conscience with regard to her children and also satisfied her own social needs. For the foreseeable future, Jeannie would live in town during the winter months and spend her summers on the farm.

The turn of the century brought a wave of optimism to the northern areas of British Columbia. With news of the building of the Grand Trunk Pacific Railway to Fort George and Prince Rupert came increased activity on the Cariboo Road and, consequently, to the roadhouses. For these reasons, Harry Moffat began an ambitious building program in the fall of 1902, which included a new roadhouse, two new barns, and several outbuildings on Lansdowne farm.

October 8, 1902
Frank Elliot hauling logs.

The logging went on until spring, when a new house was started on the upper side of the road, close to the creek. The daybook contains Harry's triumphant announcement:

Wednesday, April 15, 1903
James Craig, by commencement of work on house. We started to grade the foundation of the house this morning, and laid the first cornerstone with the assistance of God and a bottle of Scotch which we drank and implored God's blessing to rest over it and all who might occupy it. H.M.

The design of the new house followed that of many of the houses built in Eastern Canada in the nineteenth century; but, instead of being built of brick or stone, it was built of logs.

June 7, 1903
James Craig and Lyne started work on the kitchen.

James Craig, a young man from Clinton, Ontario, had first met Harry Moffat on a ship bound for Victoria in 1875. A few years later, the two met again in Quesnel and became lifelong friends. "Lyne" was Johnny Lyne, whose brother, William Lyne Jr, had settled at Deep Creek a few years earlier. *(See Chapter 5, Lyne's 170 Mile House, 1895–1935.)*

The logs of the new house, squared by hand with an adze, gave the walls a flat surface. At this time women, even in the rural areas, were not content to have round log walls in the interior of their homes, for they caught the dust and were hard to decorate. Instead, they preferred

flat walls upon which they hung cheesecloth and wallpaper. In the
Moffat daybooks are several mentions of the papering of the walls in
the roadhouse. To complete the interior of the house, Harry exchanged
a considerable amount of grain for tongue-and-groove lumber hauled
from the Reid and Johnston sawmill at Quesnel. Shingles for the roof,
cut at the same mill, were shipped downstream aboard a sternwheel
steamer and delivered to a landing at the north end of Lansdowne farm:

> *Monday, June 8, 1903*
> *Hauled shingles from river, James Craig and Russell working on*
> *house getting up rafters. [Russell was Jim Craig's son.]*

Craig had married Kathleen Duhig of Quesnel in 1884. Steve Hilborn and
John Strand also worked on Moffat's new house. Prior to its completion,
the original house was moved up from the field in 1904. The logs were
all numbered as the building was dismantled, then put back in place as
it was rebuilt directly behind the new house. The two buildings were
pegged together in the upper storeys. Years later, in the 1970s, when
David Moffat began to restore the buildings, he had to put cement sills
under the original house in order to prevent it from sagging.

The winter of 1903 was another cold one, and, after spending
Christmas in Quesnel, Harry Moffat returned to the farm, taking
Roddy and Henry to help him for the remainder of the school holidays.
With the New Year came snow and extreme cold. Harry wrote:

> *Sunday, January 31, 1904*
> *I am alone on the ranch, very cold ... 40 below.*

> *Sunday, 7 February 1904*
> *Ah Wing Chineyman cook commenced to work at $1.00 a day.*
> *Still very cold.*

With the end of the school year in April, Jeannie and the children
returned to the farm, where they moved into the new roadhouse. One
of Jeannie's first projects was to paper the several upstairs bedrooms.
The house was far from finished (in fact, it was still being worked on
in 1907) when the upstairs balcony was painted.

That fall, when the subject of a local school came up again,
Jeannie wrote:

> *Monday, 24 October 1904*
> *Harry went up to a meeting of the school, but Windt would not*
> *have it halfway. He wants to have it at his place. J.M.*

The Henry Windt family had settled in the area in 1901 and built a log home just two miles north of the Moffats. With several additional children in the neighbourhood, it was hoped that a local school could be built; but, obviously, the two families could not agree on a location.

Over and over again, between the myriad entries regarding family activities, haying, and harvesting, the Moffat House daybooks record the endless succession of stoppers:

Monday, October 17, 1904
Mr. John Bowron and Mr. Bonner, to stopping overnight.
One horse, hay and grain . . . . $ 2.00
Two men to 4 meals and 2 beds . . . . $ 3.00

Thursday, October 27, 1904
Robert Walker, teamster. To 2 teams overnight.
To 13 horses, hay . . . . $ 6.00
100 lbs. oats . . . . $ 4.25
4 meals and beds . . . . $ 2.50

November 5, 1905
I went down to McInnes House to report about the petition in circulation to stop McInnes's liquor license.

November 6, 1905
Windt, Webster and I went down to Soda Creek to give evidence as to the respectability of McInnes House. H.M.

With regard to the last two references, it would appear that Alexander D. McInnes, proprietor of McInnes House, had been accused of supplying liquor to Chief Sam of the Alexandria Reserve. As justice of the peace for the area, Harry Moffat was authorized to investigate. The outcome of this incident, not related in the Moffat daybooks, was revealed by Alvin Johnston in his unpublished manuscript of 1959: "Although Chief Sam was taken to court in Quesnel on a drunk charge, he would not divulge the name of his supplier. Consequently McInnes could not be charged. It was later found that a jealous neighbour of McInnes had started the rumour."[22]

While it is evident that neither Henry nor Jeannie were personally opposed to liquor, it is interesting to note that Moffat House did not include a saloon or barroom, nor did it ever serve liquor to the general public.

The year 1905 saw the building of two large barns at Lansdowne farm:

May 15, 1905
John Lyne commenced to work on barn today by contract for $240.00.

One of these, built of sixty-foot logs, was the largest barn in the country constructed of single logs. With the completion of the new barns in 1906, Henry Moffat was able to take a contract for the care and feeding of the BX horses over the following winter.

Friday, November 2, 1906
B.X. horses came at noon today.
9 horses and driver with Sandy McPhail.
Meals for 2 men . . . .$ 1.00

This was the first of several years of boarding the BC Express Company horses. Obviously, it was a monotonous and physically demanding job, but it did pay well; accounts from November to May 1906 amounted to nearly $1,000 (and to over $1,400 in succeeding years). The boarding contract seemed to bring more business to the roadhouse, for Moffat House was never busier than it was over the winter of 1906–07.

During the summer of 1906, Moffat House was filled with Jeannie's relatives, who had arrived from overseas in May to attend the September wedding of Jeannie's brother, John Roddie, to Agnes McQuarrie of Scotland. Strange as it may seem, Jeannie Moffat did not return to Quesnel that fall. While the older children went back to school in February, Jeannie and the younger children remained at Moffat House. It began in June of 1906, when Harry Moffat wrote this rather vague statement in the daybook:

June 29, 1906
I am going to Quesnel to attend court on Saturday to exonerate my wife's character.

Harry and Jeannie were gone for five days. Apparently, Jeannie had become involved in some indiscretion and was too embarrassed to return to Quesnel. It was April 1907 before she left home to have her last baby, delivered by Dr Beech, the resident physician:

Sunday, May 18, 1907
Born at Quesnel, a son James Levi. May His blessings rest upon his head. H.M.

Harry was always delighted when a son was born. It was more than just male chauvinism; it meant there would be yet another

Moffat House, front part built 1904.

Presbyterian in the family. Through the many years of their marriage, religion continued to be a source of conflict for Harry and Jeannie.

Just after moving Jeannie and the new baby down to Lansdowne farm, Harry received word that he had been appointed District Road Superintendent. The job was, of course, a political plum, and it lasted until December 1916, when the Liberal J.M. Yorston won the Cariboo seat. Harry was certainly the right person for the post, as his years as a freighter had made him intimately familiar with every inch of the Cariboo Road. In the years that followed, Harry Moffat laid out and supervised the building of many of the Cariboo's secondary highways.

In the absence of Jeannie Moffat for seven months of each year, a succession of Chinese cooks held sway in the kitchen of Moffat House — (1901–02 alone saw Ah Wong, Ah Chow, and Ah Hoy). Few of these ever remained for more than a few months, except for Sidoo, who was there constantly. Later, there was Ah Yen, Wing Sing, and Foo Fang Song, affectionately known as "Dear Song." Many years later, Roddy Moffat reflected upon those times and, in particular, upon the rice pudding served by the Chinese cooks at the roadhouse. As there was always lots of milk, and as rice was cheap, this dessert was served quite often. Brought in from the barn, the milk was poured into shallow enamelware pans to allow the cream to gather on the top. Left in a cool place, usually on the dining-room table, the milk collected generous numbers of drowned house flies. At the table, Roddy always passed up the pudding, as it was hard to tell the flies from the raisins. Another of Roddy's vivid memories of life at Moffat House was of the freighters, who stayed over on cold winter nights. Gathered around the big box heater in the front room, they dried their clothes, chewed their snoose, and sewed the "poppers" (silk tassels) back on to their horse whips.

By 1907, the eldest sons, Alex (sixteen), Roddy (fifteen), and Henry (fourteen) were beginning to seek their independence, and, within the next two years, each left school to take his respective place in the adult world. Alex left home first, to work for surveyor Sidney Williams; while he was gone, Roddy remained on the farm and accompanied Harry on his long freighting trips. Before long, Roddy was freighting on his own:

April 12, 1908
Roddy left for Quesnel with 600 lbs. potatoes, 2001 lbs. wheat, 150 lbs. flour, 1 doz. chickens, and 20 lbs. pork.

Between the freighting business and his duties as superintendent of roads, Harry Moffat, at age fifty-four, was an extremely busy man. His wife Jeannie, however, did not sympathize with him, for he was seldom home. In her frustration she wrote:

April 20, 1909
Spring work, Roddy disking, Henry Jr. rolling, planting potatoes, Eveline, May and Jeannie planting garden.

May 4, 1909
The Boss has not come home yet. Everyone else has their crops in, only us trying to run the ranch with only two boys here this year.

That winter, Harry Moffat took a trip back east to the place of his birth. Jeannie, who stayed home, wrote in the daybook:

Thursday, December 14, 1911
Henry Moffat, Roddy and Frances all went to Pembroke Ontario today.

They remained for only a week, as Harry found everything so changed that he did not enjoy it. In February 1915, Harry and Jeannie took a trip together to the Coast, where they stayed for two weeks. It was Jeannie's first trip away from home since her arrival in the late 1880s.

When Harry took on the mail contract for the Alexandria area in 1914, a post office opened at Moffat House. Located in a room to the left of the front door, the service continued, off and on, until 1951. As they grew up, each of the three older Moffat sons took a turn operating Lansdowne farm. In 1914, Roddy and Henry Jr rented the farm for $200 per year for five years. Taking it all quite seriously, they even charged their own father for an overnight stay at Moffat House:

Sunday, September 13, 1914
H. Moffat, to stopping.
2 horses, hay and oats . . . .*$ 2.50*
3 meals and bed . . . .*$ 1.50*

Roddy did a fair bit of freighting between 1910 and 1915, and, on one of his return trips from Quesnel, he transported 800 bricks for Moffat House, where a chimney was built during the summer of 1915 by Charles (Brick) Leonard. That fall, Henry Hudson Moffat joined the ranks of the Quesnel contingent to serve overseas in the First World War. He was gone for three years. On his return in 1919, Henry took over the Sisters Creek farm, purchased by Harry in 1909.

Retiring from his post as road superintendent at age sixty-five, Harry Moffat continued to work on the farm. During a day of rest that summer, Harry, in his unmistakably bold hand, wrote in the daybook:

Sunday, August 17, 1919
We all remained at home all day, being tired and wanting rest —
Thank God for that day set aside for man and beast. Haying,
stacking, six men hauling — hot weather.

Early in 1920, Roddy Moffat was cutting ties for the approaching crews of the Pacific Great Eastern Railway; a foreshadowing of the time when the railway, improved roads, and automobiles would bring about the demise of the roadhouses.

Moffat House was still catering to the occasional guest in 1921:

June 27, 1920
Mr. Vaughan stuck on ferry road, stayed over,
also dinner . . . .*$ 2.00*

April 17, 1921
To 2 men, 2 meals, beds . . . .*$ 4.00*
2 horses, hay overnight . . . .*$ 2.00*
100lbs. oats . . . .*$ 5.00*

The SS BX sternwheeler was built at Soda Creek in 1910.
This picture is taken at Moffat's landing, where freight was being unloaded.

In 1920, just two years after his return from the First World War, Henry Jr left home once again, this time for Vancouver, where he had been offered a good position with Rogers' Sugar Company. The following year, Henry was married to Catherine Bates, a young woman whom he had met earlier. Finally, in the spring of 1923, Henry, his wife Catherine, and their baby Harry returned to take over Lansdowne farm. Henry Moffat Sr continued to live and work on the ranch until his death at age ninety-seven on 15 March 1947. Jeannie Moffat died at her home in Quesnel in 1951 at the age of eighty-two.

Today, David Moffat (a great grandson of Henry Moffat), his wife Margaret (nee Jacques), and their two children run Lansdowne farm, which has become an efficient, modern operation. While David's mother, Kathryn (nee Moxley) Moffat lives nearby in a smaller modern home, David and his family have moved from the old roadhouse, but return to live there several times during the year, especially during the haying season. With its thick log walls the house is pleasantly cool during the hot days of summer.

WEBSTER'S RANCH, "SUNNYSIDE" WEST BANK, FRASER RIVER, 1869
Lots 96, 97, 98, and 100, G.1., Cariboo

William Adams and William Morrison, two successful miners on Lightning Creek, acquired by sale and pre-emption, a large acreage on the west side of the Fraser River during the late 1880s, and there they operated a roadhouse. Situated seven miles north of Fort Alexandria, the land had been part of the Hudon's Bay Company farm "Stornsa," where packhorses were wintered during the fur-trading era[26]

In 1869, following the abandonment of the Hudson's Bay Company lands at Alexandria, George McGregor, a company employee, pre-empted 160 acres of the farm, through which ran a brigade trail. McGregor kept a store, selling farm produce and accommodating travellers in his cabins beside the trail. At this time, the route was busy with miners and pack-train operators making their way to Quesnel and the Omineca goldfields.

During the latter part of the 1880s, William Morrison, the well-to-do miner, bought McGregor's land and, with his partner William Adams, acquired several adjoining parcels, where they started a farm of about 1,000 acres. Crown granted in April 1886, these became lots 96, 97, 98, and 100, G.1., Cariboo. Having spent their energies amassing fortunes in gold, Morrison and Adams were no longer young. Realizing it would take a younger man to develop the ranch, they invited Morrison's nephew, William Leith Webster of Wingham, Ontario, to become a partner.

Webster, his wife Margaret (nee Rintol), and small daughter Emily had moved west in 1887. While living in Clinton, William spent a few years freighting goods between Ashcroft and Barkerville. A son, John, was born there in 1889. Settled on his uncle's ranch in 1891, it took Bill several more winters of freighting to pay for the partnership.

One of Bill's first projects was to improve their living accommodations. With lumber and supplies that were hauled from Ashcroft, the two original cabins on the property were joined into a single residence; and, when a second storey was added, the building became the largest in the community. For many years there was no insulation in the walls of the house, and Emily Webster, who slept upstairs, later recalled the terrible heat of summer nights and the numbing cold of winter.

During the Klondike gold rush, the Webster's ranch house became, once again, a stopping house where miners and packers, including the famous "Cataline," remained overnight. (Cataline, whose real name was Jean Caux was born of French parentage in the Cataluna region of Spain. From this came his sobriquet. Arriving in British Columbia prior to the gold rush, he was, for many years a packer for the Hudson's Bay Company, serving its northern posts, and performing many prodigious feats of pack-train transportation. Cataline died in Quesnel in 1922.)

*Sunnyside Ranch, west of the Fraser River, was completed by
William L. Webster in early 1900s, and still stands.*

The store on Webster's ranch was also busy, selling farm produce
and beef to travellers and to Native people from the nearby reserve. An
old ledger from the 1890s lists the sale of butchered beef at 3c a
pound, barley at $1.12 for 100 pounds, wheat at 2.5c a pound, and oats
at $40.00 a ton. In 1901, Webster sold 28 pounds of bacon and 2 sacks
of flour for $5.00 each. During the early 1900s, crops of hay, grain,
and beef were sold and shipped via the riverboats on the Fraser River
to buyers at Quesnel and Fort George.

Without hope of a local school, the several Webster children
received their elementary education at Quesnel, where Margaret
Webster lived and kept house for several years. By the 1920s, John, the
eldest son, was managing Sunnyside Ranch. Although the store had
been closed, the door to Webster's house was always open, with everyone in the region calling by on his or her trips to town. Saturday-night
dances were standard practice, and, in between, whenever three or
more were gathered for supper, it was cause for an evening of music
and dancing. Bill Webster Jr passed away in 1952, but his wife Janet
continued to live on the ranch with her son and his wife Myrtle (nee
Tingley). With the death of young Bill in 1964, the family sold
Sunnyside Ranch to David and Audrey Cummings.

Notes to Chapter 5

1. Bishop George Hills, Diary, 16 July 1862, Anglican Provincial Synod of British Columbia Archives, Vancouver, BC.

2. G. B. Wright to Colonel R.C. Moody, RE, 13 May 1863, Colonial correspondence, F.1924a, BCARS.

3. Ibid.

4. Sergeant John McMurphy, RE, Diary, 16 July 1863, E/B/M221, BCARS, 38.

5. *Cariboo Sentinel*, 7 May 1866, 2.

6. McMurphy, Diary, 27 July 1863, 39.

7. Louis LeBourdais, "The Harry Jones Story," addit. MSS 676, vol. 7, BCARS.

8. Alex P. McInnes, *Chronicles of the Cariboo* (Lillooet, BC: Publishers Limited 1938), 6.

9. *Cariboo Sentinel*, 9 July 1868, 2.

10. *Cariboo Sentinel*, 13 July 1868, 3.

11. *Cariboo Sentinel*, 23 June 1869, 3.

12. *Colonist* (Victoria), 31 August 1869, 3.

13. A.P. McInnes, *Chronicles of the Cariboo*, 27.

14. Robin Skelton, *They Call It the Cariboo* (Victoria: Sono Nis 1980), 172.

15. Sarah Crease, Diary, 15 September 1880, A/E/C86, BCARS, 9.

16. Ibid., 3 October 1880, 21.

17. McInnes, *Chronicles of the Cariboo*, 27.

18. Interview with Tom Pickard in Naniamo, 1981.

19. Louis LeBourdais, Add. MSS 361, Letters of Harry Jones, originals, 1925–1935.

20. *Cariboo Sentinel*, 11 October 1873, 3.

21. Crown grant #4386/99, Ministry of Lands and Parks, Legal Surveys Branch, Victoria, BC.

22. Alvin Johnston, "Birchbark to Steel," unpublished MS, property of H. Albert Johnston family, Quesnel, BC, 1959.

23. W.H. Gurney, "My First School, Cariboo Style," 1971, BCARS.

24. Interview with Roddy Moffat, 1974.

25. Ibid.

26. Lieutenant H. S. Palmer, RE, Map, Sketch of Part of British Columbia, February 1863, "Stornsa," between Tower Point and Narcosli River, NW/971M/P174ro BCARS.

27. Selected passages from the Moffat House Daybooks, Moffat family private collection, 14 January 1889 to 17 March 1921.

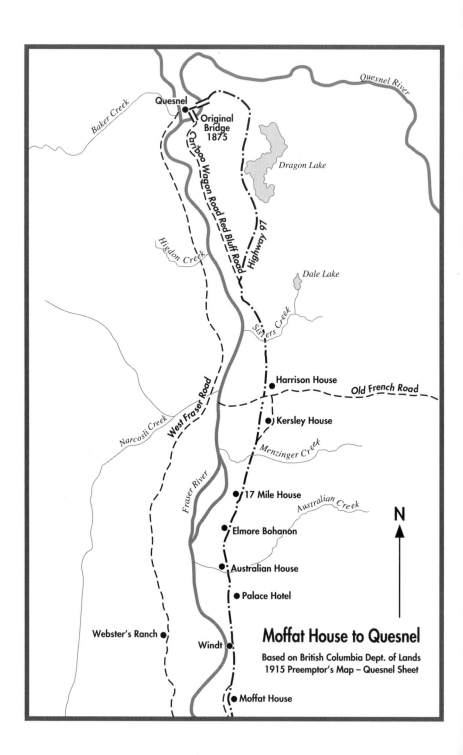

Moffat House to Quesnel

Based on British Columbia Dept. of Lands
1915 Preemptor's Map – Quesnel Sheet

CHAPTER SIX

Australian Ranch to Harrison House

THE AUSTRALIAN RANCH, 1863
Lots 3, 4, and 5, G.1., Cariboo

The Palace Hotel, 1863

The history of the Australian Ranch, twenty-one miles south of Quesnel, includes the existence of three separate roadhouses over a period of more than ninety years.

As a young man, Andrew Olson left his home in Sweden in 1851 for the Australian goldfields, where he remained for ten years. With news of a gold rush in British Columbia, "the Australian," as Andrew became known, and his partner George Oscar hurried across the sea to Vancouver Island and Victoria. Early in 1862, Olson and Oscar travelled to the Cariboo, where they mined on Antler Creek without much success. High prices and a lack of funds forced them to return to Victoria for the winter, where Andrew found work. Very discouraged at this point, George Oscar left for San Francisco, where he thought he could do better for himself.

While at work building Cary Castle that winter, Andrew Olson met George Cook, who had also been in Australia, and two English brothers,

William and Stephen Downes. On hearing of Andrew's experiences in
the Cariboo, where vegetables were scarce and overnight accommodations
few and far between, the three men persuaded Andrew to return there
with them the following spring, not for gold but for arable land where
they could establish a farm and operate a roadhouse. On his way south
in 1862, Andrew had noted several such locations not too far from the
mines. In particular, he had been impressed with an area twenty miles
south of Quesnelle Mouth, in a broad valley "where gentle slopes rise
from the river to the levels of table lands, interrupted here and there by
flats of varying extent, and a few prairies of rich meadow grass and
productive soil, already the scene of incipient farming enterprise."[1]

During the winter, the four men prepared for their forthcoming
journey, gathering all the equipment and supplies necessary. They also
built their own means of transportation. From good hardwood they
fashioned two barrows with four-foot wheels, not unlike those designed
and used in China hundreds of years ago. On each side of the wheels
were shelves, two feet wide and five feet long, upon which their supplies
were loaded and strapped down. While it took two men to manoeuvre them,
as much as 400 pounds of supplies could be transported on each barrow.

Many years later, when describing the journey of 1863, Andrew
Olson recalled vividly the frustrations of handling the barrows through
creeks and down steep hills. The journey by steamboat to Port
Douglas, and on foot along a good road as far north as the 150 Mile
House, had been comparatively easy; but from there on the route
became a narrow, muddy trail through the woods. As the four men

*A replica of the barrow used by the pre-emptors of the Australian ranch in
the 1860s on their journey from the coast.* (COURTESY L. LEBOURDAIS)

struggled along under their heavy loads, they were jostled by passing pack-trains, splattered with mud, and laughed at by those who made fun of their unique method of transportation.

By 17 June 1863, the four companions had reached an area about twelve miles north of Fort Alexandria. There beside the brigade trail Andrew Olson and the two Downes brothers pre-empted several parcels of land, which, when Crown granted, became lots 2, 3, 4, and 5, G.1., Cariboo. Lot 2, the most southerly of the group, was abandoned in 1879 and later became Lot 3141, which was acquired by Henry Windt in the early 1900s.

Of the several pre-emptions, the partners chose first to develop what became Lot 3, close to the brigade trail, and where a sizeable creek ran through the property. Amongst several improvements made that summer was the building of a single-storey log cabin they named the Palace Hotel, which served as a roadhouse. With seeds they had brought with them, a small garden was planted; but, due to the unworked soil and summer frosts, their harvest was very disappointing. The roadhouse business was not much better, due to the fact that the wagon road ended near Fort Alexandria, and not much traffic passed through to Quesnelle Mouth until 1865 when the road was completed. In the meantime, most travellers took the steamer from Soda Creek. One of very few visitors to the Palace Hotel in 1863 was Judge Begbie, who became a frequent guest over the years. Supplies for the roadhouse were purchased from the packers who frequented the brigade trail during the summer; but, once winter set in, the "Australians" had very little contact with the outside world. Deep snow and cold weather in the first week of January put an end to most travel. During their first winter the four men lived on woody turnips, boiled beans, and rabbits. On Christmas Eve, with their last ten dollars, Andrew snowshoed south to Fort Alexandria, a long day's journey, and arrived back with a ten-pound sack of flour. Pancakes were the Christmas dinner treat that year.

Realizing the agricultural shortcomings of Lot 3, the men decided to try one of their other pre-emptions located a mile north. There, on the lower benches of the Fraser River, the partners set to work to clear a few acres in time for spring planting in 1864. The work involved was monumental. Heavy timber covering the chosen area was felled with crosscut saws, and the ground was broken with mattocks fashioned from English spades found at Fort Alexandria. It was May before an area of nine acres was ready for planting. The first harvest yielded 5,000 pounds of potatoes, several hundred pounds of turnips, and a quantity of grain.

Hardly had they completed their harvest when a trader came by offering to take the valuable crop on consignment for sale to the miners of Williams Creek: "I kin git you more'n a dollar a pound for them spuds. I expect to unload some of my freight at 'the Mouth,' so I kin pack 'em to the Crick reasonable."[2] A deal was made, and, with the precious cargo loaded aboard the trader's mules, the Australians bid him God speed and a fast return. But wait as they did, they never saw the trader again — much less any returns. Later, they heard that the scoundrel had sold the vegetables and left for the Coast by way of Antler and Keithley creeks. The loss of the cash crop was cause for a serious quarrel amongst the partners, and this resulted in the departure of George Cook. As Andrew Olson and the two Downes brothers settled in for another winter of turnips and beans, they cursed both the unscrupulous trader and their own naivety.

With the arrival of spring, resentment was replaced by renewed hope for another season. Realizing that oxen were needed if the ranch were to be developed further, it was agreed that the Downes brothers would work on the ranch while Andrew Olson took a job clerking in Danielson's store at Quesnelle Mouth for seventy-five dollars a month in summer, and fifty dollars a month in winter. Over a period of several years, four oxen were purchased from Thaddeus Harper for $500, with interest set at 2 1/2 per cent annually. By the time the animals were paid for, the oxen had cost the partners $1,500.[3]

Australian House, 1867

With the building of the wagon road to Quesnel in 1865, the site of the Palace Hotel was bypassed. Consequently, the ranch headquarters was removed to the flats of what became Lot 4, where the Cariboo Road crossed a large creek (now known as Australian Creek). Here, in 1866, a substantial two-storey log roadhouse was built. Located beside the Cariboo Road, Australian House was the first of several buildings at this site. For many years, the ranch was a BX horse-change stop, and, while fresh horses were being harnessed, there was usually time for the driver and his passengers to enjoy a home-cooked meal at the roadhouse. Occupied as it was by three bachelors, the kitchen of the roadhouse became the domain of hired cooks, usually Chinese, while Native women from the nearby reserve cleaned and kept house. Several pieces of furniture used in the roadhouse were built by Andrew Olson, including a very large dining table and several benches. Made from local fir and having doweled joints, this furniture lasted for many years. With Judge Begbie as a frequent visitor to Australian House, the one downstairs bedroom was kept exclusively for his use.

As the Australian Ranch continued to develop on through the 1870s and 1880s, large fields of grain, hay, and vegetables were harvested and sold to markets in the goldfields. Not taking any chances on repeating the disaster of the 1860s, Andrew Olson made the deliveries himself. In the dead of winter, when both vegetables and fresh beef were scarce and most expensive, "Andrew's locomotive" (a tent equipped with a stove mounted on a sleigh) kept the loads of perishables and the driver warm en route to their destination. The increase in the annual crops of hay allowed for larger herds of cattle and milk cows on the ranch. As a result, a slaughter house was built, where beef was prepared both for sale and for use in the roadhouse. Dressed beef at this time sold for fifty cents a pound.

By 1872, Barnard's Express & Stage Line was operating a twice-weekly stage from Yale to Barkerville. On the morning of 15 June, William Downes boarded the stage from Australian Ranch and headed for Victoria. Two days after his arrival, he was dead. Apparently he had had tuberculosis for some time; he was only forty-two years old.[4] Downes died intestate, but the courts allowed the remaining partners to buy his shares in the ranch. This made Andrew Olson and Stephen Downes equal partners in what had become the largest and most progressive ranch in the upper country.

As the years fled by, the relationship between the two partners deteriorated. Stephen Downes became morose, moody, and resentful of Andrew, and often left him with the brunt of the ranch work. At one point, he even tried to prove that Andrew was not legally a partner in the enterprise. Andrew retaliated by submitting a bill for the years of wages he had not collected, if, indeed, he was an employee and not a partner. This changed Downes's attitude and the whole matter was dropped.[5]

In 1886, while Australian House was enjoying a resurgence of business, the large BX barn caught fire and burned to the ground. With a strong wind blowing at the time, the fire consumed the building at a frightful rate, making it impossible to save anything — even the several favourite riding horses.[6] In order to keep their contract with the BC Express Company, Olson and Downes had a new barn built immediately, on the same site.

Stephen Downes, who lived to be sixty-seven, died at the Australian Ranch on 21 June 1898 and was buried in the old Quesnel cemetery.[7] With the death of his last partner, Andrew Olson began to think seriously of selling out. The ranch, with its diversified operations, was becoming too much for Andrew, who had himself reached the age of sixty. For a number of years now, he had been suffering from severe bouts of arthritis.

While the Downes brothers had never married, they had several nieces and nephews, all of whom were now encouraging Andrew to sell the ranch. In his will, Stephen left his share of the property to Andrew, who was to sell out, keeping half the returns for himself, with the remainder to be divided amongst Stephen's heirs. Before it could be sold, however, the property had to be surveyed and Crown granted — a formality that had been hitherto neglected. To handle the legalities, Andrew engaged John A. Fraser of Quesnel. In surveying the property, it was a big shock to Andrew to discover that the ranch headquarters was not legally part of the ranch. Fortunately, it was possible to rectify this oversight.[8] Two years later, after several disagreements with the Downes heirs, the ranch was put up for sale.

Following Stephen Downes's death, Andrew received a visit from his brother, Sam Olson of Sweden, with whom he had kept in touch through the years. It was said that Andrew's family thought him to be

Andrew Olson and brother, Sam, sit near the Australian House fireplace in 1903, shortly before Andrew sold the 1500-acre ranch.
(COURTESY BCARS)

a rich man and sent Sam to persuade him to return home with all his money. Little did they realize that by the time all the legal expenses had been paid, the fortune had dwindled considerably.

Stationed at the 150 Mile House in 1900 was John (Jack) McKay Yorston, express agent and assistant superintendent of the BC Express Company. Jack and a younger brother Robert, who also worked for the BC Express Company, had been looking for a good farm on which to settle down. When they heard about the Australian Ranch, they decided it was just what they were looking for. The price, which included 1,492 acres of land (200 of which were cleared), 200 head of cattle, and other livestock, was $10,000 — a considerable sum at that time. When the Yorstons took over in November 1903, they invited Andrew to remain on the ranch with them. They knew that his knowledge and expertise would be invaluable.

Free at last of all responsibilities, Andrew relaxed and indulged himself in the luxury of reading the newspapers in his comfortable chair beside the fireplace of Australian House. A photograph of Andrew and his brother Sam, in just such a pose, was taken in 1903. In his retirement, Andrew visited Quesnel more often, where he enjoyed games of euchre with old friends at the Occidental Hotel and attended the dances held there. Although he was a shy man with women, Andrew loved to dance, dressed in his gumboots, which he wore constantly. Each year on Dominion Day, when an annual parade was held, the Yorstons assisted Andrew to wheel the one remaining "Australian barrow" down the streets of the little village of Quesnel.

Once the ranch was sold and Andrew's affairs were put in order, Sam began to pressure him to return to Sweden. Having lived and worked in the Cariboo for forty years, Andrew was very reluctant to leave; he had even forgotten most of his mother tongue. It took a lot of persuasion, but finally Andrew gave in.

At the steamboat landing at Quesnel, where the Olsons began their long journey back to Sweden, most of the population turned out to see them off. Admired and respected for his industry, integrity, generosity, and dry wit, Andrew might have noticed the tears falling from the eyes of those around him, had his own not been so dimmed.9 Less than a year later, so it was said, Andrew Olson died of homesickness.

Upon resigning from his job with the BC Express Company, Bob Yorston joined his brother Jack at the Australian Ranch in the spring of 1904. Once again, the ranch was owned and operated by bachelors. Jack Yorston had been married earlier but lost his wife in childbirth at

This pre-1906 photo of Australian Ranch show both Australian House and Bob Yorston's house to the right. (COURTESY BCARS)

Lillooet in October 1898. The two Scotsmen had arrived in Canada from the Orkney Islands during the 1890s. Brought up in stoic Scottish fashion, they were hardworking and self-sufficient.

The Australian Ranch was not to remain a bachelors' domain for very much longer. Soon after arriving in Quesnel, Bob Yorston met Ethel Robertson, the local schoolteacher. Following two years of teaching, Ethel married Bob in January 1906 and became the first bride to live on the ranch. In preparation for his wedding, Bob built his own two-storey log home, right beside Australian House. They had lived there only a few months when both houses were destroyed by fire. Almost everything was lost, but amongst the few items saved were Andrew Olson's dining-room table and a couple of his benches.

Yorston's Roadhouse, 1906–1955

Almost immediately after the fire, a contract was made with local builder John Strand, and soon a big crew of carpenters was busy constructing a large, two-storey frame house on the site of the old Australian House. While it was being built, the Yorstons lived in a big log cabin across the yard, where Ethel set up a kitchen to feed the building crew. Assisting her was her younger sister Janet, who had arrived from the Coast to give her a hand. It was fall when they moved in. Built specifically as a roadhouse, the large building contained twelve rooms. Typical of the early 1900s, when sawn boards replaced logs, the precise

Bob Yorston built this grand home for his bride, Ethel Robertson, in 1906, after fire razed the original house. A flood ravaged this home in 1955. (COURTESY BCARS)

modern construction had an air of sophistication not formerly possible. The architecture, with its several upper-storey gables and seven white columns supporting a covered verandah, reminded one of the early mansions of the southern United States. As a fire precaution, the exterior of the building was covered in sheets of embossed tin painted a slate blue. Once the house was completed, the Virginia creeper that had grown so prolifically up the south and west walls of the old house again came to life and grew up over the verandah.

On approaching the front, or west end, of Yorston's roadhouse, it was only a few steps across the wide verandah to the front door. Manufactured of solid hardwood, the door contained a large pane of opaque green pebbled glass. Inside the spacious entrance hall, coats and other items of clothing hung on cast-iron pegs, and a handsomely carved set of stairs with twenty-six steps led up to the several bedrooms on the second floor. The ornamental bannister, with its smooth, wide railing, was a great source of entertainment to the Yorston children, especially on confining winter days. To the right of the hallway, the cheerful atmosphere of a large sitting room made it a favourite gathering place for guests and stagecoach passengers. Bathed in sunlight during the day (the two windows faced south and west), at night the sitting room's cast-iron heater gave off a friendly warmth while guests relaxed in the several brown leather couches and Morris chairs. Beside the heater was Bob Yorston's carved wooden rocker, in which he dozed all night as he kept the fire going during extreme cold spells. The little private parlour on the north wall, with its carpeted floor and rosewood furniture, was appreciated more by female than by male travellers. In later years, the Christmas tree was set up there, and, for a time, it became a schoolroom for Jean, Jack, and Don Yorston and their teacher, Mrs Fisher.

Although indoor plumbing was never installed, a room situated between the sitting room and the dining room was used as the bathroom. As the name implied, the room contained a large, cast-iron bathtub, complete with lion's-paw feet. Filled with water heated on the kitchen range, the tub's fine porcelain finish could be slippery, but the luxury of its size more than compensated for this hazard. In summer, the bathwater drained out through a pipe under the house, but in winter ... well, who took baths anyway?

With the death of Judge Matthew B. Begbie in 1894, the one down-stairs bedroom of Yorston's roadhouse, which had been reserved for the eminent judge, was now kept for government representatives, political leaders, and ministers of the church. In later times, when he became badly crippled with arthritis, it became Bob Yorston's bedroom.[10]

The dining area, a very large room behind the front hallway, contained "old Andrew's" table, at which twenty or more could be seated. A survivor of the devastating fire of 1906, the old table continued to serve, not only at mealtime, but also during an evening of whist or bridge, crokinole, or chess. During the winter it became the focal point of family quilting bees and dressmaking projects, when paper patterns were laid out across its surface. A large roll-top desk, the only other piece of furniture in the room, stood beneath the twin windows facing the front yard. Here Bob and Ethel Yorston kept their accounts and wrote their letters.

In the large kitchen, which occupied most of the northeast end of the house, the activity centred around the big McClary cook-stove. This was the heart of the roadhouse, and from this steel and cast-iron monster came forth many substantial meals served to the family, the stagecoach passengers, and the hired hands. The chrome-finished warming-oven doors, above the stove top, were often open to reveal a batch of rising bread or drying herbs from the ample kitchen garden located behind the house. The big woodbox near the stove was painted red, a fact well remembered by the Yorston children, whose duty it was to keep it full. During the summer, when water was carried from an irrigation ditch behind the house, the children were also expected to keep two bucketfuls on a bench by the kitchen door. In winter, barrels of water were hauled to the house on a stone-boat from nearby Australian Creek or from the

Fraser River, over a mile away. During the cold weather the kitchen floor could be like a skating rink; without any foundation under the house, any water that was spilled froze immediately.

In the pantry, a room built into the north verandah, metal-lined bins held 100 pounds of flour, sugar, and cereals. Much of the food served at the roadhouse was prepared here, on a table under a small window. In summer the window was kept open, with a tight screen over it to keep out the flies. Perishable food, such as meat, was kept cold in a sawdust-filled ice house, while milk, butter, and cheese were kept in the dairy, a room built into one end of the ice house.

Flour, when it was first milled in the Cariboo at Soda Creek in 1868, was marketed in large wooden barrels. By the 1880s, William Pinchbeck's mill at Williams Lake produced flour in 98-, 49-, and 25-pound sacks made from unbleached cotton. Sugar, an imported product, was available in 50-pound sacks of fine, white cotton. The sacks, and the cotton string used to sew up the flour and sugar bags, were much prized by housewives who used the cloth to make everything from sheets and pillow cases to tablecloths, underwear, and even blouses. The fine cotton string was especially treasured and was used mostly for crocheting. The sugar sacks, woven from a softer, finer cotton, made nice underwear and excellent jelly bags.

For a long time the flour mill stamp, or maker's name, was dyed right into the sacks, making it almost impossible to remove. Later sacks had the maker's name printed on paper and glued, making it easy to remove. During the 1950s, some manufacturers sold flour in coloured, patterned sacks; however, in the 1960s, increased production costs brought about the use of paper sacks.

The seven upper-storey bedrooms of Yorston's roadhouse, with their ten-foot ceilings, were cool enough in summer; but, due to the lack of insulation in the walls, they were hard to heat in winter. Two rooms on the southwest side were for many years the private apartment of the Bob Yorston family. Heated in winter by the brick chimney connected to the downstairs stoves, it contained bedrooms and a playroom for the children.

Most of the interior of the house was finished in planed tongue-and-groove lumber, hauled from the Reid and Johnston mill at Quesnel. Above the four feet of dark, stained wainscoting, each room was wallpapered. The floors, made of wide fir boards, were usually treated with linseed oil. In later times, a khaki coloured "battleship" linoleum was installed in the living room and hallway. Kerosene lamps hung from the ceilings of most rooms, with candles being used in the bedrooms. "Moore" lights came into use around 1910. These might be considered the forerunner of the Coleman lantern, in that they operated on white "naphtha" gas and had mantles and clear glass globes. A central air tank that pumped up to forty-five pounds of pressure was kept outside the house. In a household where two or three lamps burned for perhaps eight hours on winter nights, only a gallon of gas was consumed per week. The electric lighting system installed in the early 1930s was said to be the first in the district.

The absence of a saloon did not affect the popularity of the road-house. The Yorstons felt that, as strong supporters of the Presbyterian Church, the operation of a saloon was contrary to their moral obligation to the public.

The building of the third roadhouse only a few years prior to what became known as "the railroad era" in northern British Columbia, turned out to be a wise move. Plans for the building of a railway line from Vancouver to Prince George began in 1912, when the Grand Trunk Pacific reached Prince George from eastern Canada. This initiated a land boom in the area between Quesnel and Tete Jaune Cache. For many years prior to, and after, the First World War, the upper Fraser River region swarmed with surveyors, engineers, and land speculators. This, of course, created a resurgence of business for the roadhouses on the upper portion of the Cariboo Road.

The visit of Janet Robertson in 1906 was, for her, the beginning of a lifelong association with the Australian Ranch. In addition to helping Ethel at the roadhouse, Janet was also the schoolteacher and, for a while, taught the Hilborn children and Tom, the youngest of the Windt boys. Lessons were held at the Hilborn farm, a mile north of the Australian Ranch. By April 1909, Janet had married John M. (Jack) Yorston, and remained in the Cariboo for the rest of her life.

The busy proprietors of the Yorston roadhouse, Ethel and Bob, were soon blessed with two lovely children, Edith and Edgar. When little Edgar was only five months old in 1910, an epidemic of dysentery swept through the country, taking with it the lives of both children. Within the next several years, three daughters were born: Jean in 1913, Jessie in 1915, and Mary Ethel (Sue) in 1917. Six children were born to Janet and Jack Yorston: John (Jack) Robert in 1911, Donald in 1913, Keith in 1915, Margaret in 1921, and a set of twin girls, Kathleen and Eileen, in 1924. These twins were said to have been the first to survive infancy in the Quesnel area.

During the winter of 1913, the northbound stage often brought supper guests to the roadhouse. As a small boy, Jack R. Yorston was given the job of watching for the arrival of the stagecoach. While his aunt Ethel and his mother busied themselves in the kitchen, Jack was kept from underfoot at his post in front of the dining-room window. From there, he could spot the carbide lamps of the stage as the horses crossed the bridge over the creek leading to the roadhouse. Breakfast was an extremely busy time. The twice weekly southbound stage left Quesnel at 4:00 a.m., arriving at Yorston's for breakfast at 7:00 a.m. Sometimes there was an extra coach with it, and, with all the guests in the dining room, as many as twenty were served.

Automobiles appeared on the Cariboo Road in 1910, but they were a rare sight. Shortly after this, the BC Express Company, which had the mail contract, put eight Winton Six touring cars into service on the road between Ashcroft and Barkerville. They ran well in dry-road conditions, but, when it rained, the narrow-tired cars bogged down in the deep ruts made by the horse-driven vehicles. On too many occasions schedules were not met, and, by 1913, the company had lost the mail contract to the Inland Transport Express Company. With this loss, the BC Express Company sold its equipment to the successful bidders, but, when the Inland Transport Express Company also failed, the contract was returned to the former, which transported the mail aboard its sternwheeler, the *SS BX*, to Prince George. By 1914, and the start of the First World War, freighting on the Cariboo Road came to an abrupt standstill. Naturally, the roadhouses suffered, and only those with farms and cattle to support them were able to carry on.

At Yorston's ranch, young George Johnston of Quesnel took a contract to clear 100 acres of additional land for grain and pasture. The large crew of men hired on the project lived in a tent camp set up on the ranch, where a Native woman did the cooking. During the building of the Pacific Great Eastern Railway to Quesnel (1912–21), hundreds of labourers lived in camps near their worksite. Beef, vegetables, and dairy products from the local farms were purchased by the railroad cooks. At Australian, where an enormous wooden railway trestle was built, 100 men were camped near Yorston's ranch. This considerable source of income was lost when the railway was completed in 1921. A short-lived resurgence occurred in the 1930s, when several business syndicates attempted to promote and develop coal deposits in the Alexandria, Australian, and Bowron Lakes districts of the Cariboo. This caused quite a stir at the Australian ranch, where Yorston's roadhouse enjoyed a brisk business catering to mining engineers, surveyors, and speculators.

By now, time was taking its toll on the older members of the Yorston family. John McKay Yorston died at home in 1937, and Robert Yorston died as a result of a massive heart attack in 1943. Following Bob's death, Ethel Yorston remained at the roadhouse for about a year before moving to Quesnel, where she lived with her sister Jessie McLure in a house on Reid Street.

While it was never again to be a roadhouse, the old house continued to be useful — even during the 1940s, when several hired men and their families shared the facilities. Following his return from the Second World War in 1946, Don Yorston lived with his bride Carrile (Moxley) in the front part of the old house. During this time, Don installed running water, a convenience never provided while it was a roadhouse. In 1955, an unforeseen freak of nature caused the demise of Yorston's last roadhouse.

The winter of 1954 brought lots of snow to the Cariboo. Sudden warm temperatures that spring resulted in unusually high water levels, and heavy June rains added to the problem. By the end of June, the high water had washed out a number of bridges in the Quesnel District. At Australian Creek, the water normally flowed off the hill and under the highway on its way through the ranch to the Fraser River. That spring, it was soon evident that the culvert carrying the water under the highway was entirely inadequate. The first sign of trouble was the lake of water in the gully above the road. It would only be a matter of time before the pressure loosened the roadbed and broke through, unleashing a flood of water onto the flats below — the site of all the buildings on the Yorston Ranch. Pumps brought in and set up by the Department of Highways had little effect on the steadily rising water. It was the morning of 26 June when the inevitable occurred.

Prepared for the worst, Jack and Don Yorston had spent several days moving all the livestock from the ranch flats, including ninety head of cattle ready for shipping. Valuable farm machinery came next. As they waited up on the road for the water to break through, the Yorstons kept thinking of other items that should be saved, and several more quick trips were made. For a little while the water trickled over the road and down the hill; but suddenly, at about 4:00 p.m., the undermined roadbed broke through, releasing a wall of water fifty yards wide. It travelled downhill at an awful rate, flattening all the buildings in its path and carrying some for several hundred yards. At a depth of twelve feet, the water almost covered the big barn roof, and when it hit the roadhouse, it splashed up against the upper-storey windows; strangely enough, they did not break. Mud, rocks, and water battered the old house off its moorings and swept it across the road to where the roof got hung up on the telephone wires. Only the weight of the two brick chimneys steadied it, bringing it to rest. Inadvertently, in its dying moments, the old house did one good turn. In moving across the road it was exposed to the full force of the flood, which it diverted, thus saving both Don's and Jack's homes, which were directly behind it. The flats of the Australian Ranch were totally devastated that day, and they have never been the same. The creek that roared out of its banks had to be rerouted, and a new creek bed had to be constructed.

For a whole year the old house sat in its dilapidated condition. Roadhouses in general had been obsolete for years, and, with the second generation of Yorstons all grown up and having homes of their own, there was no use for it. For all these reasons, the old house was demolished. Today, its only remnant is a small, twelve-by-fourteen-foot frame building with slate blue, embossed metal siding, which served as a meat house during the roadhouse era. At the time of the great flood of 1955, the water had passed right over the little building, filling it with mud and debris. Several other artifacts from the roadhouse are still to be found in the three households on the Yorston Ranch today. Among these is a hardwood bannister from the original stairway, now part of the Bob Yorston home; and, in the hallway of Don and Carille Yorston's house on the hill, there are several of the original cast-iron coat hooks — still in use.

THE BOHANON RANCH, 1862–98
Originally Lots 6, 7, 8, 9, and 10, G.1., Cariboo

Directly north of the Australian Ranch, and for the next several miles, the land was known as the "Grande Prairie" and the "Round Prairie." By 1868, these lands had become part of the holdings of the Bohanon Ranch.

James Madison Bohanon of Minneapolis, Minnesota, the son of a well-to-do grain farmer, left home in the early 1850s to seek a fortune in the California gold rush. With the discovery of gold in the British Columbia Interior, Bohanon moved north in the early 1860s and began to operate a pack-train between Yale and the Cariboo goldfields. Anticipating the larger profits that might be made from produce grown on his own farm, Bohanon and a partner, Robert L.

Shaw, began to acquire several parcels of land fifteen miles north of Fort Alexandria.

The most southerly portion of the eventually 1,100-acre ranch, (Lot 6, G.1, Cariboo) a farm of 320 acres, had been pre-empted in 1862 by Francois Choteau and Samuel Briley, two miners from Keithley Creek. By April 1864, these lands had been sold to Marvin Perley Elmore, an entrepreneur from Truemansburg, New York. Within a year, Elmore, having made considerable improvements to the property, wrote to Magistrate Henry Ball at Quesnelle Mouth, requesting that his lands at Grande Prairie be surveyed. A sketch enclosed with the application marked the locations of the existing buildings and the crops planted.[11] It is not known if Elmore's "House," a two-storey log building situated beside the Alexandria to Quesnelle Mouth trail, was a roadhouse at this time. Having experienced some success as a merchant in California, Elmore had continued in this vocation at Lillooet in 1859. Soon after this he married a young Lillooet woman, Catla, and two daughters were born. The building of the Cariboo Road to Alexandria in 1863 prompted Elmore and his family to move north, where, in addition to establishing a trading post and fur depot at Quesnelle Mouth, he also acquired the property at Grande Prairie. By 1866, Elmore had conveyed his farm of 320 acres to Jerome Harper, who, in turn, sold it that same year to James Madison Bohanon.[12]

Marvin & George Elmore. Marvin P. Elmore bought the original Bohanon ranch in 1864 from two miners. By 1866, Elmore had conveyed the land to Jerome Harper who in turn sold out to James Madison Bohanon, also in 1866. (COURTESY QDMA)

The 17 Mile House (from Alexandria), 1862

To the north of Lot 6 are lots 8 and 9, a parcel of 780 acres located 17 miles north of Alexandria and originally pre-empted by Colin Campbell Mackenzie, John Saunders, Alexander Gardner, and D. Cain in the spring of 1863. Here, beside the Hudson's Bay Company brigade trail, Mackenzie operated a roadhouse and store. That this enterprise was actually in operation in 1862 is verified by several diaries and journals.

Bishop George Hills, in his diary of 1862, mentions John Saunders and Colin C. Mackenzie, both servants of the Hudson's Bay Company at Alexandria: "The 17 Mile House from Alexandria is kept by a young man (named Mackenzie) brought up at Red River under Bishop Anderson and afterwards went to Cambridge where he took a Bachelors degree. He had Indian Blood."[13] Harry Guillod, who remained overnight at this location in August 1862, also made note of the roadhouse: "Slept in the House, but it was not yet floored, and hard and lumpy ground does not make a comfortable bed, in fact it is pleasanter in the woods, if you can find a respectable tree."[14] On his return south a few weeks later, Guillod mentioned the store: "My shoes hurt me so that I was left quite behind; J. waited for me at Mackenzie's Grande Prairie Ranch, where I got rid of my old shoes and bought a pair of moccasins of which I now had my first experience."[15]

Bohanon–Shaw & Company

With the purchase of these 1,100 acres, James M. Bohanon and his partner Robert Shaw directed the operation of their ranch from what became Lot 6, at the south end, where the main ranch house (or roadhouse, as it became at this time) was the same building as that which was occupied by Elmore in 1864. Bob Shaw, as ranch foreman, saw to land clearing, planting crops, and maintaining the livestock. The operation of this sizable ranch required many labourers, amongst whom were Chew, the Chinese cook at the roadhouse, and a Mexican named Issac Lebraw. James M. Bohanon, commonly known as "Big Dick" Bohanon, lived with a Native wife, Mary Ann, in a cabin behind the roadhouse.[16]

Two references to the stopping house at Bohanon's ranch, neither of them very flattering, were made by George Sargison in his diary of December 1871. Sargison, on his way to Barkerville to become manager of the Barnard's Express Company office located there, was travelling by coach. He made the following observations: "Reached Bohanon's at

7.00 p.m. Sunset over the hills at 3.45 p.m. Chilly, we waited patiently for two and a half hours for supper, the only meal since morning."[17] On his return soon after, Sargison wrote: "Cold day, 25 to 30 below zero, Reached Bohnanon's at 7.00 p.m. Slept better than last time we were here."[18]

With the discovery of gold in the Omineca region in 1869, Marvin P. Elmore, who was still operating a profitable trading post and fur depot at Quesnelle, embarked on a partnership with James M. Bohanon to establish trading posts in the new, but short-lived, gold-rush area. Within two years, these enterprises brought financial disaster to the Bohanon Ranch, which had underwritten them. Both the high cost of transporting goods to the Omineca and the non-payment of credit which had been extended to the miners left a heavy debt — one that was virtually impossible to recoup. In spite of these setbacks, Bohanon and Shaw continued to function; but, undoubtedly, the burden of debt weighed heavily upon the physical and mental health of James Bohanon. While on a business trip to San Francisco in the summer of 1871, he suddenly fell ill. Just before his death, he had sent a telegram to his brother, Samuel Hall Bohanon in Maine, but by the time Sam reached James's side, it was too late.

Sam and his several brothers had not heard from James Madison for years, and they were totally unaware of his move to British

James Madison Bohanon died only five year after buying his ranch in 1866.
(Courtesy QDMA)

After arriving from Maine, Ellen Bohanon and Samuel Hall Bohanon operated the ranch Sam's brother James, bequeathed them in 1871. Life in the Cariboo of the 1870s was a traumatic change from thier home in the USA but they persevered for twenty years. (COURTESY QDMA)

Columbia. From papers found in his effects, Sam learned of James's involvement in a large ranch in the Cariboo, and he travelled north to investigate. It did not take Sam long to realize that the property, operating under the title of Bohanon & Shaw, was encumbered with a debt amounting to $28,000. In spite of this, Sam and his wife Ellen, who had already reached middle age, decided to sell their farm in Maine and to assume James M. Bohanon's interests in the Cariboo. On taking over the operation in 1875, Sam and Ellen could see its potential, but it took many years of hard work and sacrifice before the debt was finally repaid. With an annual interest of 2 per cent, the total amount of the debt had grown to $50,000[19]

During this time, the Bohanon ranch was not a regular roadhouse stop on the stagecoach run, but it did provide occasional accommodation and stable room to teamsters. In 1876, not long after he had assumed control of the ranch, Sam Bohanon enlarged the acreage by purchasing another 160 acres to the north. These 160 acres were known as "The Kersley," after Charles Kersley, who pre-empted the land in 1867. However, as will become clear in the following section, Kersley was not the original pre-emptor of this site.

Wing and Phillips Farm, Grande Prairie, 1862

Situated sixteen miles south of Quesnelle Mouth, this land was first pre-empted by Henry Wing on 27 June 1862.[20] As Bishop Hills proceeded north on his journey to Williams Creek in July of that year, he and his companions came across Wing and his partner Phillips and noticed that they had started to develop a farm:

> *"It is an extension of Grande Prairie, consisting of excellent land. The young men are living in a tent, and are about to erect a log house. They are about one and a half miles back from the river. A stream meanders through the property, proceeding from a lake. There is excellent feed for animals; grass and wild tare. Height above sea level, 1394 ft."*[21]

Although they lacked the capital to develop this property, Wing and Phillips were hard workers, having planted a vegetable garden and a plot of potatoes. While Hills was still there, the one important drawback to the area became evident: "This morning [21 July] the frost formed ice on the ground. The potatoes so carefully raised by Phillips received what he fears will be their death blow."[22]

Just how long Wing and Phillips remained at this property is not known, but by August 1867 Charles Kersley made application to pre-empt the same ground, which appeared to have been abandoned. Attached to Kersley's application of 19 July 1867 was the following note made by Frank Trevor, land recorder at Quesnelle: "This land

The Bohanon Ranch at a time after 1900 when Steve Hilborn owned it.
(Courtesy Steve Hilborn)

having been pre-empted and abandoned by one 'Wing' — has had the notices, required by law, duly posted for one month."[23]

In 1894, after nearly twenty years of struggle and perseverance, Sam and Ellen Bohanon were ready to dispose of their large ranch and to retire to Quesnelle. While the main holdings were sold to Stephen Hilborn in 1897, the Kersley ranch was sold in 1894 to James Shepherd, a young Englishman who had worked on the Bohanon ranch for some years.

KERSLEY HOUSE, 1895–1955
Lot 10, G.1., Cariboo

Born in Lancashire England, James Shepherd was only a school boy when he and his brother became orphans. When his brother was adopted by an aunt, James made up his mind to travel to British Columbia, where his uncle, Abraham Barlow, had settled at Quesnel in the 1870s. Working his way overseas on a sailing vessel, Jim, who was only seventeen, landed at San Francisco in 1890 and made his way north.

Jim's first jobs in the Cariboo were at John B. Hobson's hydraulic mine at Harper's Camp and, later, at Joseph P. Patenaude's ranch at Williams Lake. By 1896, Jim had made enough money to return to England, where he married his cousin Sarah Barlow of Smithybridge, Lancashire. She agreed to move with Jim to the Cariboo.

Abraham Barlow was the first of the the large Barlow family to arrive in the Cariboo in the 1870s. Starting as a tea merchant from England, Barlow became a pioneer entrepreneur, owning land and numerous business interests in the area. (COURTESY BCARS)

James Shepherd, proprietor of Kersley House, married Sarah Barlow in 1896, in Smithybridge, Lancashire, England. (COURTESY EILEEN SEALE)

Back in the Cariboo, Jim found work on the Bohanon ranch, but it was always his ambition to start a ranch of his own. When, in 1897, it became evident that Sam Bohanon was on the point of retiring, the 640-acre Kersley ranch was sold to Jim for $5,000 with a five-year mortgage. During the first year, Jim and Sarah lived in a sod-roofed cabin while Jim and Bill Kilby, an old-time axeman, built a large, two-storey roadhouse. Cut from fir logged on Green Mountain, east of the ranch, the original "square" of the house, measuring about forty by forty feet, contained a living room, lounge, kitchen, dining room, and one bedroom on the main floor. The single brick chimney in the peak of the house carried the smoke from both the barrel heater in the lounge and the range in the kitchen. The approximate cost of building this twelve-room house was between $1,500 and $2,000.

Within a few years, Kersley House had become a popular stopping house, where teamsters and stagecoach passengers enjoyed Sarah Shepherd's excellent cooking. So great was the demand for the Shepherd brand of hospitality that it became necessary to add a dairy and to extend the kitchen along the west side of the house. The need for more help to operate the roadhouse and farm encouraged other members of the Barlow family to emigrate to Canada. Amongst these

*Bob Barlow, Frances Moffat, Mrs John Strand, and Jack Barlow
pose at Kersley House. (COURTESY BCARS)*

were Sarah's sisters (Agnes and Mary) and several brothers (Robert, Walter, John, Levi, and Joseph), most of whom spent the rest of their lives in the Quesnel area.

As travellers approached Kersley House from the south, they passed through open meadows where the Cariboo Road wound along the west side of a pleasant valley and crossed a bridge over a clear, flowing stream named for Charles Kersley. On rounding a corner, Kersley House came into view — a large, whitewashed log dwelling surrounded by a number of barns and assorted outbuildings. Facing the east, the house afforded a magnificent view of open fields and the gentle slopes of Green Mountain. Typical of many Cariboo roadhouses, Kersley House was built with a wide, covered porch extending out over the windows and doors on two sides of the main floor. Not so typical was the sharp-pitched shake roof, which allowed for a generous attic containing three dormer windows facing east. Presumably, these windows let in a lot of cold air in winter, for, in later times, they were covered over with a zigzag-patterned material that looked quite out of keeping with the rest of the house.

On entering Kersley House by the front door, one immediately stepped into a very large lounge, or sitting room, where large wooden beams reminded one of an old English country inn. The flat log walls of the interior had been papered over with gaily decorated wallpaper, which, due to the constant settling of the house, would crack and have to be replaced almost every year. The many framed photographs and paintings depicting English scenery were of great interest to visitors. Covering the dark-stained floorboards were large Axminster rugs, and, in one corner, there stood a collection of rifles and shotguns cradled in a rather unusual gun-rack made of several sets of cow horns. In winter, the focal point of the room was the large barrel heater, where various chairs, including Jim Shepherd's favourite leather-covered Morris chair, were drawn up close.

In 1900, the Kersley post office opened in the sitting room, and Sarah Shepherd was postmistress for a number of years. Later, other family members took over and kept the service going until 1950. The sitting room also contained a player-piano, a wide-faced grandfather clock, and a wind-up Victrola gramophone. Over the years, these accommodating facilities became the scene of many weddings, anniversary parties, and community dances.

In the big dining room behind the lounge, a long handmade dining table and chairs occupied the centre of the room; but by far the most interesting pieces of furniture were the two corner china cabinets. Also

Interior of Kersely House. (COURTESY ANN BARLOW)

handmade, the oak doors had been fitted with concave glass. On display were prized family heirlooms of willow-patterned chinaware and cut-glass decanters. Although plumbing and running water was never installed in Kersley House, the kitchen had been built over a deep well. This made for easy access to water, which was especially appreciated in winter. Baths were taken in the downstairs bedroom, where a full-sized, porcelain-finished steel tub had been installed.[24]

In the dairy, situated behind the kitchen, milk was put through a separator and butter was churned and stored in the well. Of great curiosity in the dairy was a chopping block, made from a single block of fir (four feet in diameter) and used in the butchering of large carcasses of beef.

At the head of the stairway in the second storey of Kersley House was Jim Shepherd's hobby room, where, as an amateur taxidermist, he worked during long winter evenings. Of the three upstairs bedrooms, the largest (on the southwest side of the house) was used by teamsters and labourers, with the other two being reserved for stage passengers.

With hard work and good management, Jim Shepherd and his family produced many fine crops of hay and grain from the fields of Kersley ranch. Alex Barlow, son of Levi and Edith Barlow, grew up

Kersley House. (COURTESY QDMA)

and worked at the ranch and remembered the seasonal harvests of 600 bushels of wheat and oats. The threshing was done by the Batiste boys, who, having the only machine in the area, contracted to thresh the grain on all the neighbouring ranches. Each fall they arrived with their families (women, children, and dogs) to work. Somehow, they always managed to stage a machinery breakdown while working at the Kersley ranch; some said this was just so they could enjoy Sarah Shepherd's blueberry pies for a few extra days.

Jim Shepherd, who believed in making the most of his grain crop, was known to turn out a distilled moonshine that packed an awful wallop. Once the liquid was poured off, the remaining mash was thrown out for the pigs and chickens, who for the next several days could be seen weaving around the farmyard in gay abandon. Having consumed the mash, the pigs turned a fluorescent pink and lay down in a stupor. On one occasion, Sarah Shepherd had to stay up all night to keep an inebriated nursing sow from smothering her offspring. The fact that "Uncle Jim" had a still and made moonshine was not common knowledge to the several nephews and nieces who grew up at Kersley House. Beatrice Kew (nee Strand), who spent much of her childhood there, recalled the teamsters gathered around the living-room heater on cold winter days. What she was not aware of, until much later, was that the teamsters weren't just warming their hands; they were busy catching the drips from the still on top of the heater.

During the 1920s, Jim and Sarah Shepherd were able to leave the ranch in the care of Levi Barlow while they took several trips home to England. On one occasion, the journey was delayed for three months while Jim recuperated from an unfortunate accident.

By this time, the BC Express Company had replaced the horse-driven stages with a fleet of six-passenger Winton touring cars, which, because of the bad roads, gave the company a lot of problems. It was in June, on the first leg of their trip abroad, when Jim and Sarah boarded the car to get to Ashcroft, where they would catch a train to the Coast. Everything went well until they rounded a bend by the Bonaparte River near Cache Creek; just then the steering wheel went awry, sending the car careening off the road and down a steep, ten-foot bank into the river. As it fell, the car turned upside down. Judge Calder and his wife and son, three of the seven passengers, were lucky to have been thrown clear of the car before it went over. Down in the river, Sarah Shepherd was the first to rise to the surface, and all she could think of was her new hat, which was fast disappearing downstream. Jim Shepherd, who was pinned under the car for a while, had his arm broken at the shoulder. The hero of the hour was Bishop de Pencier, another of the passengers, who not only rescued Jim but also two female passengers from their watery confines. Suddenly, Sarah Shepherd realized she no longer had her purse, which contained $600 in cash for the trip. Without hesitation, the bishop plunged back into the river, bringing up the missing purse and several other articles. Just then, Willis West, manager of the BC Express Company, arrived on the scene. When the stage failed to turn up on schedule, he had gone looking for it. It wasn't until after the accident that Jim and Sarah found out they had been riding car number thirteen, which had a record of breaking down. Following an operation conducted by Dr Gerald Baker at Quesnel, Jim convalesced at home. In time, and through effort and determination, he regained the full use of his arm.[25]

Kersley House continued in operation until the early 1930s, when increasing poor health and diabetes forced Sarah Shepherd to give up her role as cook and homemaker. She was almost blind when she passed away in the Quesnel hospital on 1 February 1936. Jim Shepherd made one last trip to Smithybridge in 1937. On returning home, his health failed, and, after a lengthy illness, he died on 23 October 1948.

Following Jim Shepherd's death, Kersley House did not remain in the family for very long. Levi Barlow, who was ready to retire when he inherited the property, sold the ranch to Fred Fridlington and his son Ernest. Early one morning in February 1955, a barking dog awakened Ernest, who rose to find the attic of Kersley House engulfed in flames. The dry old building burned with such speed and fury that the owners considered themselves fortunate to have escaped with their lives.

HARRISON HOUSE
Lot 609, G.1., Cariboo

Situated less than a mile north of Kersley House, Harrison House was built in 1905 by Jack Barlow for Harrison, a freight driver who operated a farm there. While serving as the farm house, the two-and-a-half-storey squared-log building also provided straw-mattress accommodation for the overflow traffic of Kersley House. In 1910, following Harrison's death, his widow, a Native woman, sold the farm, which included thirty cleared acres, to Robert Barlow for $2,000. It was Bob Barlow who added the "ginger breading" to the roofline and eves. When surveyed, this property became Lot 609, G.1., Cariboo.[26]

Built in 1905 for Harrison, a freight driver, this house still stands. Upon Harrison's death, his widow sold out to Bob Barlow, who in turn sold it in 1940 to Walter Edwards. The Edwards family still operates the farm and Walter and his wife, Betty, remain in the old house. Later improvements include a cement basement and a well-built, squared-log addition on the rear of the house. (COURTESY QDMA)

In 1940, F. Walter Edwards and his family purchased the farm, and where they continue to live in the old roadhouse. Over the years it has been kept in good repair, and still stands beside the original wagon road, close to a barn of the same vintage.

Notes to Chapter 6

1. Lieutenant H. S. Palmer, RE, Report of February 1863, Survey from Lac La Hache to Fort George, NW/971M/P174ro BCARS, p. 4.

2. Louis LeBourdais, "The Australians in the Cariboo," *Family Herald & Weekly Star*, 28 December 1927, 36–37.

3. *Ashcroft Journal*, 27 August 1904, 1.

4. *Cariboo Sentinel*, 22 June 1872, 3.

5. Janet Yorston, Aural History, Imbert Orchard Collection, tape #380, Item #20, BCARS.

6. Alvin Johnston, "Birchbark to Steel", unpublished manuscript, 1959.

7. *Ashcroft Journal*, 9 July 1898, 3.

8. Dept. of Lands, Legal Surveys Branch, Victoria, BC, papers pertaining to Crown Grant #4376/99.

9. *Ashcroft Journal,* 27 August 1904, 1.

10. Information obtained from Catherine (Macalister) Yorston.

11. Marvin P. Elmore, letter, 15 April 1865, Colonial Correspondence, 523a, BCARS.

12. Legal Surveys, Victoria, BC Crown Grant #977/97.

13. Bishop George Hills, Diary, 17 July 1862, Anglican Provincial Synod of British Columbia Archives, Vancouver, 92.

14. Harry Guillod, Diary, 13 August 1862, E/B/G94A, BCARS, 31.

15. Ibid., 49.

16. Mark S. Wade, *Cariboo Road* (Victoria: Haunted Bookshop 1979), 175.

17. George Sargison, Diary, December 1871, E/C/Sa7, BCARS.

18. Ibid.

19. Legal Surveys, Victoria, Crown Grant papers #977/97, letters of S. H. Bohanon to S. A. Rodgers.

20. GR827, Lillooet Land Recording, vol. 1, 27 June 1862, Henry Wing, pre-emption of 160 acres at Round Prairie.

21. Hills, Diary, 19 July 1862, 92.

22. Ibid., 21 July 1862, 93.

23. GR1182, Cariboo Land Records, Charles Kersley, 19 August 1867, Lot 10, #309, folio 167, BCARS.

24. Information from Alex and Ann Barlow, Quesnel, BC.

25. Louis LeBourdais, Add. MSS 676, vol. 2, folder 6, BCARS.

26. Ronald Woodall, *Magnificent Derelicts, A Celebration of Older Buildings* (Vancouver: J. J. Douglas 1975), 136.

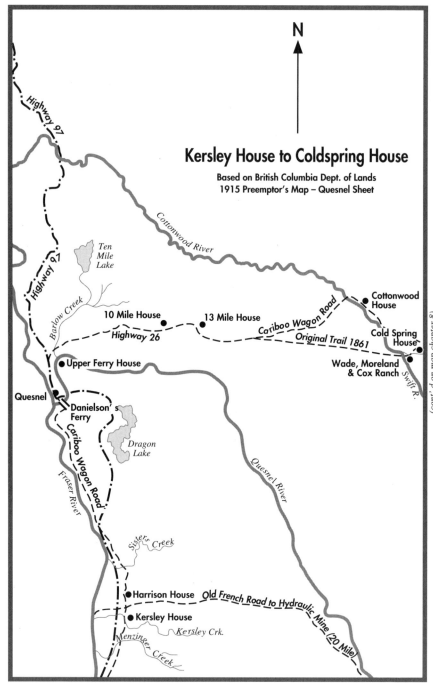

N

Kersley House to Coldspring House

Based on British Columbia Dept. of Lands
1915 Preemptor's Map – Quesnel Sheet

Highway 97

Cottonwood River

Ten
Mile
Lake

Barlow Creek

Highway 97

10 Mile House

13 Mile House

Cottonwood
House

Highway 26

Cariboo Wagon Road

Original Trail 1861

Cold Spring
House

● Upper Ferry House

Wade, Moreland
& Cox Ranch

Swift R.

Quesnel

Danielson's
Ferry

Cariboo Wagon Road

Dragon
Lake

Quesnel River

Fraser River

Sisters Creek

● Harrison House　Old French Road to Hydraulic Mine (20 Mile)

● Kersley House

Kersley Crk.

Menzinger Creek

(cont'd on map chapter 8)

CHAPTER SEVEN

Quesnelle Mouth to Cold Spring House

DANIELSON'S FARM, ROADHOUSE, AND FERRY
Quesnelle Mouth, 1860
Lot 48, G.1., Cariboo

Among the hundreds of miners on the Fraser River above Lillooet in the summer of 1859, was an enterprising Norwegian, Charles Danielson. Close to where they had been mining on Ferguson's Bar, thirty miles north of Fort Alexandria, Danielson and a fellow miner, James Snelgrove, came across many acres of arable land at the confluence of the Quesnel and Fraser rivers. This was the opportunity they had been looking for. Tired of the rough, uncertain life of the prospector, the two men decided to settle at this site, where they marked out two pre-emptions of land on the south bank of the Quesnel River. There they built a log cabin and a store beside the Hudson's Bay Company brigade trail, a quarter of a mile from the river's mouth. The delta of meadowland at the confluence of the two rivers was well-suited to agriculture, and, by spring of 1861, the partners had planted a field of turnips and another of potatoes. At harvest time, when hundreds of miners from Quesnelle Forks arrived on their journey south for the winter, many of them were sick with scurvy — the result of poor diet, and in particular, a lack of vegetables. To these men Danielson's crop of turnips was more valuable than gold. Ranging in price from twenty-five cents to one dollar a piece, they sold quickly, netting Danielson and Snelgrove a tidy profit of $3,000.

Across the Quesnel River was another, much larger and heavily forested flat of land, where, in 1861, pack-trains had started to arrive and two Chinese stores, a saloon, and a gambling tent had opened for business. Early the following year, the government placed a reserve of land in this area, which was fast developing into a supply depot for miners en route to the goldfields. To accommodate the increasing traffic arriving from the south, Danielson built a rope ferry on the river bar, close to the buildings. At the cabin, which by this time had become a roadhouse, meals and accommodation were available to passing travellers.

One of these was Harry Guillod, a young Englishman who was travelling with his brother George and one other companion in August 1862. On reaching Danielson's Ferry House: "We had a meal of tea, sugar, bread and beans — but no meat, the fellow had the conscience to charge us two dollars each."[1] For several years there were few cattle or milk cows in the Cariboo, but by 1865 Danielson and his partner were building barns and corrals on the farm, where cattle were sold to the mining camps. That same year, Danielson wrote to the resident magistrate, Henry Ball, requesting a survey of his property at Quesnel and proposing to construct a bridge across the Quesnel River to replace the ferry. Both requests were refused. While several landowners had applied to have their land surveyed, it wasn't until the 1880s that the government got around to surveying in the Cariboo. On the subject of bridge building, Danielson was told that such an undertaking would have to go to public tender. In the meantime, in 1866 and 1867 Danielson's ferry and farming accomplishments were mentioned from time to time in the *Cariboo Sentinel*.

By the spring of 1867, Charles Danielson had lost his ferry contract to Marvin P. Elmore, storekeeper and fur trader at Quesnel. It had been only two years since the wagon road was built, but already heavy traffic had rendered it almost impassable. In his application, Elmore had offered to "put the road into good order in exchange for the ferry contract."[2]

That fall, Danielson sold his interest in the farm at Quesnel to Jerome Harper, pioneer cattleman; but this was not the last of Danielson's enterprises. In 1868, he applied for, and was granted, a charter to build a bridge across the Quesnel River, ten miles upstream from the mouth. From a trail branching off the wagon road at Dog

Prairie, a few miles south of Quesnelle, Danielson built a road running northeast to the Quesnelle River. Here he constructed a roadhouse as well as a bridge to connect with the wagon road to Williams Creek, bypassing Quesnelle entirely.

DANIELSON'S BRIDGE AND ROADHOUSE, QUESNEL RIVER, 1869

Evidence of the building of Danielson's road from Dog Prairie, the bridge across the Quesnel River, and the roadhouse on the south bank are found in a letter dated 8 May 1869 as well as in an advertisement dated 12 June 1869. Both appeared in the *Cariboo Sentinel*: "Mr. Charles Danielson: Sir: I arrived safe from Cariboo and found your new trail much better than I expected, and good feed half a mile from the bridge. I had no trouble in getting through. It is a good deal shorter than by ferry. The bridge is good and strong. Yours most respectfully, A Burnett.[3]

"Mr. Charles Danielson desires to inform the Traders, packers, Travellers and others, that the road from Dog Prairie to the 13 mile-post beyond Quesnelle Mouth is now open and in good condition for pack trains and stock, and that there is an abundance of good feed throughout. There is a house of entertainment at the bridge."[4]

Following this audacious beginning, nothing more was heard of Danielson's bridge or of his roadhouse. Obviously, it did not flourish, due, perhaps, to the start of the Omineca gold rush. To reach the Omineca, traffic went by way of Quesnelle. A further tidbit of information concerning Charles Danielson appeared two years later: "Charles Danielson of Quesnelle Mouth is dangerously ill. Dr Chipp of Barkerville is to visit him."[5]

In the meantime, Danielson's ranch, now owned by Jerome Harper, continued as a pasturage for cattle and other animals destined for the slaughterhouse in Barkerville. The roadhouse and store continued to function until 1875, when the first bridge was built across the Quesnelle River, rendering those services redundant. Some years later, a fire destroyed all but the bottom logs of the old roadhouse, which were still visible in 1900.

By 1885, Thaddeus Harper, who succeeded his brother Jerome, was getting rid of his many land holdings in the Interior, including the comparatively small acreage at Quesnel, which was sold to William Albert Johnston, originally of Masham, Quebec. At this time, the property was Crown granted and became Lot 48, G.1., Cariboo, containing 216

William A. Johnston, his wife Roxelina and son Alvin, taken about 1902.
(COURTESY W. A. JOHNSTON FAMILY)

acres. It was on part of this land that W. A. Johnston, in partnership with James Reid of Quesnelle, operated a flour mill from 1887 to 1892. With the advent of cheaper sources of flour elsewhere, the mill was converted into a sawmill, which operated until 1912. Although over the years most of the original acreage has been disposed of, the Johnston family still reside at this site.

QUESNELLE MOUTH, 1862–1916

That Quesnelle Mouth would become an important supply centre for the Cariboo gold rush was determined in 1862, when Lieutenant H. S. Palmer of the Royal Engineers visited the area. In a report of his findings concerning a practical route for the Cariboo Road, made public early the following year, he recommended a "western route" by way of Quesnelle Mouth and east to the mines of the Cariboo.

When the government placed a reserve at Quesnelle Mouth in 1862, it cancelled three pre-emption applications made earlier that year. In response, the applicants, Donald McBride, Thomas Brown, and Hugh Gillis, wrote to Colonel Moody of the Department of Lands and Works, complaining that "they had already bought plows, teams of horses and other farming equipment at a cost of $4,000."[6]

While a dozen buildings had already been built along the river front, in June 1863, Sergeant McColl of the Royal Engineers began to survey a townsite that included ten blocks, each with at least sixteen lots. To make way for a street, the dozen buildings along the river had to be moved back. With the survey completed by June 22, the first lot sold, Lot 1 of Block 4, went for 40 pounds sterling.[7]

OCCIDENTAL HOTEL
Lot 3, Block 2, Townsite of Quesnelle, 1864

Despite the setback in their plans, Thomas Brown and Hugh Gillis became leading businessmen in the tiny community of Quesnelle Mouth. Beginning in 1863 with a store located next to the steamer reserve, the following year they opened a hotel further up the street on Lot 3, Block 2, of the new townsite.

Among the many visitors to the Occidental Hotel that summer was young Harry Jones, who had arrived from Soda Creek aboard the *SS Enterprise.* While everyone else headed straight for the barroom, the bashful young Welshman hung around the lobby until proprietor Tom Brown came by. Just as he had arranged with Peter Dunlevy to watch out for Harry at Soda Creek, Captain Evans had also asked Tom

The original Occidental Hotel at Quesnelle built in 1865 by Thomas Brown and Hugh Gillis. This building was torn down in 1909 to make way for a new hotel, built by Edward Kepner.

to see that Harry was looked after at Quesnelle Mouth: "He showed me the big dining room, and told me that when the bell rang I was to go in and take a place at the table."[8] At bedtime, when Harry went to use his own blanket, Tom would not hear of it, insisting that he sleep in a proper bed. Harry did not argue the point, for his bones were still aching from many nights spent lying on hard floors.

In providing separate bedrooms and beds in 1863, the Occidental Hotel, a two-storey log structure with accommodation for twenty guests, was several years ahead of most roadhouses and hotels in the Cariboo; and for some time it was considered to be the best in the country. However, despite its sophistication, there were some who found fault with the facility. Appointed to replace J. Boles Gaggin as Stipendiary Magistrate at Quesnel in the spring of 1865, Henry M. Ball took up residence at the Occidental Hotel. Following his arrival, Ball wrote in his diary: "Quesnelle Mouth, Brown's Hotel ... Very dirty ... rather disappointed after all that has been said about it, but suppose I shall get used to it in time."[9] He also mentioned two prostitutes, "Big Bell" and "Florence," both of whom were "about fifty years of age." Board and lodging at Brown's hotel was twenty-seven dollars per week.

Quesnelle was, at this time, experiencing an economic slump due to the temporary exodus of the mining population to a gold rush in the Kootenay District. Consequently, Henry Ball found things "awfully dull" in his new surroundings, where he had "no house, no office, and very little to do."[10] By the spring of 1869, business at the Occidental Hotel was so slack that reduced prices were announced:

Occidental Hotel, Quesnelle Mouth.

The Proprietors of this well known House tender their sincere thanks to their friends and the travelling public generally for their past liberal patronage and beg to inform them that in order to insure a continuance of the same,

BOARD & LODGING has been reduced to $3.50 per day, and SINGLE MEALS to $1.00.
All the luxuries that the country affords are constantly kept on the table.
PRIVATE PARLOURS & SUITES of rooms for families.
THE BAR is stocked with the best brands of Wines, Liquors & Cigars.
THE STABLE is well supplied with the best Timothy, Oats, Hay and Grain.

Brown & Gillis, Quesnellemouth, May 12, 1869.[11]

In 1870, the economic climate changed dramatically when Quesnelle Mouth became a supply centre for the short-lived gold rush in the Omineca. By 1872, with the excitement over, Thomas Brown's partner, Hugh Gillis, committed suicide on the trail from Manson Creek. It was rumoured that Gillis had been financially ruined in the Omineca gold rush. Following this tragic event, Brown took Alfred Carson as his hotel partner but soon bought him out. When Brown died in 1881, his widow, Sarah, married John McLean, the rough and ready miner of 1858, who retired to Quesnelle. Sarah, a woman of refinement, spent years helping John assume the genteel ways of a man about town.

Upon their retirement in 1900, the hotel was rented until 1907, then sold to Edward Kepner, an American from Seattle. Kepner tore the original building down in 1909 but kept the two annexes for his new Occidental Hotel, built by John Strand. The pride of the community, it was the only four-storey structure in Quesnelle until the building of the courthouse in 1965. With two ballrooms, a bar, restaurant, barbershop, travellers' display rooms, and rooms for 100 guests, it was by far the most fastidious facility on the Cariboo Road.

CARIBOO HOTEL, 1890s

During the 1890s, a second hotel opened on Front Street, a few doors from the Occidental Hotel. This was the "Cariboo," a single-storey, false-fronted log building operated by Edward Hopwood. Following Hopwood, Archibald McNaughton owned the Cariboo Hotel until his death in 1900. McNaughton's widow Margaret sold the building in 1909 to John Strand, a Norwegian carpenter and construction engineer. By the following year, Strand had rebuilt the original hotel into an imposing three-storey facility, adding to it one of Quesnel's first movie houses, the Empress Theatre, in 1913.

It was near dawn on a cold, January morning in 1916 when fire broke out in the theatre and quickly spread north and south along the block. The lack of water and manpower, as well as the extreme temperature, made it impossible to subdue the fire, which destroyed all of the buildings between Barlow and Carson avenues, including both hotels. Although new facilities were soon built on the same sites, the romance, elegance, and gaiety of Quesnel's first river-front hotels seemed to die in that fire. The hotels had been the social centres of the little community, and while the Occidental and Cariboo have become synonymous with Quesnel's history, there were others, not so well known, that came and went through the years.

John and Sarah McLean stand on the second floor of a
white Occidental in 1907 shortly before it was sold to
Edward Kepner. McLean, (right) was one of the five
original prospectors to reach the Cariboo.

Mid-page, Edward Kepner and family are seen in front of one of
the annexes which surround the original Occidental. Below, the
second four-storey Occidental draws a crowd while John Strand'
Cariboo Hotel sits in the background. (COURTESY QDMA)

Archie McNaughton, (middle right) a pioneer Overlander, bought the original Cariboo Hotel from Edward Hopwood who poses in front of the 1890 entrance with his sister and niece in the foreground. In 1910, John Strand incorporated the old hotel into his New Cariboo Hotel and three years later, he added the Empress Theatre to make Front Street the focal point of the community. (COURTESY QDMA)

WHITEHALL'S RESTAURANT AND STORE, 1862

In his diary of a journey down the Fraser River from Tete Juan Cache in 1862, the Overlander Robert B. McMicking mentioned his arrival at Quesnelle Mouth, where he and his companions "ate their supper off a table for the first time in four months" at Whitehall's Store, and paid $1.50 each for it.[12]

FASHION HOTEL, QUESNELLE MOUTH, 1864

This establishment was visited by Governor Frederick Seymour on his trip to the Cariboo mines in 1864.[13]

COLONIAL RESTAURANT, 1865

This restaurant was operated by P.L. Johnson, and advertised as a place "where music and good cooking [was] available at all hours."[14]

ARMSTRONG HOTEL, 1890s

This hotel was "newly fitted and refurbished — a quiet Boarding & Lodging House."[15] Situated on Front Street, where later stood the Rex Theatre, the Armstrong Hotel went out of business in 1898. Moved by Alfred Carson to his ranch on the banks of the Quesnel River, the building was eventually washed away.

NUGGET HOTEL, 1900

The turn of the century saw the start of the long-standing Nugget Restaurant in Quesnel. Financed by a consortium of Chinese merchants, it began as a hotel situated on the north side of Barlow Avenue, between Reid and Front streets. Following an all-consuming fire in the 1920s, the Nugget Restaurant (with lodging rooms in its upper storey), opened on the south side of the street. During the 1960s, under a restructured partnership, the Greenleaf Restaurant opened on the site of the old Nugget, where it continues to this day. For a few years the original name was perpetuated in another restaurant on McLean Street, the New Nugget.

STANHOM LODGE, 1920–71
Lot 1, Block 11, Townsite of Quesnel

A boarding house located at the foot of McLean Street in the 1920s was named for its two proprietors, Grace Stanton and Dora Homan. Arriving in Quesnel in 1910 to assist Edward Kepner in the operation of his new Occidental Hotel, the two women found themselves out of

A woman of many talents. Dora Homan spent decades in the lodging business. She was noted for her psychic powers and spent evenings charting horoscopes. (COURTESY QDMA)

Originally the Anglican Church boarding school — this building became the present Quesnel Hotel. After the fire on Front Street in 1916 Mr. Ewing moved this building from the upper end of Kinchant Street to the site of the former Occidental Hotel.

work when the hotel burned down in 1916. In 1920, as Quesnel's population increased, the women bought and opened their own private boarding house, Stanhom Lodge, which they operated until 1925 when they leased the BA (Quesnel) Hotel from Charlotte Ewing. During the 1930s, when the hotel was sold, Stanhom Lodge was reopened.

Both well-educated and liberal-minded, these two independent women are remembered for their experimental backyard garden, where Grace Stanton, a botanist, was assisted by Dora Homan in the growing of walnut trees, new varieties of apple trees, melons, and even grapes. Dora, who called herself a psychic, was recognized by the townspeople as an astrologist. In a collection of her documented effects housed in the Quesnel and District Museum and Archives, it is clear that towards the end of her life Dora Homan stayed up almost every night, working on other peoples horoscopes.

Stanhom Lodge continued in operation until the early 1960s. The building was destroyed in 1971 to make way for an access road to the Moffat Bridge, completed in 1972.

TRAVELLERS REST, 1920–44
Lot 9, Block 1, Townsite of Quesnel

With the closing of the Hudson's Bay Company trading post in Quesnel in 1919, the company sold off lots 8 and 9 of Block 1, on which stood the trading post, a residence, dairy, barn, and two warehouses.

Gustavus Wright stopped road building long enough to complete this Quesnelle residence in 1863. Like many such structures it would have its day as a hostelry. (COURTESY QDMA)

The trading post, on Lot 8, was purchased by Charles Allison, druggist, while the old residence on Lot 9 was sold in the early 1920s to Sarah (Sally) Agnes Thompson, who opened a boarding house which she named the Travellers Rest. The two-storey log building, originally constructed in 1863 by entrepreneur G. B. Wright, contained seventeen rooms, where for many years Sally kept house and provided meals for many local bachelors. Following the sale of the building in 1944, it became a storage depot and was allowed to deteriorate. At this time, the age and historical value of the building was not realized. Gutted by a fire in 1959, the building was soon demolished.

FIRST TRAIL TO LIGHTNING CREEK, 1862

When Wright failed to establish a steamer on the upper Fraser River in 1862, Magistrate Thomas Elwyn, pressured by merchants and packers, came to the decision that a trail of some sort had to be started immediately. Foregoing the original plan of a trail from the mouth of the Cottonwood River, it was arranged for a contractor, a Mr Kyse, to build a trail from McDonald's Bar, four miles up the Quesnel River, to Lightning Creek. By the middle of June 1862, miners and mule trains were crossing the Quesnel River by way of "the upper ferry" from where they travelled along an excruciatingly bad trail. Soon after it was built, Harry Guillod, on his way to Van Winkle, judged it "a bad and hilly trail, a conglomeration of mud, stones, and trees fallen in every direction."[16]

FOUR MILE HOUSE, THE UPPER CROSSING, QUESNEL RIVER, 1862

Upon leaving Phillip and Wing's farm (later Kersley's) at 7:30 a.m. on 21 July 1862, Bishop George Hills and his entourage headed north for sixteen miles along "a new trail" to the "Upper Crossing" of the Quesnel River, four miles upstream from its mouth. In his diary, Hills describes the crossing:

This river, flowing in a westerly direction towards the Fraser, we crossed a few miles from its mouth at a place called the upper crossing, kept by a southern American named Cook [sic. Should be Cock]. Our horses were driven over the stream which is about 80 yds. wide ... The river being rapid they were carried down some way by the current. It was curious to witness the ten heads all above water with ears pinched up and snorting noses, pressing for the opposite land.[17]

Henry D. Cock, ferryman and proprietor of the roadhouse at the Upper Crossing, is not to be confused with Mortimer Cook, who, with his partner Kimball, established a ferry crossing on the Thompson River in 1859. This is clarified by reading F. W. Laing's 1942 article, "Some Pioneers of the Cattle Industry," wherein Henry Cock is mentioned in a detailed account of an 1861 cattle drive (organized by a Major Thorp) from Washington Territory to the Cariboo. Near Kamloops, Thorp and his men overtook several other herds being driven north from the same area. One of these was led by Henry Cock and his associates, who immediately joined forces with the Thorp expedition. Many setbacks hindered the progress of the cattle drovers. Upon reaching Kamloops, they met with scores of miners heading south for the winter. Realizing they were too late to sell their cattle in the Cariboo that season, they elected to winter the cattle in the Bonaparte River Valley, northwest of Kamloops. Here they met with two other cattlemen, Snipes and Murphy, who were also wintering a large herd of cattle. It was at this time that Henry Cock became involved in a near lynching. As F. W. Laing relates, the earliest mention of the affair is found in the *Fort Kamloops Journal* of 28 September 1861:

> I omitted mentioning yesterday that a party of Americans, three in number, called here, Murphy, Stevenson and Cook [sic Cock] inquiring how they should act towards another American who it was strongly suspected had stolen from Murphy in gold dust and coin something over $200.[18]

Six days later, another entry in the journal stated: "The Americans camped on the opposite side held a trial yesterday of the party suspected of stealing money from Snipes & Co."[19]

The final outcome of these events, which Laing discovered in an account written much later by A. J. Splawn (one of Thorp's men), gives the reader an idea of the casual disregard for law and order shown by the Americans of that time.

> The frontiersman's court convened, consisting of six men — I was one of that number. The prisoner was brought before us. He was unable to give any account of his suddenly acquired wealth, in fact he had a sullen, hang dog expression we did not like. After talking it over we decided he had a thief's face anyway, and that if he was not guilty of this particular theft it was probably because he had not had the right opportunity. We thought he had better

hang to avoid future complications. As the rope was being prepared a former Magistrate of Fort Kamloops, a Mr. McLean appeared and demanded an explanation. Mr. Cock gave it. To hang a man on that kind of evidence was hardly safe, Mr. McLean thought, and he advised that we give the prisoner the benefit of the doubt. Not being wise to British laws we turned him loose.[20]

On leaving the Bonaparte Valley in May 1862, the herds of Major Thorp and Henry Cock proceeded north without further incident, except for a delay "north of Soda Creek," where a trail of ten miles had to be cut through the timber due to a slide beside the Fraser River. This was the "new trail" to the Upper Crossing on the Quesnel River, mentioned by Bishop Hills in his description of his journey north from Phillip and Wing's farm. Upon reaching the Quesnel River, "Cock sold his cattle and commenced to operate a ferry."[21]

At Cottonwood Crossing, between Quesnelle Mouth and Van Winkle, good grazing was found, and from there, several head of cattle were driven each week to Lightning Creek, where the meat was sold for $1.50 per pound. The offal brought an even higher amount due to its popularity with Chinese miners.

Lieutenant H. S. Palmer's map of the land reserve at Quesnelle Mouth in September 1862 includes details of the Quesnel River, from the mouth to the Upper Crossing, showing the location of Cock's ferry and roadhouse on the south bank and "Cock & Co." pre-emption claims of 320 acres "from house downward."[22] It would seem that Henry Cock did not remain long at the Four Mile Creek ferry crossing. A year later, in October 1863, Dr W. B. Cheadle, who arrived at Quesnelle Mouth by way of the *SS Enterprise*, mentioned in his diary that he "walked to 4 Mile House ... we stayed there all night. Packers playing cards. Proprietor one of those Canadians who had come overland and down the Fraser last year — gave a fearful account of hardships, especially on the raft."[23]

A further reference to Four Mile Creek and the Upper Crossing was made by Bishop Hills in his diary of 25 July 1862:

On passing the upper Ferry of the Quesnel we met a return train of some 50 horses. Their owner was an Oregon farmer who had taken bacon up to the mines. He is called "Bacon Brown," and his pack train the "Bacon Train." He left Oregon on the 13th of May and reached Cariboo in exactly two months and cleared $5,000. His bacon sold for $1.00 lb.[24]

The man described was Michael C. Brown, one of the party of explorers on Williams Creek early in 1861.

While the pack trail from Four Mile Creek on the Quesnel River sufficed for the time being, Palmer's study of 1863 also suggested that a wagon road should link up with the road from Alexandria by way of Quesnelle Mouth rather than by way of the Upper Crossing. Built by contractor Allen Smith, a ten-foot wide trail from Quesnelle Mouth was completed later that year, bypassing the Four Mile Crossing and the roadhouse located there. Four Mile Creek was later renamed Barlow Creek, after Abraham Barlow, a pioneer settler of the Quesnel area in the 1870s.

THE 10 MILE HOUSE, 1887–1924

Prior to the late 1880s, the flat of land ten miles northeast of Quesnel had been a campground used by early fur traders and packers and, in 1862, by the Royal Engineers. Charles Laronde, a powerfully built man of French and Cree parentage, was born at Fort Garry, Manitoba, in the 1840s. As a trapper and buffalo hunter, he lived outdoors for many months of the year, cooking over campfires and sleeping under the stars. Rumour had it that he had taken part in the Louis Riel rebellion. In British Columbia, Charlie became a packer along the old Hudson's Bay Company trails and, in the 1880s, was employed by a mining company on the Cottonwood River. It was at this time that Charlie settled on the old campground ten miles east of Quesnel, where freighters rested and pastured their horses before starting up the steep, three-mile hill to the 13 Mile House. As a result of the arrival of the Canadian Pacific Railway in Ashcroft in 1885, freighting on the road to Lightning Creek was particularly brisk, with thousands of tons of machinery being hauled in to where large European and American syndicates were investing in mining properties.

As the need arose, Charlie Laronde began to provide meals to the teamsters, cooking at first over an open fire and, later, in a cabin built beside the road. The cabin exemplified Charlie's skill as an axeman; it had tight, dove-tailed corners and, on the roof, hand-cut cedar shakes. Companion and assistant to Charlie was his wife, Marie Boucher, a Native woman from the Stone Reserve near Fort George. Of small but wiry build, Marie was a good cook, a competent ranch hand, and well versed in the art of trapping. The Laronde trapline, one of the first to be registered in the area, extended from the Quesnel River north to Cottonwood.

With business on the increase in the 1890s, Charlie added a larger log cabin to the original, and by 1900 had added two others, making for a strange assortment of roofs. Last but not least was a summer kitchen lean-to, which was added on at the rear. Some distance from the roadhouse were two log barns facing each other, one on either side of the road. Among her many duties on the homestead, Marie kept a milk cow, and, when cream was plentiful, she served it whipped on top of her wild berry pies. Small wonder freighters like young Roddy Moffat always planned to stop for a meal at "the Ten."

Charlie Laronde, one of the last of the old-time fiddlers, often played for dances in Quesnel. For just a token payment, he rendered quadrilles, schottisches, and polkas, his favourite being the "Hudson's Bay Jig." At midnight, after passing the hat, Charlie played on until 4:00 a.m., standing in his moccasins on a makeshift platform and stamping out the time with one foot. As he grew older, Charlie was besieged with rheumatism, the result of carrying too many heavy loads on his back. As the problem worsened, Marie took over the trapline, snowshoeing out over the rough winter trails. Left at home to keep the fires burning, Charlie skinned the furs and catered to the one or two teams that came by. Where Marie's cooking had delighted those who stopped at the roadhouse, Charlie's left much to be desired. Occupied much of the time with his skinning and hide stretching, when travellers called in for a meal, Charlie put aside his work to mix up a pan of biscuits, his hands still covered in skunk oil or some other offensive concoction

10 Mile was built and expanded through the 1890s by Métis trapper Charlie Laronde and his wife, Marie.

used in the preservation of animal hides. Needless to say, business soon came to a standstill.

Towards the end of his life, Charlie decided to make a will, naming his wife as his beneficiary. Realizing he had neglected to get clear title to his property, Charlie sought the assistance of John Boyd of Cottonwood House, who put the matter in the hands of his lawyers, Crease & Crease of Victoria. Six months later, after quite a few ten-dollar bills had changed hands, Boyd made a special trip from Cottonwood House to see Charlie. Apparently, his lawyers advised him that the problem would be more easily resolved if Charlie and Marie were legally married (of course, according to Native customs, they already were). "By Jove," exclaimed Charlie, "you know, we were on our way to see the priest about twenty years ago, but we got snowed in. The next spring we were too busy, and after that I plumb forgot."[25] In due time, Charlie's property was Crown granted and became Lot 223, G.1., Cariboo. Following her husband's death, Marie inherited the property, and, upon her own death in 1924, the land went to a niece.

The buildings of the 10 Mile House were still standing in 1960. The owner of the farm at that time, Charles Schmidt, had built a new house, and, although he was loath to destroy the old buildings, he realized they had outlived their usefulness. As the bulldozer worked to demolish the old roadhouse in June 1960, it became apparent that the logs, most of which had been cut in the 1880s, were still sound. A year earlier, the main road, which had always gone right through the 10 Mile property, was relocated to the southeast, bypassing the farm by a quarter of a mile. Today, the site of the 10 Mile House is still visible from the highway, across a cleared field and behind a small lake.

THE 13 MILE HOUSE, 1864
Lot 389, Cariboo, G.1

Built in 1864 by E. T. Dodge & Company (a freighting company in Lillooet), the roadhouse at the 13 milepost from Quesnelle Mouth was leased by Overlander Richard S. Cormack until 1866, when it was taken over by Alexander Wallace, an ex-Royal Navy man. Wallace, a crusty bachelor, rented the property for several years before purchasing it in the 1870s.

Shortly after settling there, Wallace was seriously wounded by a Chinese gambler, who attacked him with an axe after robbing the cash box in the restaurant of the roadhouse. Fortunately, Wallace was able to gain control of the axe, which he used to subdue his assailant.

Sandy and Jean Locke's "13" on the right faces his newly cleared meadow that runs down to Wallace Lake. (COURTESY BCARS)

Leaving the Chinese for dead outside the front door of the roadhouse, he managed to get to Quesnel, where he notified the authorities. Attended by the local physician, Dr Trevor, Wallace's life hung in the balance for some time. Upon investigation, it was concluded that the oriental, a large, tall man from northern China, was a compulsive gambler down on his luck. While paying for his coffee at the roadhouse, he had seen the money in the cash box and decided to rob Wallace.

During the many years of his tenure at the 13 Mile House, Alexander Wallace became known for his brusque manner, and, although he gave his customers fair exchange for their money, the roadhouse lacked the feminine touch. Road Superintendent William A. Johnston, who knew Wallace very well, judged him to be a man of differing moods. On one occasion when he stopped for supper, Johnston washed his hands before sitting down to his meal. Obviously, Wallace was in a foul mood that day, and when Johnston requested a clean towel, he snapped: "You married men are so fussy, you make me sick. That towel has been there for two weeks, and you're the first one to complain!"[26]

Sarah Crease, on the other hand, saw quite a different side of the old Scot's nature when she and her husband stopped by in 1880: "Wallace's farm ... where we watered our horses — Wallace a jovial, good natured, good looking man ... very pleased to see Henry."[27]

Ready to retire in 1899, Alexander Wallace sold the 13 Mile Ranch and roadhouse to Alexander Locke, a local stagecoach driver.

Site of 13 Mile House, 1992.

"Sandy" Locke, originally of Ontario, had arrived in the Cariboo in the 1870s. While driving the BX stages between Quesnel and Barkerville, he became acquainted with the well-known Kelly family of Barkerville and, in 1893, married Elizabeth Ingels Kelly (popularly known as Jean).

On purchasing the 13 Mile property, Sandy had the original road-house torn down and replaced by John Strand, who built a comfortable, two-storey log house on the same site. While Jean cared for her growing family, managed the roadhouse, and catered to the passengers aboard the stages, Sandy worked hard to develop the property. During this time further hayland was leased at 15 Mile, and a meadow was cleared by the lake.

As a young man in 1910, Alvin Johnston worked in the family freight and livery stables at Quesnel. To him, a trip to deliver goods to the Locke family at the "13" was more like a visit with old friends than a night spent at a wayside house. Arriving in time for supper, and with the outside chores attended to, everyone gathered in the parlour for an evening of comradeship and entertainment. While Laura, the eldest girl, played the piano, her mother, a talented performer, led the singing.

Several of the seven Locke children were born at the 13 Mile House, but, by 1912, when the youngest reached school age, the family sold out and moved to Quesnel. The Lockes were the last to operate the "13" as a roadhouse.

Alexander Locke and his children at 13 Mile House. (COURTESY QDMA)

The site of the 13 Mile House, on top of a knoll and beside the original wagon road, is today occupied by a modern residence. Bypassed by the present highway, it can still be seen against a backdrop of dark trees behind Wallace Lake, named for the long-time proprietor of the original stopping house.

CAMERON'S HOUSE, 1862, THE 15 MILEPOST FROM QUESNELLE
Lot 361, G.1., Cariboo

Following the arrival of the McMicking party of Overlanders to Quesnelle Mouth on 12 September 1862, all but a few of the group left the very next day. The others, Robert and Thomas McMicking and four companions, decided to walk out to "the mines," where, despite the lateness of the season, they might find work. On a journey that took two days, they got only as far as Wade's ranch at Cottonwood, twenty-four miles out, before they realized, through talking with people they met along the way, that the mining season was over. Although it was a wasted trip, the party made the acquaintance of the Cameron family, who kept the roadhouse where they stayed on both nights of their journey. As Robert McMicking wrote in his diary: "They were very clever and kind Canadians and we enjoyed our nights well."[28]

Settled at this site early in 1862, William Cameron and his sons built a roadhouse beside the trail and, in August, pre-empted 160 acres of land "on the trail half way between Cottonwood and the Mouth of

Quesnel."[29] "Cameron's" is also noted on Lieutenant H. S. Palmer's map of 1863, from a survey made the previous summer. Later in 1863, the Cameron family gave up their pre-emption and moved to Richfield on Williams Creek, where they operated a hotel.

COTTONWOOD CROSSING, 1862–64
Wade & Company Farm, Roadhouse, and Store
Lots 437 and 438, G.1., Cariboo

With the building of the first twenty-five miles of pack trail from Quesnelle Mouth to Van Winkle in 1862, the increasing numbers of miners and pack-trains reached a wide, fertile valley known as Cottonwood, about thirty-five miles from Richfield. This was an area bounded by Lightning Creek and the Swift and Cottonwood rivers; the soil was fertile and the feed plentiful — a natural cattle-holding point and stopover site for pack trains.

First to recognize the commercial potential of the area was George Cox, a packer who pre-empted 160 acres at the junction of Lightning Creek and Swift River on 14 June 1862. By July, Cox had found two partners, Dudley Moreland and Jim Wade. Together, they pre-empted 320 acres of adjoining land, which later became Lots 438

The eroding bank in this 1890s photo probably explains why Lightning Creek was diverted a quarter mile south of the property at Cottonwood House.
(COURTESY BCARS)

and 380, G.1., Cariboo. Operating under the title of Wade & Company, this threesome virtually gained control of all the arable land in the immediate area. Lieutenant H. S. Palmer, who was at the site in July 1862, described the commercial developments already in operation: "Cottonwood farm, a small thriving settlement composed of a butchering stall, a restaurant, and a store."[30]

Bishop Hills, who also passed through the area that summer, left some rather interesting notes regarding his visit to Wade & Company's farm:

Reached Cottonwood at 2.00 p.m. and forded that stream about 40 yards wide, then forded the Lightning on the north. Here the strange sight of camels presented itself, and I moved my horse some distance, lest it should take fright. These camels were brought from California. Originally they were from the Amazon ... At the Cottonwood Crossing there are several houses and stores. The liveliness of the mines seems to start here, and we were greeted by several friends. On passing by one of the butcher stores, the owner on seeing Mr. Knipe, threw down his knife, left his waiting customers, and came out with a hearty welcome. He had met Mr. Knipe last year at Antler Creek, and had come to respect him. At that time he was a partner in a sawmill, but now turns his hand to butchering. In this he is a true American, versatile.[31]

While Magistrate O'Reilly had reported illegal land speculating at Van Winkle earlier that year, by the end of July, the developers of the Cottonwood property were being similarly accused. In an article that appeared on the front page of the New Westminster *British Columbian* concerning "three shrewd Americans who had pre-empted 360 acres of land at Cottonwood," Moreland, Wade, and Cox, without legal right, were said to have "marked off portions of the land into town lots, which they were actually selling for $250 each."[32]

The full impact of these indiscretions, known as the "Cottonwood Scandal," came to the public's attention when it appeared that Judge Begbie had accepted a gift from George Cox consisting of twenty acres of land at Cottonwood. Apparently, when Cox applied to O'Reilly for a certificate of improvement on his pre-emption (Lot 438), it would have given him the legal right to subdivide; but O'Reilly had refused, believing that Cox's pre-emption was about to become part of a government land reserve. Cox then complained to Begbie, who happened to be in the neighbourhood at the time; and Begbie, who wanted to purchase twenty acres from Cox, ordered O'Reilly to issue the certificate. The incident grew to include a court case against John Robson, editor of the *British Columbian*, who had published an article accusing Begbie of accepting a bribe. In the trial, Begbie sentenced Robson to jail for contempt of court, where the latter remained until he made a public apology. The case against Begbie was never proven.

In the meantime, business continued at Cottonwood Crossing, and, in July 1862, Wade & Company submitted a proposal for the building of a toll bridge across the Swift River — a bridge which would greatly benefit the commercial developments on that property. But this was not to be, for by this time the Royal Engineers had conducted another survey with regard to the proposed route of a wagon road to Richfield, and had found a more suitable site for bridging the Cottonwood River. Unfortunately for Wade & Company, this route was four and a half miles downstream from their property, but that was not the worst of it; the new route put Wade & Company's developments on the wrong side of Lightning Creek. In spite of this, Wade & Company built its own bridge across the Swift River. However, the adoption of the new route and the building of the bridge downstream in the summer of 1863 virtually killed their enterprises. That summer Moreland, Wade, and Cox began mortgaging and selling off their property.

Although business continued on as usual, by the fall of 1863 Wade's ranch had been sold to Matthew Corothers and James Spencer, entrepreneurs and miners at Williams Creek. In spite of being bypassed, traffic bound for the mines continued to flow through this original route. In a daybook kept by Wade & Company in June 1863, and kept up by various changes in management to December 1864, records show repeated sales of goods from the store: fresh beef, root vegetables, and a host of basic essentials used by miners and packers. Also shown are the many meals served at the roadhouse at two dollars each and the many drinks, at fifty cents a shot; but there were no beds, which most roadhouses were now routinely offering their guests. References to pack-trains are also numerous, some of which included a great number of animals. The largest of these, "Scott's Train," consisting of seventy-nine horses and mules, was charged $39.50 for pasturing overnight. Throughout the pages of the daybook are scattered the names of many patrons, all synonymous with the early history of the Cariboo: Gustavus B. Wright, Frank Way, Mike Hagarty, Black Jack, Jim Sellers, Half-Breed Dick, Dutch Charlie, Ned Toomey, Tom Manifee, Peter Dunlevy, Dancing Bill, Major Thorp, the Reverend Knipe, William Ballou, A. S. Bates, Hankin, Liverpool Jack, and so on.

Also mentioned in the daybook is the name Charles Heath, appearing first on 23 October 1863. Heath was a lawyer and was involved in the courts in the Cariboo. In June 1866 Heath was foreman of the grand jury during the fall assizes at Quesnelle Mouth. By early 1864, Heath had acquired James Spencer's two-thirds share of the old Wade & Company Ranch. This included the "houses, out houses, and other buildings," indicating that by the end of May, Heath had assumed full ownership of the property, the total cost of which was $2,200.[33] Although these changes in ownership are not mentioned in the daybook, it is interesting to note the several different styles of handwriting in which the entries appear. On 30 May 1864, another new hand began to fill the pages — a strong disciplined hand, obviously trained in penmanship — the hand of John Boyd, Charles Heath's junior partner/manager.

BRIDGE HOUSE
DuPuis & Company, Cottonwood River, 1863–65

Following the resurvey of the trail to Van Winkle, on Lightning Creek, and the building of the first toll bridge across the Cottonwood River in the summer of 1863, a roadhouse built by DuPuis & Company, known as "Bridge House," was soon in operation at the "far end of the bridge."[34]

That summer, when young Harry Jones reached the Cottonwood area, he went by way of the new trail and across the bridge to the roadhouse: "where I was in lots of time for supper, and did more than justice to the good things that were set before me on the table."[35]

There Harry remained overnight, continuing his journey to Van Winkle the next morning. Along the way, where the trail ran beside Lightning Creek, he watched a group of miners working in the clay bedrock of the creek, where they had found rich deposits of gold. Less than a year later, the bridge over the Cottonwood River was washed out by the spring freshet of 9 May 1864. DuPuis & Company lost no time informing the authorities and offering to build a replacement, as its roadhouse business was dependent on the bridge. The request was refused, as Captain Grant and his engineers had decided on yet another site for a bridge across the Cottonwood River. In the meantime, DuPuis & Company operated a ferry across the river to the roadhouse.

With the completion of Wright's wagon road to Cottonwood in the fall of 1864, DuPuis and Company's Bridge House had been bypassed. Although DuPuis sold out the following year, the new owner, J. T. Laurior, continued to operate the facility.

COTTONWOOD HOUSE, 1863–74
Lots 380 and 379, G.1., Cariboo

Part 1: A Hard Beginning

Of the many overland freighters on the trails between Yale and the goldfields of the Cariboo, John Ryder was one of the earliest. With teams of eight and twelve head of oxen pulling heavy loads over 400 miles of rough trails, it was imperative that adequate pasturage be provided for the animals at the end of their long journey. By 1863, good farming land was becoming scarce in the Cottonwood area (the only arable land close to the mines), but on 27 March 1863 Ryder pre-empted 160 acres of land " situated on the north side of the Cottonwood River, about 4 miles below the mouth of Lightning Creek."[36]

In addition to this was a further 160 acres of adjoining land, pre-empted by Ryder and his partner Allen Smith, the contractor on the second survey of the trail to Van Winkle in 1862. With the new survey that summer, the road, when it was built, passed through Ryder's land, making it a very strategic property. By 1863, the ranch, known at first as "Ryder & Smith's" had become "Smith & Ryder's." A certificate of improvement issued to John Ryder in December 1863 allowed him to transfer Lot 380 to Allen Smith. At this point, Ryder left the country to develop another property at Cheam in the Lower Mainland.

Magistrate Peter O'Reilly, on his way to Quesnelle Mouth on 2 October 1863, mentioned this roadhouse in his diary: "Reached Smith & Ryder's at 6.00 p.m. Pitched tent, house not finished and very uncomfortable."[37] Presuming that Ryder built a single-storey cabin on Lot 380 when he first settled there in March 1863, the house referred to in O'Reilly's diary was probably the cabin attached to the southwest corner of Cottonwood House, known today as the parlour of the roadhouse. Two of the first references to meals served or to overnight stays at "Smith's" are found in the diary of Captain John Evans, the leader of the group of Welsh miners, where he had "supper and breakfast at Smith's," for which he paid three dollars on 12 September 1864.[38]

To enable him to continue work on a larger, two-storey roadhouse started in 1864, Smith mortgaged lots 380 and 379 from a local businessman, August Hoffmeister, for $5,000 in November 1864. Although a substantial two-storey log roadhouse was operating at Cottonwood by the spring of 1865, Smith defaulted on the mortgage, and, as of 1 July 1865, the ranch and "all its appurtenances" were lost.[39] Several factors contributed to Smith's failure. In the first place, he put himself into a vulnerable position with a short-term mortgage that had to be paid back in seven months; but, as it was later revealed, this was common practice for Hoffmeister, who gained title to several local roadhouses and hotels in much the same manner. Two other factors were the declining local economy, and the delay in the completion of the wagon road from Cottonwood to Richfield. Hoffmeister, it appeared, was one of three partners in a consortium known as Laumeister, Hoffmeister, and Steitz, whose business interests ranged between Quesnelle Mouth and Barkerville. It soon became apparent that this company had substantial debts of over $26,655.72, all of which was owed to the Bank of British Columbia.

Upon forfeiture of Smith's property, Hoffmeister and his partners put the Cottonwood Ranch and roadhouse up for auction, hoping to obtain at least $5,000. An article concerning the event, published in the *Cariboo Sentinel*, disclosed the fact that the ranch, "which two years ago would have found a purchaser for $10,000 to $15,000," realized only $4,400 and was purchased back by the partners. The article also described the roadhouse:

> A most commodious dwelling house has lately been erected on the premises, but is not quite finished. We regret the fact that the unfortunate mechanic who erected it has not been paid, and he claims to have expended $2,200 upon it. This undoubtedly shows plainly the need for a Lien Law in the Colony.[40]

Unable to settle their indebtedness with the bank, the partners Laumeister, Hoffmeister, and Steitz were forced to convey the titles of their several properties (Beaver Pass Ranch, Fenton Hotel on Lot 9 in Richfield, and the Cottonwood Ranch) to the bank. Shortly after this, the partners dissolved their alliance, and, although Hoffmeister continued to have his "fingers in the pie," Cottonwood Ranch was held by the bank for the next nine years under the watchful eye of its agent, W.C. Ward. Following the bank's acquisition, it is thought that one of the Edwards of nearby Pine Grove House was hired to operate Cottonwood Ranch until October 1866, when John Pelletier took over. Although somewhat embellished, Pelletier's advertisement in the *Cariboo Sentinel* gives some particulars regarding the accommodations at Cottonwood House at this time:

> Cottonwood Ranch
> NOTE. The undersigned having purchased from Mssrs. Hoffmeister
> & Co. this splendid ranch, together with the commodious two

storey house known as the Cottonwood Hotel, is now prepared to afford every accommodation to the travelling public and hopes by strict attention to business to merit a share of the patronage bestowed on the former proprietors.

COTTONWOOD HOTEL
This is one of the most comfortable Hotels on the road, containing as it does warm and well furnished bedrooms and good beds.
The TABLE is supplied with every delicacy possible to procure in the upper country.
The BAR is stocked with the best liquors and the choicest Cigars.
Meals, $1.50 Each
The stabling for Horses is all that could be desired, and the charges very moderate.
Hay for horses per day, $2.00;
Oats and Barley at the cheapest market rates.
John Pelletier, Proprietor.[41]

While the advertisement stated that Pelletier had "purchased" the Cottonwood Ranch, he had, in fact, only leased it from the Bank of British Columbia. Part of the agreement had been that Pelletier would complete the building of Cottonwood House. An enterprising fellow, Pelletier remained at Cottonwood until October 1868, when, with his contractual obligations completed, he left to manage the Richfield Hotel.

Until 1874, the bank continued to mortgage, lease, and repossess the Cottonwood Ranch and roadhouse from a parade of unsuccessful purchasers. One of the last of these was John Hamilton, the freighter, who at this time owned the Pine Grove stopping house a few miles up the road. With the departure of Pelletier, Hamilton negotiated a mortgage of $3,500 to purchase Cottonwood Ranch. Having already attained a good reputation as a roadhouse proprietor, Hamilton's ambition was to establish a dairy at Cottonwood; and this he did, even at the expense of importing a herd of fifty pure-bred milk cows from Oregon. In spite of this brave beginning, so well applauded by the editor of the *Cariboo Sentinel*, Hamilton also failed to keep up his mortgage payments, losing tenure to the ranch on 16 January 1871. Following this, the firm of Josiah Beedy and Jochum Lindhard, merchants of Van Winkle who had subleased Cottonwood from Hamilton, stepped in and put down a deposit of $500 on the ranch, at the same time assuming a mortgage of $3,000. By September 1871, Beedy and Lindhard had dissolved their partnership, and, while Lindhard assumed the financial obligations of their mutual interests, Beedy supervised the operation of the road-house and ranch.

Lindhard, who was only thirty-eight years old, was dying of Bright's disease, a serious kidney ailment. A trip to California to seek medical aid did nothing to relieve the affected organ, and Lindhard died at his home in Van Winkle on 9 June 1873, leaving his widow Caroline as his heir. Lindhard's mortgage against the Cottonwood property was lifted in November 1873, giving clear title to the property. A year later, on 19 March 1874, John Boyd of Cold Spring House bought Cottonwood Ranch and roadhouse for $5,000.

The early history of the Cottonwood Ranch reflects the uncertain economy of the mining community in the Cariboo of the late 1860s. However, by the mid-1870s, with the introduction of lode mining, confidence was restored and the economy eased.

COLD SPRING HOUSE, 1865–74
Lot 443, G.1., Cariboo

John Boyd had arrived in the Cariboo in 1862 as one of a second wave of miners from California. Originally from Belfast, Ireland, John's parents, Adam and Mary Ann Thomas Boyd, were Protestants. An architect by profession, Adam Boyd had died of the black plague. Well-educated and possessing a keen sense of business, John was only fifteen when he left home for the United States, where he spent some years working in the California goldfields. Married at Marysville in 1860 to Elizabeth Mullen, Boyd became a widower a year later, when his wife died giving birth to a daughter, Mary Ann. Leaving the infant in the care of guardians, Boyd followed the rush of prospectors to the Cariboo in 1862, where, for two years, he was foreman of the Cunningham claim. He then settled into a more secure occupation as co-owner and manager of Charles Heath's ranch at Cottonwood Crossing.

Although the new trail to Van Winkle, built in 1863, bypassed the old Wade & Company Ranch by two miles, account books of 1864 indicate that heavy traffic was still passing by way of the old trail, through what was now Heath & Boyd's ranch. Of particular interest was the fact that pack-train operators were being charged to cross the private toll bridge and that hay, beef, and vegetables were still being sold, not only to stores at Williams Creek, but also to DuPuis & Company, Edwards at Pine Grove, and the nearby Smith ranch. Many of these same commodities were also sold to G. B. Wright & Company during the 1864 season, when over 520 men were employed in the building of the Cariboo Road from Quesnelle Mouth to Cottonwood.

With the completion of the road, and the beginning of stagecoach service to and from Quesnelle Mouth late in 1865, Heath and Boyd realized that if they expected to compete in the lucrative roadhouse business, they would have to relocate their ranch buildings to a site beside the Cariboo Road. The area chosen was open land, two miles northeast of Wade's old ranch and four miles from Smith's ranch. It was also the junction of a trail leading to the Swift River, along which many miners travelled. Through the property ran Cold Spring Creek, a year-round source of water flowing out of Cold Spring Lake. (A spring from this source still stands today in the little BC Forestry park, a short distance down the Swift River road.)

While records show that developments began very early in 1865, there was no formal application for land at Cold Spring until 6 July of that year, when Boyd and Heath leased "a piece of ground containing one acre more or less for building purposes," for which they paid an annual fee of $60.[42] The account books for this period indicate the

John Boyd's Cold Spring House. The man on the left, has been confirmed as John Boyd by descendants of the family. This is the only known photo of Cold Spring House. (COURTESY BARKERVILLE HERITAGE PARK)

many activities taking place on the ranch, including the building of a "new House." An entry for 23 January 1865 shows that Antoine Malbauf, a trapper and nearby landowner, was hired "at $100 a month with board (idle time to be deducted) to cut down and snake out trees [from nearby stands of spruce] suitable for building." In an entry for 12 June 1865, Malbauf is "credited with $59.40 for 3,300 shakes cut @ $18.00 per 1000"; and in an entry for 24 June 1865, a notation in the margin reads: "Antoine Malbauf commenced working on a new house this morning."[43]

Building continued through the summer and winter, with the inclusion of bedrooms being one of the main features of the new roadhouse. Cold Spring House and store opened for business early in May 1866, and, to mark the occasion, the *Cariboo Sentinel* carried this advertisement:

Cold Spring House
Boyd & Heath, Proprietors.
This House is situated beside the wagon
road 26 miles from Quesnellemouth.
The proprietors have lately fitted up bedrooms, with good beds
and are now prepared to offer every accommodation for travellers.

The table is furnished with all the luxuries that can be procured.
The bar is well supplied with the best brands of Liquors and Segars.
Good stabling, Hay, Oats and Barley.
The cheapest House on the Road.[44]

While there were no official changes to the management of the ranch until 1869, the fact that Boyd's name appears first in the list of proprietors indicates that he was beginning to gain a controlling interest in the partnership. In the Cold Spring House Daybook there are references to two of the first overnight customers:

Wednesday, May 10, 1866
Mr. Thomas Poole.
To bed and breakfast . . . .$ 2.50

Thursday, May 11, 1866
To Andrew Lewis. Dr. to 3 days
board and lodging, 2 meals $14.00

Lewis, a Black miner from the Aurora claim on Williams Creek, was ailing, and fell seriously ill while at Cold Spring House. A relative, T.B. Lewis, arrived to attend the sick man, who was said to be suffering from "mountain fever." The patient lingered on all summer, and, in August, a grave was dug at the foot of a long hill, now known as Mexican Hill (see story of Antoine Parody later in this chapter). In the account book a bill is recorded:

To T.B. Lewis,
Dr. to attending A. Lewis during his sickness,
death and burial . . . .*$ 25.00*[45]

From this time on, through hard work and involvement in a wide variety of enterprises (i.e., roadhouse keeping; trading in merchandise and livestock; and supplying hay, beef, and fresh produce), Boyd and Heath began to acquire financial success and independence. Boyd practised strict adherence to rigid, detailed, bookkeeping; he, himself, accounted for every last penny on both sides of the ledger. Through the many years of business between 1864 and his death in 1909, John Boyd kept his accounts in dozens of ledgers, daybooks, cash books, and letter books, both with regard to Cold Spring House and to his later acquisition, Cottonwood House and ranch. Of these various account books, the daybooks are the most interesting, containing not only the day-to-day accounts, but also the many "memos" — personal tidbits concerning not only Boyd's business affairs but also his friends and associates. From the pages of these books, one gathers that John Boyd was a fair and honest man, with typically Victorian social attitudes.

On 2 June 1866, the stagecoach rumbling into the yard of Cold Spring House was an object of much conversation, as down stepped Andrew Niles of San Francisco, followed by a bevy of fair and buxom maidens. Quickly word was passed around that these were the "Hurdies," the young German dancers who were back for another season to entertain the miners in the saloons at Barkerville. The Cariboo Road also brought freighters, some of whom remained overnight, others of whom merely bought a hot meal or items from the store. Typical of dozens of entries in the daybooks was that for A. S. Bates's freighter "Hixon" and his swamper from Soda Creek.

Saturday, 4 January 1868
To 2 suppers . . . .*$ 3.00*
5 drinks, (at cards) . . . .*$ 1.25*
2 beds . . . .*$ 2.00*
917 lbs. hay . . . .*$ 45.60*
Horse feed, hay, oats . . . .*$ 4.00*

2 breakfast . . . . *$ 3.00*
                                            $58.85

Among the more familiar names to appear in the Cold Spring House and, later, the Cottonwood House books were those of Angus McPhail and John Yeats, trusted employees from the late 1860s who remained to work for John Boyd for the rest of their lives.

When gold was first discovered on the lower end of Lightning Creek in the early 1860s, it attracted many Chinese miners who lived and worked in several small communities along its banks, all of which were in close proximity to Wade's old ranch and Cold Spring House. From the records of Frank Trevor, mining recorder at Quesnelle Mouth, are three samples of dozens of claims registered by Chinese miners:

30 December 1864
Lightning Creek. Recorded in favour of Ah Ching #418, one claim of 100ft., about 2 miles above Jim Wade's old House, on the north side of the river.

11 June 1866
Recorded in favour of Ah Twon, #498, Ah Yow, #499, Ah Tune, #500, 100ft. of ground each (in bed of Lightning Creek) at the mouth of the Canyon and 1 mile above Boyd & Heath's House at Cottonwood.

25 June 1866
Recorded in favour of Ah Ay, #29, and Ah Way, #196, 2 claims of 100ft. each of mining ground situated about 6 miles above the mouth of Lightning Creek, and taking in the bed of the said creek and 50ft. on each side from the centre thereof.[46]

From these Chinese communities came a steady supply of labour for the local roadhouses and ranches. First in a long list of Chinese cooks at Cold Spring House was Ah Fatt, who was hired in September 1865, prior to the opening of the new roadhouse, at forty dollars per month plus board. Ah Fatt was a likeable, generous chap who had many friends, some of whom he entertained during the long winter with meals, drinks, or a bed for the night in the cook's quarters. John Boyd was soon on to this, and Ah Fatt was charged accordingly. During busy times, roadhouse cooks served meals at all hours, having only a little while in the evenings for relaxation. The primitive kitchen of the roadhouse (where fresh water was packed in and dirty water was packed out, firewood was packed in and ashes were packed out) was a constant round of chores. It is with some pleasure that we think of Ah Fatt and his friends enjoying a few hours of leisure. A typical entry on the debit side of the ledger reads:

4 January 1868
Dr. to Ah Fatt, 8 drinks (at cards) . . . .$ 2.00
2 plugs of tobacco . . . .$ 2.50

And the next day:

1 small bottle of pain killer . . . . .75cts.

While nothing nice was ever said about the bedrooms at Cold Spring House, the roadhouse soon became known for its hospitality. The quality of meals in all roadhouses depended on the standards set by the proprietor. At Cold Spring House, John Boyd realized he faced stiff competition for the stage clientele from neighbouring roadhouses — not from Cottonwood House, for it was always in a state of upheaval, but from the proprietors of Pine Grove House and Beaver Pass House, who had both already gained a fair reputation. In view of this, the dining room of Cold Spring House offered a wide and varied menu, which included such delicate foodstuffs as canned oysters and caviar imported from San Francisco and delivered by the freighters E. T. Dodge of Lillooet. In addition to this, the farm produced many varieties of fresh vegetables, several kinds of meat, and dairy products.

From the sudden change in handwriting and from various entries in the account books during the winter of 1867, it is evident that John Boyd was away.

13 February 1868
John Boyd, to draft on Bank in San Francisco .$ 300.00.
to exchange on same . . . .$ 9.00

13 April 1868
John Boyd, to draft on Victoria bank . . . .$ 303.00

During his stay in Victoria, John Boyd courted Janet Fleming, the sixteen-year-old daughter of Thomas and Mary Fleming of the San Juan Islands. Originally from the British Isles, the Flemings had settled on the island in the late 1840s, during the disputes over the boundary between British Columbia and the United States. Following their marriage in Victoria on 18 April 1868, Boyd returned to Cold Spring House, while his bride remained at the Coast until June. Young Janet must have been warned of the vast changes she would face in the Cariboo of the 1860s; not only to the primitive living conditions, but to a world almost devoid of female companionship. It is said that she took with her six laying hens "to keep her busy."[47]

The fact that few White women travelled to the Cariboo prior to the 1870s is clear from the masculine names which appear in the Cold Spring Daybooks (where any women mentioned were usually married). One of the first women to appear in the daybooks was Mrs Nason, who, with her husband Ithiel B. Nason and their children, spent a night at Cold Spring House in July 1870. In the books, a married woman travelling with her husband was always referred to as a "Lady," while a married woman travelling alone used her husband's name. Such was the case with "Mrs. Allen," whose name appeared as an overnight guest at Cold Spring House in February 1870. More familiarly known as "Scotch Jenny," "Big Jenny," or Janet Morris (from her first marriage), this beloved pioneer of Williams Creek died in a tragic accident the following September.[48] (See Chapter 8, Cottonwood House to Richfield.)

Quite unlike his friend, Henry Moffat of Lansdowne farm, John Boyd seldom mentioned his wife or family in the records, the exceptions being brief memos regarding trips taken to Barkerville or Quesnelle Mouth, or the announcement of the birth of one or another of their ten children. The first of these children was a son, John Charles, born at Cold Spring House on 29 October 1869 and baptized on 1 December 1869 by the Anglican priest, the Reverend J. Reynard. John Boyd was enormously proud of his little son; in fact, he was proud of all his sons. On John's second birthday, a memo tucked in between two small business entries reads:

Saturday, 28 October 1871
John C. Boyd Jr. two years old this morning.
Cash to boy, birthday present . . . .$5.00.

The author Emelene Thomas, in her 1947 narrative entitled *Cottonwood Picture*, had obviously read the Boyd daybooks, but she was unaware that the family did not move from Cold Spring House until 1886. Supposing them to be at Cottonwood, she describes a trip taken by Boyd and his little son, which not only illustrates Boyd's pride in his first born, but also his increasing success as a businessman:

Now that Johnny is a big two year old, his father thinks him sufficiently grown up to take along on a business trip to Williams Creek. His mother agreeing, father and son set off, both well wrapped, the sleigh bells jingling merrily signal their departure. Securely tucked away in the sleigh is $500.00 in gold, destined for the bank. A further $421.00 in gold is collected along the way. At Last Chance Claim the travellers stop for the night, the miners making much of the boy. Next morning on "the Creek," Johnny, with money in his pocket to spend has a wonderful time in the Hudson's Bay store, while his father checks the list of goods requested by Mrs. Boyd, overshoes, slippers, mittens for John, and apples. With the purchase completed, its over to the barber shop where both father and son are attended to."[49]

The early 1870s were slow times for Cariboo roadhouse keepers. While improved roads had lowered freight rates, the recession caused by the exodus of miners to the Omineca had forced proprietors to charge less for their services. Bed and breakfast could now be had for $1.50.

6 February 1871
Barnard's Express Co.
Mr. Freeman, driver, to dinner . . . .*$ 1.00*
4 passengers, to dinner @ $1.00 ea . . . .*$ 4.00*

All through February, business was extremely slow. Ah Fong, who had replaced the jolly Ah Fatt in the kitchen, was suddenly taken ill, putting Janet Boyd to work until another cook could be found. For these services, Janet was duly paid. The substitute cook, Chee Kim, proved very competent; in fact, he proved indispensable. From this time on, there would be two cooks at Cold Spring House. John Boyd believed in paying anyone who laboured on his behalf, even his own children (seven sons and three daughters), all of whom were always paid for any chores they performed. Mary Ann, Boyd's daughter by his first wife, who spent much of her early life at school in San Francisco, rejoined her father and his family in the late 1870s. In 1884, while the eldest son, John, attended a finishing school in Victoria, the younger children were tutored at home by Mary Ann, who was paid ten dollars per month — a fee which Mary Ann herself later reduced to five dollars per month.

At times the infinite details of Boyd's bookkeeping appeared to go to extremes. When he took his dog with him on a two-day trip to Barkerville, even the cost of feeding the animal was entered in the books:

John Boyd, taken in 1889 at the birth of his son Chester on the San Juan Islands.
(COURTESY BILL BOYD, 3RD GENERATION, SON OF ALBERT BOYD)

29 April 1871
To meat for dog on trip . . . .*25cts.*

Business transactions were scarce during this period, and Boyd was thankful for the few that came his way. That spring, a deal was made to keep Gerow & Johnson's horses at Cold Spring Ranch (Gerow & Johnson had the mail contract). While Janet Boyd was away on a trip to the Coast that summer, John Boyd renewed a magazine subscription to *The London Illustrated News,* and for his wife, who was fashion-conscious, he ordered *Leslies' Ladies Magazine.* In spite of the fact that they were rather out of date by the time they were received, these well-known and respected publications provided informative and entertaining reading for the Boyds and their guests at the roadhouse.

Cold Spring House had quite an assortment of visitors. On a crisp November evening in 1870, the Boyd family gathered to greet a neighbour, George Hyde, the proprietor of Beaver Pass House. In his spare time, George was a talented taxidermist, and he had called to deliver a beautifully stuffed owl—a work which John Boyd had commissioned for five dollars. Later that year, Ah Whan, a merchant leaving Barkerville at the approach of winter, arrived at Cold Spring House escorting four Chinese prostitutes on their way to the Coast. With teeth chattering, they piled into the house to warm up before continuing their long stagecoach journey.

The 1870s saw John Boyd rise to the peak of his business career. By the fall of 1871, Charles Heath had relinquished all claims to both the original Wade & Company Ranch and to Cold Spring Ranch, giving Boyd clear title to both properties. Now in his forties and in the prime of life, Boyd began to expand his holdings and, where possible, to eliminate his competition. The first opportunity came in the spring of 1872, when John Hamilton, owner of Pine Grove House and ranch, ran into serious financial difficulties, which forced him to sell out. Boyd acquired the 191 acres of land, the roadhouse, and all its contents for a mere $450. Plainly, Boyd was not interested in the Pine Grove property for the hay meadows or the crop potential, for the soil there was light and the harvest sparse compared with the land he owned in the Swift River-Lightning Creek area. It was Pine Grove House itself that Boyd wanted; and, with its acquisition, it was promptly closed and dismantled, leaving Cold Spring House and store as the only facility of its kind for miles around. Cameron and Hyde's Beaver Pass House, fifteen miles east of Cold Spring House, also stood to gain from the closure of Pine Grove House.

In 1874, with the purchase of the Cottonwood House estate from Caroline Lindhard, Boyd's dream of empire came true. Not only had he gained control over any serious competition to his store and road-house, but, with over 1,000 acres of land at his disposal, he was able to produce even larger supplies of saleable hay and to increase his services in "ranching"—a word often used in Boyd's account books to signify the boarding of animals:

2 October 1874
Indian Charley, shepherd, began ranching here, [Cold Spring] on the 1st. inst. MEMO: 67 sheep began feeding in the field this morning.

15 October 1874
4 cows belonging to P. Phair were brought here this evening to be fed and cared for until spring, also one cow belonging to J.C. Beedy.

While the Boyd family remained at Cold Spring House, Boyd's brother-in-law, John Fleming, managed Cottonwood Ranch and roadhouse.

It was during the winter of 1874 that a Mexican packer, Antoine Parody, hauling a load of oats and hay to Barkerville, left the 13 Mile House one morning and reached Cold Spring House at noon. From that point, he had hoped to reach Beaver Pass House by nightfall. Towards evening, a team of horses without a driver appeared beside the barn at Cold Spring House. On investigation, they were found to be Parody's lead team, still hitched to the doubletrees and dragging the lead chain, which had broken away from the sleigh. Realizing there was something wrong, Angus McPhail and another hand hitched Parody's team to a sleigh and drove it up the road. There they found Parody's wheel team, still hitched to the loaded sleigh, which was upside down and over the bank. The horses were fine, but Parody was found crushed to death under the load. When the lead chain broke part way up the steep hill and the sleigh started sliding downhill backwards, Parody had apparently jumped off on the wrong side. Antoine Parody was buried at the foot of Mexican Hill, which was so named in his memory.[50]

By the late 1870s, John Boyd had returned to his earlier interests in mining. As alluvial gold diminished, the exploration of quartz-vein deposits led to the establishment of several small stamp mills at Island Mountain, Williams Creek, and Lightning Creek, where Mr Beedy of Van Winkle had established a small mill at Perkins Gulch. The investigation of quartz ledges was also of major interest at this time, these being the concentrations of gold in quartz veins — a source hitherto unexplored. It was the quartz ledges that interested Boyd, who had obviously come across these formations on Lightning Creek, only a few miles east of Cold Spring House. During the spring of 1878, the following account appeared in Boyd's daybook:

30 April 1878
Self and Angus McPhail prospected today and found ... a quartz ledge which we have named Lightning Creek Quartz Ledge ... and staked 1500 ft. for mining purposes for ourselves, and an extension of 1500 ft. for John Fleming ... the first to be called the Cold Spring Co., and the extension to be known as the Cottonwood Co. Said ledge crosses Lightning Creek between 4 and 5 miles above Cold Spring House, running from Lightning Creek and crossing the wagon road in a north west direction.[51]

A month later, in May, Boyd made a very exciting comment in the day book: "Struck gravel overhead in the Big Bonanza Bedrock tunnel ... and found gold in the gravel."[52]

THE BIG BONANZA COMPANY, 1878
The Roadhouses at Wingdam Flat
Lot 446, Cariboo, 1904

The claims mentioned at the close of the preceding section, with some minor additions, formed the origins of the Big Bonanza Mining Company, in which John Boyd, as secretary-treasurer, played a controlling role for many years. A list of shareholders included several of Boyd's employees: Angus McPhail, John Yeates, David Allen, Boyd's brother-in-law John Fleming, Henry Moffat, John Bowron, James Craig, Saul Reid, John Naismith, and Boyd's son-in-law Alfred Carson. By 1879, the company was reported to have "sunk a shaft some 80ft., obtaining at that depth a good prospect."[53] From the very beginning, the miners could not control the water and slum that would seep into the shafts from Lightning Creek. While they were said to have struck gold in "paying quantities" in 1879, they suffered a great setback the following season, when the spring freshet washed away part of the wingdam which was holding back the water from the diggings. For years the company struggled on, always on the brink of a "big bonanza" but never able to control the seepage. By 1896, the claims of the Big Bonanza Company were sold to the Lightning Creek Gold Gravels & Drainage Company. Two years later, they were sold again, this time to the British American Gold Mining & Trading Company, which attempted to drain the old channel of Lightning Creek by digging a tunnel near the foot of what is today known as Wingdam Hill. In August 1899, in speculation of a large development, John Fleming pre-empted 160 acres on "Wingdam Flat," and, in 1904, when a Crown grant was issued, this became Lot 446, Cariboo.[54]

As early as October 1885, Boyd's daybooks mention various "houses" on this site, all of which were kept by two of the original members of the Big Bonanza Mining Company, John Yeates and David Allen. Situated almost halfway between Cold Spring House and Beaver Pass, for a number of years these roadhouses catered specifically to freighters and their teams. Roddy Moffat was sixteen years old in 1908, when he was freighting on the Barkerville road, and he remembers the two frame-built stopping houses at Wingdam. On reaching Wingdam one spring evening, Roddy fell ill with a sudden high fever; this turned into measles and delayed him for ten days.

Despite the apparently unconquerable problems of water and slum, mining has continued off and on at Wingdam for the last ninety years, with a score of different companies expending their financial capabilities to the limit in pursuit of the rich gold deposits in the bedrock. In 1938, when a cave-in occurred in one of the underground tunnels, two miners risked their lives to save two others, who would otherwise have drowned. Very recently, yet another company optioned the Wingdam properties, where they engaged in tunnelling to bedrock on the south side of Lightning Creek before exhausting the shareholders' money.

By 1879, the "quartz excitement" in the Cariboo was over and was replaced by large hydraulic operations. In the Barkerville region, where there were several such mines (including the Waverly Hydraulic Company on Grouse Creek), Cold Spring House had become a halfway point for the managers, whose administrative centre was at Quesnel. That year a daily average of five guests, some of whom remained overnight, ate supper at Cold Spring House; and, in the barns, up to ten horses were fed each night. Among the stoppers was an assortment of freighters, including the energetic Chinese, Ah Foke; Barnard's Express & Stage Line drivers and passengers; and a steady trickle of government officials (e.g., Magistrate Henry Ball, Gold Commissioner John Bowron, and police sergeant James Lindsay). Boyd's old partner, Charles Heath, was also a frequent visitor, as were Barkerville merchants Van Volcunbergh, Charles Oppenheimer, W. A. Meacham, and I. B. Nason.

Following Judge Begbie's last circuit in 1878, he was replaced by Judge Henry Crease, who presided over the fall assizes held at Richfield in 1880. In her diary, Sarah Crease, who accompanied her husband on the trip upcountry, mentioned "Boyd's House" near Cottonwood, where she and the judge were guests both on 17 September 1880 and a week later, when they were about to leave the Cariboo. Sarah's remarks concerning the roadhouse, the outbuildings, the meals, and the Boyd family constitute one of the only documented, first-hand accounts of the Boyd family at Cold Spring House. While affording great praise for the meals served, her assessment of their bedroom and bed was far from flattering:

Friday, 17 September 1880
Dined at Boyd's near Cottonwood, thriving looking place, store-house, large woodshed and workshop around dwelling and wayside House. Wife, daughter, and little children nice and respectable — Mrs. B. has a sweet thoughtful face — Miss B. a round rosy, good-natured one — had a good dinner, first taste of bunch grass beef — most excellent — wild Raspberry and Huckleberry jam very good — After dinner strolled around the place with daughter and children. Bed hard, and narrow room cold, musty and comfortless.[55]

The next morning, after coffee, the Creases left for Richfield at 6:00 a.m. As they departed, Boyd made this entry in his daybook:

> Saturday, 18 September 1880
> Judge Crease and Lady. Dr.
> To 2 suppers . . . . $ 1.00
> Bed . . . .$ .50
> 2 horses, fed hay 1 night . . . .$ 1.00
> 55 lbs. Oats taken away . . . .$ 6.30
> By cash bal. a/c . . . .$ 5.75

On their return trip a week later, the Creases ate a noon meal at Cold Spring House. Of this visit, Sarah wrote: "Reached Boyd's House at 11.30 a.m. — he showed us fine gold dust brought in by Chinamen. Offered me a specimen — refused as before — Had a good dinner which refreshed us much."[56]

While seemingly blessed with success and happiness, the Boyd family, which at this time included eight children, was not entirely without sadness and tragedy. One day, near the end of September 1884, nine-year-old Ida Grace, the eldest daughter of Boyd's second marriage, fell from her horse, suffering a severe concussion. Despatched to Victoria soon after, where she received the best of medical care, Ida died on 30 January 1885 and was buried in Ross Bay Cemetery.

Twelve years after purchasing the Cottonwood farm, John Boyd and his family moved from Cold Spring House on the first day of May 1886. Although Boyd did not record his reasons for the move, the daybook entries suggest that it might first have been viewed as only a temporary arrangement:

> 1 May 1886
> Mayday ... John Boyd, Mrs. Boyd and children Albert, Alice and Agnes with sundries went to Cottonwood this forenoon intending to remain there for some time.

> 2 May 1886
> Went back to Cottonwood taking Mary Ann, William, and Henry, also sundry goods ... Closed Cold Spring House for a time and returned self and family to Cottonwood Ranch.

Certainly the location of Cottonwood House, a wide-open valley, was very pleasant. Cold Spring House, on the other hand, had been built on a narrow strip of leased land between the Cariboo Road and

Lightning Creek. John Boyd never did own the land there, and, while Cold Spring House had served its purpose, it was now time to move on to better things. From that time on John Fleming became caretaker of Cold Spring House. One further important family event, recorded by Boyd, took place at Cold Spring House in 1886:

24 May 1886
Married today at Cold Spring House at about noon by the Rev. P.W. Wall, my daughter Mary A. Boyd to Mr. A. Carson of Quesnelle, B.C. Parties present: Mrs. W.W. Dodd, Mr. Alex Locke, Mr. J.A. Yeats, Mr. W.A. Johnston, John Boyd and family.[57]

Just why Mary Ann's wedding was held at Cold Spring House is not explained. Undoubtedly, the house held many fond memories for the family, with eight of ten children having been born there. Boyd's very brief and impersonal mention of this event was consistent with others concerning his wife's or daughters' activities. From this time on, Mary Ann and her children were referred to as "Mrs. Carson and family."

While there is apparently no account of it, Cold Spring House was said to have burned down in the early 1900s. Later occupants of the site, Mr and Mrs George Berry, confirmed that the original footings of the building were blackened and charred.

John Boyd and family at Cottonwood in the 1890s. COURTESY BCARS)

Notes to Chapter 7

1. Harry Guillod, Diary, 1862, E/B/G94A, BCARS, 31.
2. GR 216, M. P. Elmore to Magistrate H. M. Ball, 15 May 1867, Cariboo, BCARS.
3. *Cariboo Sentinel*, 12 June 1869, 3.
4. Ibid., 8 May 1969, 3.
5. Ibid., 1 April 1871, 3.
6. Gordon R. Eliott, "Quesnel: Commercial Centre of the Cariboo Gold Rush," Quesnel Historical Society, November 1958, 47.
7. Ibid., 48.
8. Louis LeBourdais, "The Harry Jones Story," addit. MSS 676, vol. 7, BCARS, pp. 23, 24.
9. Henry M. Ball, Diary, 18 August 1864–27 October 1865, addit. MSS 681, BCARS.
10. Ibid.
11. *Cariboo Sentinel*, 12 May 1869, 2.
12. Robert B. McMicking, Diary, 11 September 1862, Special Collections, Main Library, University of British Columbia.
13. Margaret A. Ormsby, *British Columbia: A History* (Toronto: MacMillan 1958), 208.
14. *Cariboo Sentinel*, 29 October 1866, 3.
15. *Ashcroft Journal*, 22 January 1898, 2.
16. Guillod, Diary, 14 August 1862. p.
17. Bishop George Hills, Diary, 21 July 1862, Anglican Provincial Synod of British Columbia Archives, Vancouver.
18. F. W. Laing, "Some Pioneers of the Cattle Industry," *BC Historical Quarterly* 6:257–75.
19. Ibid., 262.
20. A. J. Splawn, *Ka-mi-akin, The Last Hero of the Yakimas* Portland, N. P., 1917, pp. 160–180.
21. Laing, "Some Pioneers of the Cattle Industry," 257–75.
22. British Columbia Department of Lands, Legal Surveys Branch, Victoria, BC, Lieutenant H. S. Palmer, RE, Map, Sketch of Mouth of Quesnel, 4 September 1862, Land Reserves 16T1 and 17T1,
23. Dr W. B. Cheadle, *Journal*, 18 October 1863, E/B/C42.1, parts 3 and 4, BCARS.
24. Hills, Diary, 25 July 1862, 101.
25. W. Alvin Johnston, "Birchbark to Steel," unpublished MS, copyright H. Albert Johnston family, Quesnel, BC, 1959.
26. Ibid.
27 Sarah Crease, Diary, 25 September 1880, A/E/C86, BCARS.

28. McMicking, Diary, 13 September 1862.

29. GR 827, Lillooet Pre-emptions, vol. 1, W. Cameron, PR#174, 15 August 1862,. BCARS.

30. Lieutenant H. S. Palmer, RE, Map, Sketch of part of British Columbia, February 1863, BCARS

31. Hills, Diary, 21 July 1862, 95.

32. British Columbian (New Westminster), 30 July 1862.

33. Department of Lands, Legal Surveys Branch, Victoria BC,Papers included with Crown Grant #1383/120.

34. Letter, 10 May 1864, Colonial Correspondence, F502-1. DuPuis to Governor Seymour.

35. LeBourdais, "Harry Jones Story," 25.

36. F. W. Laing, "Colonial Farm Settlers on the Mainland of British Columbia, 1858–1871," Victoria, 1939, 331.

37. Peter O'Reilly, Diary, 1862, A/E/or3/OR3, BCARS.

38. Captain John Evans, Diary, 1862-64, addit. MSS 2111, BCARS.

39. Papers attached to Crown Grant #4377/99, Indenture #1698, Smith to Hoffmeister, 28 November 1864.

40. Cariboo Sentinel, 26 August 1865.

41. Cariboo Sentinel, 1 October 1866, 3.

42. GR 112 Cariboo Pre-emptions, 1860–69, vol. 69, Boyd and Heath, record of 6 July 1865.

43. Cold Spring House Daybook, 1865, Special Collections, University of British Columbia.

44. Cariboo Sentinel, 7 May 1866, 2.

45. Cold Spring House Daybook, August 1866.

46. GR 216, vol. 85, pp. 3, 11, and 13, BCARS.

47. Fred W. Ludditt, Barkerville Days (Vancouver: Mitchell Press 1969), 154.

48. Colonist (Victoria), 11 September 1870, 3.

49. Emelene Thomas, "Cottonwood Picture," part 2, North Cariboo Digest (Winter 1947).

50. Alvin Johnston, "Birchbark to Steel", unpublished manuscript, 1959.

51. Cold Spring House Daybook H, 30 April 1878, 125.

52. Ibid., 31 May 1878, 146.

53. British Columbia Department of Mines, Annual Report, 1878, 373–74.

54. Papers attached to Crown Grant #1825/147, Department of Lands, Legal Surveys Branch, Victoria, BC.

55. Sarah Crease, Diary, 17 September 1880, 10.

56. Ibid., 25 September 1880, 16.

57. Cold Spring House Daybook G, 24 May 1886.

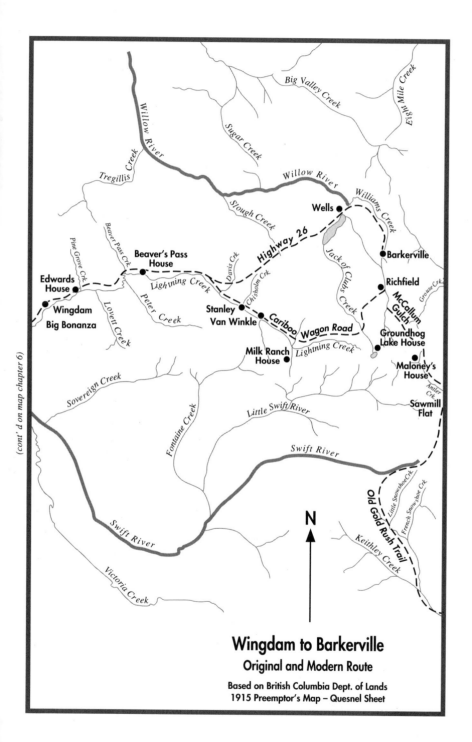

Wingdam to Barkerville

Original and Modern Route

Based on British Columbia Dept. of Lands
1915 Preemptor's Map – Quesnel Sheet

CHAPTER EIGHT

Cottonwood House to Richfield

COTTONWOOD HOUSE: THE LATTER YEARS, 1886–1961
Lots 380 and 379, G.1, Cariboo

Following their move to Cottonwood in May 1886, the members of the Boyd family continued on much as they had at Cold Spring House; their lives centred around the comings and goings of passing travellers, freighters, and stagecoach passengers. Considerably more accommodating than the roadhouse at Cold Spring, Cottonwood House was well-suited to a larger family, the staff of Chinese cooks, ranch-hands, and the ever-changing parade of overnight guests. Within the twelve-room house was a large front room, a formal dining room, a parlour, a large kitchen, and eight bedrooms.

Now in his early fifties, John Boyd was reaping the rewards of his many years of diligence and hard work. As a successful businessman, he had been able to afford good secondary schooling for his children; and, while he never allowed himself the luxury, he sent his wife and family on frequent trips to Victoria and the San Juan Islands. Daybooks from this period show that he was still an active trader and merchant:

September 3, 1886
Sold to King Sam Chan this morning, one small stove called

*Bonanza in exchange for three 10lb. boxes of No.1 Yuan Chun
Tea ... Tea to be forwarded here from Stanley. Stove came from
Cold Spring House ... Sent one hog dressed on accnt. to John
Bowron and Mr. James Lindsay by John Stevenson today.*[1]

The winter of 1886 was long and hard, with extremely cold
temperatures and deep snow. As sometimes happened when stoves got
overheated, a fire broke out in the roof of Cottonwood House.
Fortunately, the damage was minimal:

January 26, 1887
*The roof of this dwelling caught fire near the stove pipe this morning
and burnt through two or three shingles. Mercury in thermometer
congealed this morning.*

The extremely cold temperatures also had an effect on the mail delivery
system, which resulted in Boyd performing an act of compassion: "Mr.
A. Locke arrived with mail on his back, travelling on snowshoes —
had one foot frozen. Bathed said foot in cold water for some time, then
dried and rubbed it with arnica, which process restored the foot to its
normal condition." By fall of 1888, John Boyd was satisfied that the
move to Cottonwood had been worthwhile:

September 15, 1888
*Amount of butter made at this place since May of 1886 until now
is 914 lbs. Bales of hay made at hayshed 6,830.*

As had become her habit during her many confinements over the
years, Janet Boyd spent much of her time at her parents' home on the
San Juan Islands, while her husband remained at Cottonwood. One
exception to this occurred at the birth of their ninth child, Chester, in
May 1889; at this time, John Boyd left home for his first holiday since
his marriage and joined his family on the Coast. There he remained
until September, at which time they all returned.

Visitors to Cottonwood House during this period continued to
include stage passengers and drivers, both Chinese and Native
freighters, and a host of government and professional men. Among
these was the new road superintendent Joseph St Laurent, government
agent John Bowron, merchants John Peebles, Ithiel B. Nason, dentist
Dr Jones, and Dr Hugh Watt of Barkerville. Judge Clement Cornwall,
on his way to the spring and fall assizes, could be counted on to spent
at least one night at Cottonwood House, when he and John Boyd

engaged in stimulating conversation late into the night. Boyd's married daughter Mary Ann, now the mother of two sons, came only occasionally, while eldest son John Charles, employed by the Hudson's Bay Company at Quesnelle Mouth, was a frequent caller.

Christmas of 1891 was celebrated with friends and family at Cottonwood House, and Boyd, in a mellow mood, made note of the occasion:

> *December 25, 1891*
> *Invited guests here today: son John C., Mr. and Mrs. Carson and family, Mr. John Naismith, A. McPhail, R. Blair, and J.P. Fleming from Bonanza claim. The day passed pleasantly for all, each feeling pleased with each other's company.*

The delivery of mail to and from Cottonwood House had begun several years prior to the official establishment of a post office in 1895.

The Boyd Family about 1891. Seen in the picture are John Boyd with Janet Carson at his knee, Janet Boyd, the two Carson sons (with sailor suits,) Mary Anne Carson, Agnes and Alice Boyd, Alfred Carson and three Boyd sons.
(COURTESY BILL BOYD, SON OF ALBERT BOYD)

Acting as postmaster John Boyd forwarded and received letters for his own family and the local populace. Each transaction was carefully recorded:

October 15, 1887
Post office Order sent to Mrs. Ann Yeates of
Cornwall England . . . .*$ 30.00*

Ann Yeates was the mother of Boyd's long-time employee, John Yeates, who died at Cottonwood the following year.

As had happened on previous occasions during a cold spell, on 8 January 1892 Cottonwood House was threatened by fire: "A fire broke out this morning on the roof of the House, close to the stove pipe, and but for the timely aid of Andrew Allson, Abraham Barlow and Joseph Brown, it would have been serious."

Following Mary Ann's marriage and her subsequent move to Quesnelle Mouth, John Boyd hired live-in governesses to teach the younger children (Henry, Albert, and Alice). In 1895, a travelling correspondent for the *British Columbia Mining Journal*, a publication that became known as the *Ashcroft Journal*, mentioned John Boyd and how he saw to his family's education:

Mr. Boyd has a large family and thoroughly educates his children during their earlier years at home, keeping a governess for that purpose. One great trouble with this system is that he has been unfortunate in obtaining nice looking governesses and they are soon captured by the young men of the vicinity and Mr. B. has to send below for another.[2]

When gold was discovered in the Klondike at the turn of the century, Willie Boyd left home to try his luck; but, like so many others, he failed to find a bonanza. On his return to Cottonwood, Willie and his brother Harry had a serious quarrel and did not speak to each other for years. Apparently when Willie left home for the Klondike, Harry assumed Willie's role as the elder son. On Willie's return, when he attempted to regain his former authority, it created enormous friction between them. Although they slept in the same bedroom and sat at the same table at mealtime, the only form of communication between them was by notes carried back and forth by anyone who happened to be around. Typical of these was, "Tell Willie we have only two bags of oats left and he should order more." When Willie died suddenly in 1939, it was Harry who seemed to grieve the most.

Although he had been a landowner since the 1860s, it was not until 1899 that John Boyd applied to have his various acquisitions

Crown granted. It was July 20, 1901, when Boyd received Crown grants on district lots 379, 380, 388, 436, 437, and 438.

During the last few years of his life, John Boyd spent a considerable amount of time acting as a notary public for local people, advising them on everything from making wills to appealing criminal injustices. He had, at age seventy-five, become a respected and revered pioneer of the Cariboo. Yet for all his careful attention to detailed accounting and making sure that all his affairs were in writing, when he died on 28 March 1909, it became evident that he had not made a will of his own. Following a long and tiresome period during which his family provided all the documentation it could, the final settlement of the estate was very disappointing. Even though his debts were negligible, with the exception of his property, John Boyd left very little in tangible assets. He had worked hard all his life and spared no expense to keep his family in comfortable circumstances. Never was his wife obliged to work, not even in the kitchen of the roadhouses (except in unforeseen emergencies), and she had been free to visit her family at the Coast whenever she chose. The ten children were all well-educated, attending secondary schools in Vancouver and Victoria. All this must have come at considerable expense. Not every family in the Cariboo was nearly so fortunate.

In August 1909, only six months after John Boyd's death, Janet Boyd despatched her daughter Agnes to the Children's Aid Society in Vancouver, where she took custody of a little six-year-old girl, Maple Moffat. Adopted by Janet, Maple Boyd spent her early life at Cottonwood House and, at age thirteen, attended Columbia College in New Westminster. Badly spoiled, Maple would not apply herself scholastically and, after a very short time, returned home. In later years, she worked in a cafe in Quesnel.

Following the death of her husband, one of the first changes Janet made was to dismiss Ah Ling and his assistant Ah Soy, the Chinese cooks at Cottonwood House. When Agnes Boyd married Edward Somers in 1911, Alice and Janet were left to attend to all the domestic work. For his part, Willie Boyd managed the store and post office as well as a small flock of sheep. Harry, the youngest son, handled most of the outside work, including the ploughing and haymaking, which was still done with horses and hand-balers.

In 1915, when a large contingent of local Quesnel men signed up to serve in the First World War, Archibald, Chester, and Walter Boyd were among them. Walter was the only one to return.

Following her marriage to James Coreau in 1935, Alice and her husband remained at Cottonwood House, where she had become the mainstay — cooking, cleaning, and mothering her family until 1950, when she and Jim moved to Wells. While tending to the small flock of chickens out behind the house late in the fall of 1938, Janet Boyd slipped on the ice and fell, breaking a hip. Confined to a wheelchair, she lived on for another two years until her death at age eighty-eight on 10 January 1940.

The years following his mother's death were not easy for Harry Boyd, who had taken on all the responsibilities of the estate. While hired labour had been easy to find during the Depression of the 1930s, it became non-existent at the outbreak of the Second World War. Without money to update and modernize farming methods, Harry's hands were tied.

Negotiations for the sale of the ranch began in 1950, when the property was sold to Vagn and Anna Olrik. At this time, Harry moved off the property to settle in a small house down the road, where he operated the Cottonwood Post Office until his death on 14 July 1959, at age eighty-two.

Boyd family outing at Cottonwood House. The senior Mrs Boyd (Janel Fleming), Alice in a white hat, adopted daughter Maple, and little Edna Locke are all decked out for the journey. Archie is seated behind the right-side steering wheel. Harry poses on the running board while Willy opts for solid ground. (COURTESY BCARS)

In 1961, lots 1 and 2 of District Lot 380, Cariboo, was purchased from Olrik by the province of British Columbia, and, on 27 June 1963, it became Cottonwood Historic Park. Although not completed, the restoration of the roadhouse and outbuildings, which is being conducted under the direction of Barkerville Historic Park, are well under way. The roadhouse now reflects the mid-1870s, when the Boyd family first acquired it. Each summer interpreters in period costume give tours of Cottonwood House. Of particular interest to visitors are the photographs and history of the Boyd family displayed in the interpretation centre. In many ways, Cottonwood House is more authentic than are most of the displays seen in Barkerville. With the long and uninterrupted tenure of the Boyd family at Cottonwood, much of the original contents of the roadhouse were still there when it was taken over by the provincial government.

Cottonwood House: The Interior

On passing through the front door of Cottonwood House today (during its period of operation it faced the Cariboo Road), one is immediately aware of the nine-foot ceilings and the worn, hand-sawn board floor of the front room. Dominated by a large barrel heater, this room was a natural place for miners and other transients to assemble, especially in winter. It was said that this heater, large enough to burn

Harry Boyd and John Lazzarin Jr, Cottonwood House, 1930s. This car was a "stage" or taxi, that travelled between Quesnel and Barkerville.
(COURTESY BCARS)

several four-foot logs at a time, had been used in the roadhouse of the Wade & Company farm in the 1860s. Made by a blacksmith at Pitt Meadows, it was hammered into shape around a tree stump and was entirely hand-riveted. Supported by a metal cradle with legs, the heater stands about eighteen inches off the floor. Encircling this is a thin metal guard rail, which not only kept small children from getting too close, but also made a convenient footrest and sock-drying rack. A large copper reservoir, shaped to fit the round surface of the heater, sat on top of it and dispensed hot water from a tap mounted on its side. Above this was a drum (or second chamber), through which ran the stovepipe. This drum not only increased the output of heat in the house, it was also used as an oven in which to bake bread or cake. At some time, the drum was removed, but its existence is verified by a picture taken in earlier times.

Close by the roadhouse were several sources of water which could be used for domestic purposes. Less than 400 yards away is the Cottonwood River, and up the hill behind the house is a spring; but, with the exception of a handpump installed beside the kitchen sink in the 1940s, there was never any plumbing in Cottonwood House. From the earliest times, guests were expected to "wash up" prior to a meal in the facilities provided behind the front door. Here hot water from the reservoir on the heater, and cold water from a tank on the counter, were poured into enamel basins and emptied down a built-in wooden sink, finally draining out into a barrel.

To the right of the front door is a long counter, similar to an old-fashioned bar, on which are displayed a set of gold scales and various registers which were used in the buying and selling of gold and goods at Cottonwood House. Along the wall are shelves holding small store items such as canned milk, tobacco, cigarettes, coffee, and tea. Larger grocery items, such as flour, beans, sides of bacon, rice, and so on, were kept in the warehouse across the road.

While operating Cold Spring House, John Boyd had sold liquor in bottles and drinks over the bar, but with the move to Cottonwood House, the liquor licence was discontinued. Towards the back of the east wall, and close to a window, is Boyd's roll-top desk, where he worked on his accounts and wrote his letters. A set of wooden "pigeon holes" nearby are a reminder of the post office, which was established in 1895. At the far end of the front room, behind the heater, is the main stairway, a set of plain, steep, wooden stairs leading up to the landing on the second floor. Known as "the cedar cupboard," the area under the stairs was named for the delightful aroma of the furniture polish stored there. A doorway leading off the front room opens into a large room filled with six wooden cots, equipped with straw mattresses. Here slept the freighters, hired help, and any single men staying overnight. Believed to be the original kitchen, this room became a dormitory after the building of the shed-roofed kitchen on the north end of Cottonwood House. Chinese cooks and labourers also used this room, and the remains of a small Buddhist shrine may still be seen on the west wall.

A large table, and chairs to seat twenty people, is the focal point of the long, narrow, formal dining area. Prized family china, used only on special occasions, is stored in an old-fashioned dresser in a corner of the southwest wall. There are conflicting stories with regard to how meals were served at Cottonwood House. One source, originating from Harry Boyd, maintains that only the men of the Boyd family ate with the guests, and that they had to mind their manners while John Boyd presided at the table. On one occasion, when a guest reached out with a fork to spear another piece of meat off the platter, John rapped his knuckles. Later generations of the Boyd family claim that everyone ate together in the dining room, except perhaps the very small children. It is probable that both these opinions were true, but at different times. In a family of ten children, spanning a period from 1869 to 1891, when the last child, Walter was born, formalities could have changed.

A second set of steep, narrow stairs built into the northwest corner of the dining room led up to the north end of the upstairs landing. A cupboard under these stairs held the dirty linen until washday, which was every Monday morning. To the west of the dining room, the "annex," also referred to as the parlour or family room, was housed in the original single-storey cabin built by John Ryder prior to the building of the main roadhouse in 1864. Apparently, this cabin was not accessible from within Cottonwood House until shortly before the Boyd family moved there in 1886. Typical of a ladies' parlour, it contains a heater, some stuffed easy chairs, and a small oval tea table. On the walls are family pictures and, in one corner, is an old pump organ, which belonged to Janet Boyd. In later times, the family Christmas tree was set up in this room. Archie Boyd, a descendant of the original family, remembers helping to light the myriad number of little wax candles that decorated the branches, and he reflected on how easily it could have caught fire. In the shed-roofed kitchen (a large room added to the north end of the roadhouse), the enormous steel and chrome cookstove immediately captures ones attention. A facsimile of the original, the stove, with its double baking ovens, warming ovens, and copper hot-water reservoir, allowed the cook to prepare a considerable amount of food ahead of time, as was often necessary, as both regular and unscheduled meals were served. Beside the kitchen range and under a window facing west was an accommodating round table and two comfortable chairs, where the cook could visit with friends or snatch a few restful moments between chores. At some later date, a sink was built into a counter along the north wall of the kitchen, where, in the early 1900s, a handpump dispensed water from a shallow well dug out behind the house. Opposite the sink was a large, metal-surfaced table used for cutting up meat or vegetables. During the heat of summer the cooking was done in an outside kitchen, which was set up in the shade to the east of the house.

Upstairs, off the open landing, was the boys' bedroom, the girls' room, and the children's playroom (or schoolroom), three bedrooms kept for guests, and a large linen closet. In later times, Alice Boyd occupied the bedroom at the head of the back stairs, while her brothers, Harry and Willie, shared a room on the front east corner of the house.

When Maple Moffat appeared on the scene in 1909, she at first slept with Janet Boyd or Alice but later occupied a bedroom, made especially for her, in the front part of the upstairs landing. It was probably at this time that the metal bars were installed, for safety's sake, across the doorway in the upper storey.

In his memoirs of Cottonwood House, Archie Boyd mentions the old outhouses behind the warehouse, the interiors of which were liberally inscribed with interesting notations written over a period of many years. The subjects varied from the weather to memorable occasions at Cottonwood House. Typical of these are:

June 18, 1910
River flooding following 3 days of heavy rain.

April 10, 1928
Fine spring day, started ploughing in the upper field.

April 29, 1930
Grand visit of Lord and Lady Willingdon to Cottonwood House.

10 January 1931
Two feet of snow fell last night.

As the number of inscriptions grew, they provided interesting reading for the occupant of the outhouse. At one time, these unique examples of early graffiti were written about in an article (concerning historical sites along the road to Barkerville) published in the *Saturday Evening Post.*

EDWARD'S HOUSE, 1863–1866,
First Advertised as Halfway House, 1865
Later Known as Pine Grove House, 1866–1872
Lots 388 and 387, G.1., Cariboo

In 1859, Edward F. Edwards, a small man, was one of a handful of Englishmen amongst a large population of American miners at Yale. On 24 May of that year, when all loyal Englishmen celebrated Queen Victoria's birthday, Edwards was "whooping it up" in one of the many saloons along the waterfront. On shouting "Three Cheers for the Queen," Edwards was seized by several brawny Americans who took him, kicking and screaming, down to the river and dunked him. Undeterred, the spunky little man continued to praise the Queen in between dunkings. Just as he was about to drown, an unusually tall and husky Yankee ordered the dunkings stopped, threatening to shoot anyone who laid a hand on the "courageous little fellow." With that, Edwards was escorted back to the saloon and, for the rest of the day, was treated as a hero, packed around from one saloon to another on the shoulders of two strong American miners.

Arriving in the Cariboo in the early 1860s, Edwards mined for a while, married, and, in 1863, established a roadhouse at Pine Grove Creek, twelve miles east of Cottonwood on the trail to Van Winkle. A pre-emption of 160 acres of land at this location was applied for by E. F. Edwards on 29 August 1863. "Edwards House," as it became known, soon gained a reputation for good food and was possibly the most popular "restaurant" on the trail prior to the building of the Cariboo Road.

It was late in 1863 when the English tourists, Dr W. B. Cheadle and Lord Milton, reached the Cariboo and the mines of Williams Creek. On their way east from Quesnelle Mouth they stopped at Edwards House and, in his diary, Cheadle had this to say of Edward Edwards: "He had been a merchant for eight or nine years, after that mining in Australia, came to BC in the rush of 1858. He is a thorough going Englishman, and gave us several amusing stories of the first rush to this country. Although he hates Americans, he has to admire their energy ... they opened up the country in 1858 and '59."[3]

Although Edwards had come from a good family and was well-educated, he had developed the habit of continually using the word "bloody" in his conversation—so much so that he became known as "Bloody Edwards." By 1864, E. F. Edwards had formed a partnership with his brother, Walter Edwards, in the roadhouse farm at Pine Grove, where, in 1865, the latter pre-empted eighty acres of adjoining land. The land pre-empted by the two brothers later became lots 388 and 387, G.1., Cariboo.

Where most roadhouses in the Cariboo were advertised in the spring of the year, the proprietors of Edwards House at Pine Grove bought space in the *Cariboo Sentinel* in the fall of 1865. The idea was to capture the attention of those leaving the Cariboo for the winter:

Halfway House
Between Van Winkle and Cottonwood.
E.F. Edwards Begs to inform Miners & Traders going down country
that they will find the best of fare and comfort at this hotel,
good cooking, bar well stocked with the very best of liquors;
excellent accommodation for travellers.
Edwards Ranch, Sept. 29, 1865.[4]

One very wet day in April 1865, Harry Jones, the Welsh miner, and a companion walked from Quesnelle Mouth to Edwards House, a distance of thirty-five miles. The continual rain had turned the road into a sea of mud, especially the last twelve miles to Pine Grove. Leaving Cottonwood at 2:00 p.m., it was midnight before they reached

Pine Grove House was built in 1863 on land pre-empted by Edward Edwards.
It was later owned by John Hamilton family and bought by John Boyd in 1872.
(COURTESY BCARS)

Pine Grove. Cold, hungry, and soaked through, their only thoughts were of the comforts they would find at the roadhouse. To their dismay, they found the barroom floor covered with men rolled up in their blankets, every one as close as possible to the blazing fireplace. The suggestion that a space be made by the fire for the sodden travellers fell on deaf ears, until Edwards himself appeared and ordered the men to: "Pick up their bloody blankets and make room for the bloody wet fellows who didn't have an inch of dry clothing on their bloody skins."[5]

Harry Jones also approved of the meals served at Edwards House:

"After eating the best meal we ever had on the Cariboo Road, we turned in, and in spite of our wet blankets, slept until six o'clock in the morning. We made the unfortunate mistake of leaving before breakfast, and when we reached Beaver Pass House, five miles beyond, we paid $2.50 each, for the worst meal ever." [6]

Edwards Halfway House, which did not have the advantage of being part of a self-sufficient farm, could not withstand the slump in the economy; it was sold in October 1866, for $925, to John Hamilton, a freighter. By 1867, E. F. Edwards had become manager of the Fenton Hotel in Richfield. An advertisement of the sale of Edwards's property, including a list of contents of the roadhouse, gives some idea of the accommodations:

Pine Grove House was operated by the John Hamilton family from 1866–1872. (Left to Right) John Jr, unidentified, Elizabeth Muir (daughter), Mrs J. Hamilton, John Hamilton Sr, unidentified. (COURTESY BCARS)

A ten roomed House, elegantly furnished and fitted with every modern convenience. The BAR, with fixtures, mirrors, etc, THE BEDROOMS,: with "Pulu" mattresses,[7] sheets, pillows, Carpets, etc. THE KITCHEN—with splendid three oven range, "battier de cuisine" DINING ROOM: A complete set of crockery and Electro plate, Crystal ware. 20 stall stable, barley and hay lofts. 320 acres of land preempted. 8 acres of Timothy fenced. 1 acre of turnips and carrots. Agricultural implements, tools, and seeds.[8]

During the summer of 1866, a cold-blooded murder was committed less than a mile east of the Pine Grove stopping house when James Barry, an American gambler of questionable reputation, shot Charles Morgan Blessing, a decent, upstanding Canadian, in the head and robbed him of his money and a curious, skull-shaped, gold-nugget scarf pin. When this curiosity was discovered in the possession of a hurdy gurdy girl in Barkerville, Barry was pegged as the murderer. Barry quickly fled the scene, but the recently installed telegraph system assisted in his arrest at Yale, from where he was returned to Richfield to stand trial. He was found guilty and was hanged the following year.

During Hamilton's tenure, the roadhouse at Pine Grove Creek, known by then as Pine Grove House, continued the tradition set by the Edwards family for good food and accommodation. This was provided by Mrs Hamilton and her daughter Elizabeth. A son, John Jr, also lived here and was involved in the family business.

John Hamilton's ambitions did not end at Pine Grove. In December 1868, he negotiated a mortgage to purchase the Cottonwood Ranch and roadhouse. By May 1869, the *Cariboo Sentinel* was applauding John for his latest enterprise: "Mr. J. Hamilton, of the Cottonwood ranch is expected shortly to arrive from Oregon, where he has purchased between fifty and sixty head of dairy cows with a view of establishing a dairy farm at Cottonwood for the purpose of supplying Cariboo with fresh butter every week." [9]

Late that summer, a wedding took place at Cottonwood House: Hamilton's daughter Elizabeth was married to Robert Poole, a partner in his freighting business. Within two years, it became obvious that John had taken on more than he could handle. In attempting to continue on with his interests in freighting and the operation of Pine Grove House, and despite the fact that he had subleased the Cottonwood Ranch to J. C. Beedy in 1870, John Hamilton failed to keep up his mortgage payments and lost Cottonwood House early in 1871. To satisfy his debtors, he was also forced to sell Pine Grove House and property, which was picked up the following year by John Boyd for a mere $450. As mentioned in the history of Cold Spring House, John Boyd immediately closed Pine Grove House and, over the next few years, dismantled the buildings, hauling the best of the materials back to Cold Spring. Lots 388 and 387, Cariboo, the site of Pine Grove farm, remained part of John Boyd's holdings for many years, and were used primarily as pastureland.

In 1973, Lot 1 of District Lot 388, the site of Pine Grove House, was purchased by the provincial government and became Blessing's Grave Historic Park.

THE VALLEY OF BEAVER PASS
Beaver Pass House, 1862
Lots 405 and 407, G.1., Cariboo

On departing from the Cottonwood area, Bishop Hills and his party travelled in an easterly direction along the well-used trail beside Lightning Creek. "Now we are fairly in the Cariboo country," he wrote excitedly in his diary of 23 July 1862.

"where the hills on either side of the creek are said to be auriferous. We left camp [Cottonwood] at 8.00 a.m. and came 16 miles to Beaver Pass. Along the way we passed several mining claims, and stopped at one where a wingdam has been constructed, which divides the bed of the creek ... At Beaver Pass the man at the House (Buchanan) has preempted 160 acres of good land. He has turnips up, but does not think he can grow corn ... for frosts are frequent ... he has fat cattle about to be driven to the mines." [10]

The valley of Beaver Pass, at the junction of Lightning, Beaver Pass, and Peter creeks, is a low-lying, prairie-like area about ten miles west of Van Winkle, and, in 1862, was the scene of frenzied mining activity. In early spring that year, two enterprising individuals, Henry "Scotty" Georgeson and George Buchanan (a cattle drover from below the border) took up land beside the trail to Van Winkle, where they built a log cabin and store and catered to the needs of passing miners. During Bishop Hills's visit in July, Buchanan did not mention his partner Georgeson, who was away at the time registering their pre-emptions of 22 July 1862, which later became lots 407 and 405, G.1, Cariboo.

Georgeson and Buchanan developed their pre-emptions sufficiently to obtain certificates of improvement the following year, when they sold out to Stephen V. Boyce, who immediately sold to Henry Roeder, a cattle-buyer from Washington Territory. Apparently, Roeder built a new single-storey roadhouse at Beaver Pass during the summer of 1863. It was late that same year when Cheadle and Milton, on their way to Williams Creek, remained overnight in the new house. In his journal, Cheadle wrote this amusing account of the crude accommodations:

> Six miles past Edwards reached Beaver Pass where we found the Gold Escort and forty miners. I had an awful cold, sore heels, and a thirty pound pack ... awful night last night ... Wind blowing thro' cracks in walls and floor ... only one blanket apiece, twenty men in the room, one afflicted with cramp in his leg which brought him to his feet swearing every half an hour. Milton and others talking in their sleep, the rest snoring ... my nose running ... very little sleep![11]

That winter, Roeder took on a partner, Alfred Townsend, who bought a half interest in the property for the sum of $1,273. While there appears to be very little written information concerning Beaver Pass House at this early stage, two letters sent by Roeder to his wife in Whatcom during the summer of 1864 bring to light many interesting facts concerning the roadhouse and its operation. In his first letter, dated 10 July 1864, Roeder described his journey north from Washington Territory, driving a herd of cows and calves. It had gone well, with the loss of only one head and three days' delay while searching for cows missing in the dense woods at Quesnelle Mouth. Upon his arrival at Beaver Pass, Roeder found his hard-working partner Townsend busy supervising the building of a second storey on the roadhouse; this man had already planted a garden, built a milk house, and fixed fences and irrigation ditches.

> "We have had two carpenters here that were at work when I arrived, building an addition to the main House 14' X 30', a second storey to the House we built last year: and tongue and groove and relay both floors for $350.00 and their board ... It will cost us about $1000.00 before we are done. I have been putting in my spare time lately making ticks for beds, and pillows."[12]

The letters also imply that, during the winter of 1863–64, while Roeder was away, the ranch had been leased out on shares to a party who took advantage of his absence. Upon his return the following year, Roeder found that he had been cheated out of his share of the sales of hay and turnips, as well as his share of the profits of the roadhouse.

Roeder seemed to accept this, chalking it up to experience and suggesting that either he would sell out or make better arrangements for the coming winter. He was pleased with the man he brought to do the cooking: "[He] turns out to be a No. 1 cook, and so far I like him better than the Negro we had last year and pay him only half the wages." [13]

Alfred Townsend, who appeared to be the driving force on the ranch, had made arrangements to sell milk at Williams Creek for three dollars per gallon. And, regardless of the reduced price of cattle at that time of the season, Roeder intended to sell all the calves. At this point, the letter went on to mention how Henry Felker, a rancher from Lac La Hache, had sold twenty-four cows and three horses at Williams Creek for $5,000, and that he had run away after stabbing a man. Roeder was not a young man any more, and he very much regretted being separated from his wife and family, "for what is the use of being married only to live the single life." [14]

In his second letter, written at 11:00 p.m. on 15 August that same year, Roeder said that although business at the roadhouse had been slack compared to what it had been the previous year, it had recently picked up. Now, with Townsend away haying, he, Roeder, was run off his feet attending to the barroom, the stables, the woodpile, and the

Beaver Pass Ranch and Roadhouse, first pre-empted in 1862, was built by Henry Roeder and Alfred Townsend. Additions were made in the 1890s by John Peebles. This picture dates back to the 1930s when H. Jack Gardner and his family owned the property. (COURTESY H. J. GARDNER FAMILY)

milking, so he had little time for letter writing. The next part of the letter gives some insight into how business was being affected by the fact that the Cariboo Road had not yet been finished:

> Business at the roadhouse should be even better this fall and winter, after I have gone below. Business here is always better in the winter when freighters can travel on the snow and ice, rather than fight the mud in summer. I was in hopes the whole road would be built this season, but as it was started from both ends there is a stretch of 24 miles in the middle, past here, that will not be built until next season. Townsend is happy to see the House being fixed up as he intends to spend the winter here.[15]

By the following year, 1865, Henry Roeder had sold his share of Beaver Pass Ranch and roadhouse to his partner Alfred Townsend. In his ambition to develop the ranch, Townsend made the fatal mistake of taking out a short-term mortgage with the slippery moneylender August Hoffmeister; by October 1865, he was obliged to forfeit the property. As Hoffmeister and his associates, Laumeister and Steitz, were having their own financial problems at this time, Beaver Pass Ranch became an asset of the Bank of British Columbia. Following this, the bank placed several lessees on the property, and, as the *Colonist* remarked: "Beaver Pass changes hands every season."[16]

By 1869, a fellow named Daniel Nordenburg claimed title to Beaver Pass, and, on 4 November 1869, he sold the ranch to John Cameron and George Hyde for $1,250. Cameron and Hyde proved to be the first to make a go of Beaver Pass, and (after buying out Cameron) George Hyde, his wife, and their two children became the first permanent residents of the ranch. Hyde, formerly of New Westminster, was the son of Captain George Hyde of the Royal Navy. As has been mentioned, in his spare time he was also a talented taxidermist, and his work was often commissioned by his neighbours

A wedding took place at Beaver Pass House in September 1875, when Hyde's daughter Elisabeth, a young woman of twenty-two, was married to sixty-three-year old William Hitchcock, the Government Assayer in Barkerville. Apparently, this was a marriage arranged by her parents, and Elisabeth had no say. Ill-suited though it may have seemed, the union did afford the young woman some measure of dignity and financial security, for soon after this she became mistress of a home in New Westminster, where John Boyd Jr of Cold Spring House boarded while attending high school.

It was in June 1878 when George Hyde, suffering from tuberculosis, passed away at Beaver Pass House, leaving his wife and young son to carry on. Mrs Hyde was still there two years later in the fall of 1880, when Judge Henry Crease and his wife Sarah, on their way to Barkerville, stopped to pay their respects. Sarah describes Mrs Hyde as "a doleful little woman, with a nice little farm." A week later, on their return south, the Creases stayed overnight at Beaver Pass House "with Mrs. Hyde, a poor lonely widow and young son George who were very glad of our company. We sat in the kitchen while she cooked supper, which we all needed.... Gave us a soft, clean bed in a small room."[17]

Following her husband's death, Mrs Hyde hired David Allen, one of John Boyd's employees, to manage the farm, which was sold that year to John Peebles of Stanley. With their many business interests in Stanley, the Peebles allowed Mrs Hyde to continue living at Beaver Pass, which she did, even after her marriage to Warton Brunskill. John Peebles, originally of Lochee, Scotland, had arrived in the Cariboo in the earliest days of the gold rush, where he staked claims on Williams Creek in 1862. Successful in his mining ventures, by the early 1870s Peebles had not only married but had established a store and blacksmith shop in the new community of Stanley. During his tenure of nearly twenty years at Beaver Pass, Peebles made many improvements to the ranch and roadhouse.

By the late 1870s, the fields of the ranch had become clogged with tailings from hydraulic mining operations on Peter and Beaver Pass creeks, sending many tons of sand and gravel downstream. By ploughing and digging a series of irrigation ditches, the fields were brought back into production. During the 1890s, the roadhouse underwent a change in appearance, when Peebles hired John Strand of Quesnel to repair and rejuvenate the building. With its unique roofline and lattice railing, the addition of a two-storey verandah built across the front of the roadhouse distinguished it from any other log building in the area. In 1899, a passing reporter from the *Ashcroft Journal* remarked on the improvements at Beaver Pass Ranch and recommended its accommodations.

With the passing of John Peebles in early September 1899, his widow, Ellen Dickie Peebles, inherited his estate, which included not only Beaver Pass Ranch and roadhouse but also a store, butcher shop, and freight-line business in Stanley. At this time, the property at Beaver Pass was Crown granted. It was not long before Ellen was married again, this time to Mr Wormald, the owner of the Stanley Hotel.

In 1908, H. Jack Gardner and his bride Mary (nee Adams) of Hertfordshire, England, bought the Peebles' estate. They ran a general store and butcher shop in Stanley and leased Beaver Pass Ranch and roadhouse first to a Mr Bishop, a professional cook from Boston, Massachusetts, and, second, to a Mr and Mrs James Skene. When fire destroyed Gardner's store in Stanley in 1916, the building was replaced, but the Gardner family, which now included four children, left to live in Beaver Pass. Business in Stanley was at a low ebb at this time, with much of the male population overseas. At Beaver Pass, Jack Gardner was able to harvest enough hay and oats to feed a small herd of dairy cows. Marketed in Barkerville, the butter made on the ranch was sold in Jack's own one-pound, printed wrappers. At the roadhouse, Mary Gardner was kept busy looking after her growing family and the occasional passing freight team. By this time, the BC Express Company had discarded its coaches and horses for the motorized Winton Six touring cars. A trip to Barkerville could now be made in a few hours, without having to stop at places like Beaver Pass House.

During the early 1930s, the need for a new barn prompted the beginnings of a small sawmill on the ranch. This first mill, powered by an old Ford tractor, was built by sixteen-year-old Alf Gardner, Jack's

Beaver Pass House as it appeared after renovations and additions made by John Strand in the 1880s.
(COURTESY BARKERVILLE HISTORIC PARK)

eldest son. Soon the demand for lumber from nearby mines gave the Gardners the opportunity to expand their home-built hobby into a full-blown industry. Moving from Beaver Pass to Quesnel in 1928, the Gardner family was the last to occupy the old roadhouse. In the 1940s a heavy winter's snow collapsed the roof, and brought about the demise of the old roadhouse.

THE HOUSE AT DAVIS CREEK, 1862

As Bishop Hills and his entourage advanced towards Van Winkle, the aneroid (barometer) readings, taken by Hills at almost every camp, indicated a steady rise in altitude. At Cottonwood, the reading had been 1,935 feet above sea level, while at Beaver Pass, eighteen miles east, the reading was 2,769 feet above sea level. The vegetation had also changed. Where there had been cottonwood trees and fertile soil, there were now clumps of dark spruce and pine growing in thin soil and shale rock. To the southeast, they caught glimpses of snow-capped mountains. Leaving Beaver Pass early on the morning of 23 July 1862, the party took the trail along Lightning Creek for about ten miles. At a spot along the hillside three miles from Van Winkle, they came to a house "kept by a German." [18] In August that summer, Harry Guillod also wrote of the roadhouse at this location, where the proprietor served the "best coffee" he had ever tasted."[19]

Within the year the roadhouse, which was actually on Davis Creek, had been acquired by a Catherine Edwards, and, when W. B. Cheadle passed by in October 1863, he noted particularly the house of "the Irish woman named Edwards," who charged fifty cents for coffee.[20] By September 1865, following the building of the wagon road to Van Winkle, Catherine Edwards was most upset, for her roadhouse had been bypassed. In a letter to the Honourable J. W. Trutch, Commissioner of Lands and Works, Catherine, who claimed to have "suffered many hardships since [her] entry into BC in 1858," explained that she was entirely dependent on her own resources, "having expended everything [she] possessed in improvements to the House," which, upon purchasing, she had understood "would be on the new line of road." Now her investment was worthless, and she would soon be destitute.[21]

As it happened, Catherine Edwards was soon to marry Captain John Evans, leader of the Welsh miners, whose mining claims were close to Catherine's roadhouse. Following John Evans death in August of 1879, Catherine was married again, almost exactly a year later, to William Rennie, an Overlander of 1862.

VAN WINKLE TOWN, 1862

Once past Beaver Pass, the increasing activity along Lightning Creek sparked a growing sense of excitement in Bishop Hills and his companions. They had at last reached the area where thousands of men had gathered in search of gold. Unlike most others, the bishop had not come for gold but to minister to the miners and to establish an Anglican congregation in the goldfields.

At Van Winkle, the first settlement on Lightning Creek, there were already twenty-five log buildings, but Hills was more impressed with the mining:

Every portion of the stream and its banks is taken up, and each Company is engaged in some preparation ... making wheel pumps, sluice boxes, or sinking shafts into the bedrock. Tunneling into the hillsides, a new feature of the mines, is expected to provide employment through the long winter.[22]

Even as Hills looked on, one company had "washed up," and he was shown 122 ounces of course, nuggety gold, mined that very day. Anxious to reach Williams Creek, now a mere fifteen miles away, Hills and his party remained at Van Winkle only long enough for the arrival of their packs. After taking leave of Reverend Knipe, who was to remain there for the summer, Hills and his entourage set off up the creek. A month later, when Harry Guillod reached Van Winkle, he took careful note of the instant gold-rush town, leaving a good description in his journal:

Van Winkle lies in a valley shut in on all sides by high hills, with Lightning Creek running through the centre; you have the sun for only a few hours of the day. The town (every place with a dozen huts in it is a "town" here) is one street of wooden stores, restaurant, bakery, etc, and a bit of a place with "Dr. Kennedy, Surgeon", on a plate. On the side of the hill to the right is the Government encampment consisting of a few tents. We slept in a log cabin with some miners, one of whom was an old man named Noble, who has worked his claim two seasons. Went to service twice. The Minister was a young man, the Rev. Knipe.[23]

At the restaurant where Guillod and his companions paid $2.50 each for breakfast, he mentioned: "We had a woman wait on us, a pretty American, who with her husband kept the House, having a little boy two years old running about ... We also found a man and his wife with family of six, living in a tent." [24]

Another traveller to the Cariboo that year, Captain C. W. Buckley, added to Guillod's information concerning this restaurant, mentioning that the menu included "Roast beef, dried fruit pie, and Plum pudding," and that, while his wife may have been an American, the proprietor, N. L. McCaffrey, was a Scotsman.[25]

Although the deep ground of Lightning Creek proved unprofitable until some years later, several companies of miners were discovering rich placer gold on the benches and hillsides of the creek. So active were these operations in 1866 that they caused a landslide, flooding the buildings in Van Winkle to a depth of three feet. In 1864, the fact that there were several hundred miners living in this area warranted the opening of a post office at Van Winkle, where N. L. McCaffrey became postmaster. By 1865, the town included three general stores, two butcher shops, three saloons, and a new hotel:

The Van Winkle Hotel.
The above splendid hotel is now open for the public, the proprietor having taken great pains through the winter to make it the most superior House in the Cariboo. Good accommodations with suites of rooms for one or more — or private parties. Attached to this hotel is a First Class Restaurant and Bar, where can be obtained the most choice brands of Wines, liquors, cigars, etc. N.L. McCaffrey, Prop.[26]

Above Van Winkle, at Lightning Creek. Hillside trees have been cut down to provide pit props for underground mining and building. McCaffrey's Van Winkle Hotel is on the far left. (COURTESY BCARS)

The McCaffreys remained at Van Winkle for only three years, until June 1868, when the hotel and restaurant were sold to A. D. McInnis, formerly of Cameronton on Williams Creek. At this time, N. L. McCaffrey also resigned as postmaster, claiming he was not paid regularly enough for his services.

It was during the mid-1860s when two of the Cariboo's noteworthy entrepreneurs, Josiah C. Beedy and Joachim W. "Henry" Lindhard, became active in the Lightning Creek area. Both had been pioneers in 1858, and, in 1861–62 they were engaged in mining, storekeeping, and packing into all the main gold centres from Port Douglas to Williams Creek. Both these men made considerable contributions to the advancement of modern mining methods on Lightning Creek. During the late 1860s, Lindhard and his partners in the Van Winkle Company implemented a plan for a bedrock drain, which made it possible for all claim holders on the creek to pump the water out of their deep shafts. Josiah C. Beedy, another member of the Van Winkle Company, had his own "hill claims" on Burns Mountain, where he installed one of the first stamp mills in the country. In 1886, as partners, Beedy and Lindhard operated a general store in Van Winkle, and, in 1870, when the town boomed (as a result of the confidence shown in the deep mines on Lightning Creek), the partners moved a hotel that had been situated on Dunbar Flats down to Van Winkle.

Van Winkle continued as a viable community until 1885, when a new road, built from Stanley to Barkerville, bypassed the old town. By the early 1900s, most of the population had moved to Stanley. In 1910, the old townsite of Van Winkle was purchased by Lester A. Bonner, manager of the Lightning Creek Hydraulic Mine, for use as a tailing dump for his Perkins Gulch operations. At this time, all the remaining buildings were destroyed and burned.

STANLEY, BC, 1870

The year following the discoveries of rich gold deposits on Lightning Creek in 1861 "there was not an inch of vacant ground to be found on the main creek, all the way from Eagle Creek to the mouth of Davis Creek."[27] Bedrock on Upper Lightning Creek varied greatly, from 30 feet to almost 200 feet, and to reach paydirt, shafts were dug, at great expense, along the full distance. Due to the porous nature of the ground, the primitive pumps failed to keep the water out and, by fall of 1864, all these claims were abandoned.

Early in 1870 the Davis Company, with improved machinery and skilled engineering, managed to sink to bedrock. They were followed by the Ross and Lightning companies, which also obtained good prospects. The success of these companies prompted a staking rush on the creek and its tributaries. Later that year, the town of Van Winkle, which had been virtually deserted over the previous several years, sprang back to life. Two miles downstream, on ground formerly held by the Welsh company of miners and Captain John Evans but now occupied by the Costello, Vulcan, Lightning, and Clark companies, a new town was emerging. News of these happenings appeared in the *Cariboo Sentinel* of 6 August 1870: "Ground has been broken on a new town site adjoining the Eleven of England Co's claim on Lightning Creek. Beedy and Townsend, who have a store in Van Winkle will be the first store." [28]

The site, a flat of ground between the shafts of the Costello and Vulcan companies' claims, became known as Stanley, after Lord Stanley of Preston, who, in 1869, had became the Earl of Derby. By 1873, buildings were standing shoulder to shoulder on both sides of a single street. As mentioned in the *Cariboo Sentinel*, "the growth of Stanley has been astonishing!" There were saloons, general stores, private homes, bakeries, hotels, a barber, and even a bowling alley. Horseracing, a favourite sport of early "Caribooites," took place on a recently completed track, where contenders from all over competed in the "Stanley Derby." In 1875, Lightning Creek produced three times as much gold as did the rest of Cariboo put together. At the height of production, between the

The town of Stanley, a gold mining town on Lightning Creek, 1872–1945.

late 1870s and early 1900s, the combined population of Stanley and Van Winkle grew to be about 1,000.

Among the first of several hotels in Stanley was the Last Chance Hotel, Store, and Blacksmith Shop. Operated by a Welshman, Lewis Morgan, this establishment was located just upstream, opposite Clarke's Last Chance Mine on the south bank of Lightning Creek. John Boyd, Harry Jones, and George Sargison all mention this hotel. Jones wrote of it as being "one of the first, where we congregated of an evening."[29]

THE STANLEY HOTEL

First advertised by J. J. Robertson in the spring of 1871, this hotel was located close to the Last Chance Creek, but on the flat on its north side. By the fall of 1872, it was sold to S. P. Parker, the former proprietor of a boarding house in Barkerville. Unfortunately, Parker died a few months later, leaving his widow with a family of young children. Following her husband's death, Mrs Parker carried on with the hotel until May 1874, when it was advertised for sale. The hotel was purchased soon after by a Mrs Austin, who was also in poor health. Within a year, she too was forced to retire. Following his wife's death, Mr Austin sold the Stanley Hotel to John Fleming, married the widow Parker, and moved to Richfield, where he and his new family operated "Austin's Hotel." In her diary of 18 September 1880, Sarah Crease mentions the vivacious Mrs Austin: "Mrs. Austin, formerly Parker — a good looking, tall, fair, lively, woman with large family."[30]

Stanley, once a mecca of industry, has now vanished.
The Stanley Hotel and other buildings succumbed
to fire not long after this picture was taken.
(COURTESY BCARS)

On purchasing the Stanley Hotel in 1880, John Fleming and his partner Henry Moffat (who was soon to start a roadhouse in the Alexandria area, south of Quesnel) ran into financial difficulties within the year and sold it to Fleming's brother-in-law, John Boyd. Fleming remained as manager of the hotel, and, after five years, it was sold again:

August 2, 1886
Sold this morning to Mr. William Trelaise of Stanley, my Stanley Hotel, Stables and Cow House for the sum of $160.00.[31]

The last owner of the Stanley Hotel, William W. Wormald, took it over in the early 1900s and operated it until 1920, when it was torn down.

THE YORKVILLE SALOON AND BOARDING HOUSE, 1872

One of the Cariboo's more colourful characters was William W. Houseman. Originally from England, he claimed to have been one of the Queen's Own Guard. At Van Winkle he operated a butcher shop but by the early 1870s he had settled near Stanley, where he built a saloon and miners' boarding house known as the Yorkville Saloon. "Mr. William Houseman, better known as the 'Duke of York,' is building a new saloon and restaurant on the wagon road adjoining the Vancouver Company's claim, below Van Winkle." [32]

Over six feet tall (some said six feet, eight inches), Houseman was slim and good-looking, with a military bearing. Obviously well-educated, his strong English accent, coupled with his other attributes, soon earned him the title "The Duke of York." Houseman was also an excellent cook, capable of preparing and serving a banquet equal to that served by any chef in Europe. In Houseman's Yorkville Saloon, the miners of the Vancouver Company considered it great sport to watch "the Dook" slide full glasses of liquor along the polished surface of the bar, much like curling rocks, which always came to rest exactly opposite their intended customers. Although he did not charge for accommodations, the miners living at his boarding house more than made up for this through what they spent at the bar.

There are many stories about the "Duke of York," his eccentricities, and his hare-brained schemes (all of which were designed to make or save money). Apparently, he did not believe in wasting a lot of wood to heat his saloon; instead, he kept a lighted candle in the isinglass-fronted heater behind which he placed an orange-coloured paper. This gave the appearance of a fire, and, as Houseman claimed, after a few drinks the miners didn't know the difference.

As did everyone in those days, Houseman dabbled in mining and had a claim on a tributary of Lightning Creek, known first as Houseman Creek and, later, as Eagle Creek. Houseman made sure that his shaft was never bottomed, so no-one ever knew how rich it was; thus, he made a fortune promoting this claim. Although he made at least two fortunes, William Houseman could never hang on to his money, and he died a pauper in Victoria in 1922.

THE LIGHTNING HOTEL AND THE LIGHTNING INN

In 1873, when William Houseman moved his Yorkville Saloon to Stanley, he renamed it the Lightning Hotel. Continuing on as proprietor until the early 1890s, he then sold the hotel to William Ellis. In later years, the Lightning Hotel was owned, in succession, by John Lowe, William Morgan, and Len Ford. The last and longest owners of the hotel, John and Hannah Williams, operated it in the early 1900s. At this time, Stanley was booming, with a population of several hundred miners, supported mainly by the Slough Creek and LaFontaine mines. Business at the "Lightning" was brisk, due to the sincere hospitality offered by the proprietors. Hannah Williams was a real English pastry cook and kept a great variety of irresistible dainties on the long dining-room table. Roddy Moffat, still a teenager when he first began driving freight in the early 1900s, recalled purposely curtailing his helpings of meat and potatoes in order to make room for Hannah's pastries. Actually, this was a common practice and was encouraged by the cooks, who knew that desserts were much cheaper to produce than were meat dishes.

When a fire destroyed the Lightning Hotel in March 1924, John Williams bought and moved several buildings from the defunct LaFontaine Mine to Stanley, where he opened the Lightning Inn on the site of the original hotel. Business continued for many years, but the inn closed in 1947, when Hannah Williams died. One section of the old inn still stands beside the road in Stanley; in fact, it is the only building left standing in Stanley.

THE GRAND HOTEL

John Peebles, who had been in the Cariboo since the early 1860s, operated the Grand Hotel in Stanley in the mid-1880s. Still operating a decade later, the hotel was visited overnight by Luiga Yolland and her husband, an Anglican minister, on a trip to Barkerville. In her memoirs, Luiga comments: "There was no sitting room at the hotel, only a big barroom, but we were conducted to the annex, a 'lean to' known as 'the bridal chamber.' This favoured area was kept scrupulously clean and free of bedbugs, and we appreciated it fully." [33] Following the death of John Peebles in 1899, the hotel, as part of the Peebles estate, was purchased in 1908 by H. Jack Gardner. A fire that began in the attached store destroyed the building in 1937.

THE FLETCHER AND MCNAUGHTON HOTEL

During the 1880s, this hotel operated on the banks of Chisholm Creek and was supported by the workers of a nearby mine. As late as 1947, there were still two hotels operating in Stanley, one of which was the King George Hotel (which burned down that winter). By the 1950s, the town of Stanley was almost deserted. Without a single store or hotel operating, the few remaining residents were forced to shop in the town of Wells, ten miles away. The last of the miners, Tom Crawford and his wife Lil, left Stanley in 1989. Now bypassed by a modern highway, the historic cemetery and the remains of Lightning Inn are all that is left of this once bustling mining town.

DUNBAR FLATS, LIGHTNING CREEK, 1863

As Cheadle and Milton left Van Winkle and trudged up Lightning Creek in the late fall of 1863, they encountered mining operations all along the way. Bone-weary from their arduous journey, they did not linger, wanting only to reach their destination on Williams Creek. The freezing temperatures at this altitude had coated every object on the trail with ice, causing them many tumbles: "Our path was a difficult one, over endless sluices, flumes and ditches, across icy planks and logs, all getting tumbles, gum boots very treacherous." [34] At a point two miles east of Van Winkle, they stopped for a meal at Beedy and Lindhard's roadhouse where they "got a capital dinner of Beefsteak pie, beefsteak and onions, and pancakes." [35] This was Dunbar Flats, where J. C. Beedy had a hydraulic mine. Wherever a company of miners was at work, there was always a hostel close by, for hard manual labour brings on hearty appetites.

During his first trip to the Interior in the fall of 1869, the recently appointed Governor, Anthony Musgrave, was welcomed at Barkerville and, later, visited the miners on Lightning Creek. At Dunbar Flats, where His Excellency gave an address in support of Confederation, he observed a spectacular display of gold which had been mined from Lightning Creek. In replying to the governor's message, miners James

Orr, George Duff, and Ian Greig represented all the miners on the creek. After thanking the governor for his appearance on the creek, the miners, each in turn, pointed out the great wealth of Lightning Creek, and the positive effect it would have on the development of British Columbia.

THE HOTEL DE FIFE, DUNBAR FLATS, 1869

Mining had been particularly good when a new boarding house known as the "Hotel De Fife" opened on the flat. Built for Janet Allen, more familiarly known as "Scotch Jennie," the new hostel was one of several similar facilities operated by this early entrepreneur. A year later, in September 1870, Janet, a beloved citizen of the goldfields, met her death while driving her buggy through Black Jack Canyon between Richfield and Barkerville. The road through Black Jack Canyon is treacherous, a narrow, winding track cut right out of the rock. Apparently in a great hurry to reach Barkerville, Janet allowed the buggy to get too close to the steep banks of the canyon.

THE BALD MOUNTAIN TRAIL, VAN WINKLE TO
GROUNDHOG LAKE, 1862

Prior to the building of the Cariboo Road, there were two routes between Van Winkle and Williams Creek. One of these, by way of Upper Lightning and Jack of Clubs creeks, became the route of the wagon road in 1865. The original route branched off east of Van Winkle Creek and proceeded uphill over the western flanks of Bald Mountain, later named Mount Agnes, to Groundhog Lake, near the headwaters of Jack of Clubs Creek. This was only a few miles west of the headwaters of Antler Creek whence the first miners, William Cunningham, Jack Hume, and James Bell, had travelled in 1861 to discover Lightning Creek.

In their diaries, several of the earliest travellers to the goldfields via Van Winkle mention their arduous journeys over the mountain to Groundhog Lake. Among these were Bishop George Hills, Captain Cecil W. Buckley, and George Blair, who all travelled by this route in 1862. Lieutenant H. S. Palmer of the Royal Engineers, who was also at Groundhog Lake that year, referred to it as "Marmot Lake." [36]

On leaving Van Winkle on the afternoon of 24 July, Bishop Hills and his party proceeded up the trail beside Lightning Creek, headed for a campground three miles to the east. A storm that broke over them turned the trail into a sea of mud, and after two miles of steady going they reached "the meadows," where they pitched their tents. No sooner were they in their tents, than a second, more severe, storm hit, sending vivid lightning flashing across the sky, accompanied by loud claps of thunder. It was still raining the next morning when they broke camp and set off in some discomfort, due to the wet condition of their equipment. Travelling in a southeasterly direction, the trail led uphill, through boggy subalpine meadows, where the horses sank into holes up to their bellies. Hills himself was in the water up to his knees on several occasions, and once, when he tripped over a log, he fell headlong into a creek. This area, known later as the Milk Ranch, was a dairy farm in the mid-1860s. Abandoned a few years later, the land was pre-empted again in 1870 by Patrick O'Hare, who also kept a herd of dairy cows there and sold milk in Barkerville. Today, at this site, there are the remains of a few buildings and two free-standing rock walls (or ramps).

It took four hours of hard going to reach the summit of Bald Mountain, the altitude of which Hills calculated to be 5,136 feet above sea level, close to the snowline. A mile further on they came to "a House by a lake, the headwaters of a creek called Jack of Clubs, flowing north."[37] Anxious to reach their destination that day, Hills and his party did not stop at the roadhouse there but hurried downhill for several miles to where the trail "turned eastward, over a spur or divide of the Bald Mountain" towards Williams Creek.

GROUNDHOG LAKE HOUSE, 1862

Three weeks later, on 12 August 1862, Captain C. W. Buckley and his clerk Craigie followed much the same route taken by Bishop Hills over Bald Mountain. In his diary, Captain Buckley also described the meadows and the difficult climb through swamps and bogs to reach Groundhog Lake. By this time it was nearly dark, too late to continue on for another six miles to Williams Creek. Remaining overnight at the roadhouse, they found the conditions deplorable: "There was no meat in the House, so we supped on coffee, beans, and dried apples, for which we were charged twelve shillings each [$2.50] and then, spreading our blankets on the filthy floor, we went to sleep as well as we could." [38]

The proprietor of the house, one Samuel Tomkins, a miner, was a chatty sort of fellow, regaling his customers with the latest news of local happenings, appreciating the fact that one of them was Peter O'Reilly, the local magistrate. Tomkins explained that the shortage of supplies in the house was due to the rash of recent robberies in the neighbourhood. "The proprietor told us that John Towe's packtrain had been robbed of three casks of spirits while camped about two miles from here, and another 'train' at the same place had been robbed of nine sacks of flour." [39]

Of the several stoppers at Groundhog Lake House that night, one was a Frenchman, who told of many robbers and cutthroats in the country at that time. Just two nights before, while sleeping in a deserted hut at Keithley Creek, he had been attacked by two men who robbed him of fifty-four dollars and of a ring that he valued. In the struggle they had nearly throttled him, threatening to blow out his brains if he followed them.

During 1862, the year of the greatest population during the Cariboo gold rush, food supplies were very scarce. Merchants had not anticipated the arrival of so large a population, and staples such as flour were practically non-existent. Bishop Hills, in his diary of 5 July 1862, mentioned that he had been told by a reliable source that pack-trains loaded with needed provisions were being deliberately held back by some merchants until desperate customers paid whatever price was asked. Consequently, unless a miner hit a big strike, he could not afford to remain in the Cariboo.

Advertised in the first *British Columbia and Victoria Directory* of 1863, Groundhog Lake House operated for only a few years, possibly until 1865, when the Cariboo Road bypassed the Bald Mountain trail.

SAMUEL TOMKINS – GROUNDHOG LAKE HOUSE
On the Lightning Creek Trail for Williams Creek.
Every accommodation for travellers.

MEALS AT ALL HOURS
the bar supplied with WINES, LIQUORS and CIGARS
of the finest quality. [40]

THE NEGROES' INN, UPPER LIGHTNING CREEK, 1862

Had Bishop Hills taken the Upper Lightning Creek trail from Van Winkle, he would no doubt have passed by a roadhouse at the head-water of Jack of Clubs Creek and Lightning Creek. Kept by two Black men, William Lacey and his cousin, this roadhouse is not to be con-fused with the "Coloured Man's House" at the head of Nigger Valley on the flanks of Snowshoe Mountain. Seeking freedom and a peaceful way of life, these two men operated a roadhouse at this site until 1865, when the wagon road was built to Richfield and they sold out. Later mining has destroyed the cabin site, but in the remains of an old dump on the lower side of the road are the shards of "Ladies' Legs" liquor bottles and cast-iron kettles, dating back to the early 1860s. Spread over the whole area are the shattered remains of many whisky shot glasses, confirming the existence of an ancient hotel or roadhouse.

BISHOP HILLS AT WILLIAMS CREEK, 25 JULY 1862

As they rode downhill off the mountain from Groundhog Lake, it occurred to Bishop Hills that they had passed a watershed, for now the creeks flowed in a northerly direction. On reaching Williams Creek they encountered a lot of mining activity:

> *"Every conceivable obstruction hindered our progress, and we had great difficulty getting our animals along, well practiced as they had become. They were frequently mired, stuck fast in the bogs, and made all sorts of effort to free a way. At last the only course was to take them right down the centre of the stream.*[41]

On reaching the town of Richfield on Williams Creek at 5:30 p.m., Hills and his party pitched their tents next to a miner's cabin on a knoll overlooking the community. The ground here was so wet, the snow having only just melted, that "it was like settling down for the night upon a swamp." Despite this unpleasant situation, they were indeed thankful to have at last reached their destination.

Notes to Chapter 8

1.   Cottonwood House Books, Daybook H, 2 February 1887, 94, Quesnel and District Museum and Archives, Quesnel, BC.

2.   *British Columbia Mining Journal*, 20 June 1895, 2.

3.   Dr W. B. Cheadle, Journal, 1 November 1863, E/B/C42.1, parts 3 and 4, BCARS.

4.   *Cariboo Sentinel*, 29 September 1865, 3.

5.   Louis LeBourdais, Add. MSS 361, Harry Jones, Letters to LeBourdais, 1925–1936, BCARS.

6.   Ibid.

7.   "Pulu": a light, fibrous, cotton-like material, used to stuff mattresses. A forerunner of kapok.

8.   *Cariboo Sentinel*, 22 October 1866, 2.

9.   Ibid., 1 May 1869, 2.

10. Bishop George Hills, Diary, 23 July 1863, Anglican Provincial Synod of BC Archives, Vancouver.

11. Cheadle, Journal, 20 October 1863.

12. Henry Roeder to his wife, 15 August 1864, E/B/R62ca, BCARS.

13. Ibid., 10 July 1864.

14. Ibid.

15. Ibid.

16. *Colonist* (Victoria), 9 November 1865.

17. Sarah Crease, Diary, 24 September 1880, A/E/C86, BCARS.

18. Hills, Diary, 24 July 1863.

19. Harry Guillod, Diary, 23 August 1862, E/B/G94A, BCARS.

20. Cheadle, Journal, October 1863.

21. Catherine Edwards to Commissioner of Lands and Works, 16 September 1865, GR 1372, F508b, BCARS.

22. Hills, Diary, 1862.

23. Guillod, Diary, 23 August 1862.

24. Ibid.

25. Captain C. W. Buckley, RN, Diary, 1862, addit. MSS E/B/B85, BCARS.

26. *Cariboo Sentinel*, 1 July 1865, 2.

27. British Columbia Department of Mines, Annual Report, 1875, p. 608.

28. *Cariboo Sentinel*, 6 August 1870, 3.

29. Harry Jones to Louis LeBourdais, 1935, addit. MSS 361, BCARS.

30. Crease, Diary, 18 September 1880, 11.

31. Cottonwood House Books, Daybook L, 22 August 1886, 248.

32. *Cariboo Sentinel*, 16 November 1872, 3.

33. Luiga Yolland cited in Emelene Thomas, "Cherished Memories," *North Cariboo Digest* (January 1950).

34. Cheadle, Diary, 21 October 1863.

35. Ibid.

36. Lieutenant H. S. Palmer, RE, Map, Sketch of part of British Columbia, Lac La Hache to Richfield, p/6/6p/BC –P1745 1863, BCARS.

37. Hills, Diary, 5 July 1862.

38. Buckley, Diary, August 1862, E/B/B/85, BCARS.

39. Ibid.

40. *British Columbia and Victoria Directory,* 1863, published and printed by Howard and Barnett, Victoria, BC, 153.

41. Hills, Diary, 24 July 1862.

Author's Bibliography

Published Sources

Akrigg, G. P. V. & Helen B. British Columbia Chronicle, 1847–1871: Gold and Colonists. Vancouver, BC. Discovery Press. 1977.

Anderson, James. Sawney's Letters and Cariboo Rhymes. Barkerville Restoration Advisory Committee of BC 1962.

Bancroft, H. H. Bancroft's Works Volume XXXII. History of British Columbia. 1792–1887. San Francisco. The History Company, Publishers. 1886.

Boam, A. J. & Brown, A. G. British Columbia.London, England. Sells Ltd. 1912.

Brown, R.C. Lundin. British Columbia, An Essay. New Westminster, BC The Royal Engineers Press. 1863.

Champness, W. To Cariboo and Back in 1862 Fairfield, Washington. Ye Galleon Press. 1972.

Craig, Andy A. Trucking: British Columbia's Trucking History. Hancock House, Saanichton, BC 1977.

Downs, Art. "Wagon Road North". Cariboo and Northern BC Digest, Winter, 1947.

Downs, Art. Paddlewheels on the Frontier, the Story of BC Sternwheel Steamers. Cloverdale BC. BC Outdoors, 1967.

Eliott, Gordon R. Quesnel, The Commercial Centre of the Cariboo Gold Rush. Quesnel Cariboo Observer. 1958.

Forbes, Molly. Lac La Hache. Quesnel, BC 1970.

Forbes, Molly, "Alex Meiss and His Wooden Leg." Clinton Cache Creek Pioneer. March 11, 1970.

Gosnell, R.E. The Year Book of British Columbia and Manual of Provincial Information. The Government of British Columbia, Victoria, BC 1903.

Halcome, Rev. J. J. The Emigrant & The Heathen. Sketches of Missionary Life. Excerpts from the diary of Rev. R.J.Dundas. 1874.

Hong, William M. And So That's How It Happened. Recollections of Stanley-Barkerville, Edited by Gary and Eileen Seale. Quesnel, BC Spartan Printing. 1978.

Horsefly Historical Society. Horsefly, Its Early History, 1858-1915. Revised Edition. 1981.

Laing, F. W. Colonial Farm Settlers on the Mainland of British Columbia, 1858-1871. Victoria, BC 1939.

Laing, F. W. "Some Pioneers of the Cattle Industry." BC Historical Quarterly, Vol.6, October 1942.

Lindley, Joe. Three Years In Cariboo. A. San Francisco. Rosenfield, Publishers. 1872.

Ludditt, F. W. Barkerville Days. Vancouver, BC Mitchell Press, 1969.

McInnes, Alexander P. Chronicles of the Cariboo, Dunlevy's Discovery of Gold on the Horsefly. Lillooet, BC Lillooet Publishers Limited, 1938.

Melvin, G. H. Post Offices of British Columbia 1858-1970. Vernon, BC 1972.

Milton, Viscount, and Cheadle, Dr W. B. North-West Passage by Land – 1865. Coles Canadian Collection. Toronto, Canada. Coles Publishing, 1970

Moberly, Walter. "The History of the Cariboo Wagon Road." Art, Historical and Scientific Association of Vancouver, BC Papers. (1908): 75-89.

Morice, Adrien Gabriel. The History of the Northern Interior of British Columbia, formerly New Caledonia. Toronto, 1904.

Old Age Pensioners's Organization, Branch #77, Quesnel, BC A Tribute to the Past. 1808-1908. Quesnel, BC. Spartan Printers. 1985.

Ormsby, Margaret. British Columbia, A History. The McMillan Co. of Canada Ltd. 1958.

Patenaude, Branwen C. Because of Gold. NP Big Country Printers, Quesnel, BC 1982.

Pettit, Sydney G., "His Honour's Honour." British Colombia Historical Quarterly. Volume X1, No.3 July, 1947.

Ramsey, Bruce. Ghost Towns of British Columbia. Vancouver, BC Mitchell Press.1963.

Splawn, A. J. Ka-mi-akin, the Last Hero of the Yakimas. Portland, Oregon. 1917.

Thomas, Emelene. "Cherished Memories." *North West Cariboo Digest.* January, 1950.

Thomson, James. *For Friends At Home. A Scottish Emigrant's Letters from Canada, California and the Cariboo 1844–1864.* Edited by R.A. Preston. Montreal and London. McGill-Queen's University Press. 1974.

Touchie, Rodger. "Frontier Inns." *BC Motorist.* May–June 1974: 47-53.

Wade, Dr Mark S. *The Overlanders of '62.* Victoria. Memoir No. IX, Provincial Archives of BC. 1931.

Wade, Dr Mark S. *The Cariboo Road.* Edited by Eleanor A. Eastick. Victoria, BC. Haunted Bookshop, 1979.

Walkem, W.W. *Stories of Early British Columbia.* Vancouver, BC 1914.

West, Willis. *Staging and Stage Holdups. British Columbia Historical Quarterly.* Vol.12, No.3, July,1948.

Williams, David R. *The Man for a New Country: Sir Matthew Baillie Begbie.* Sidney, BC. Grey's Publishing. 1977.

Whitehead, Margaret. *The Cariboo Mission: A History of the Oblates.* Victoria, BC. Sono Nis Press. 1981.

Woolliams, Nina. *Cattle Ranch.* Vancouver, BC. Douglas & McIntyre. 1982.

Unpublished Sources

Alexander, Richard H., "Diary", April, 1863. E/B/A1 3.2A British Columbia Archives & Records Service, Victoria, BC.

Ball, Henry M., "Diary", August, 1864–Oct., 1865. Add.Mss. 681 BCARS.

Blair, George, "Diary", Jan.1862–Dec. 1863. Add.Mss. 187. BCARS.

Boss, Martha W. "A Tale of Northern BC to Cassiar" Add.Mss.771. BCARS.

Bowron, Lottie, M., Scrapbook, Reminiscences of Barkerville. Add.Mss. 44. BCARS.

Boyd, Archie C. "Memoirs of Cottonwood House." Barkerville Historic Park, Barkerville, BC.

Boyd, John C. Daybooks, Cold Spring House, May,1866–May,1886. Howay Collection, Special Collections Library, U.B.C. Vancouver, BC.

Boyd, John C. Daybooks, Cottonwood House. 1874–1901. Quesnel and District Museum, Quesnel, BC.

Buckley, Captain C. W.,"Diary", July, 1862. E/B/B85. BCARS.

Cheadle, Dr W. B. "Journal", 1863. E/B/C42.1. Parts 3 and 4. BCARS.

Clapperton, John. "Diary", 1862-1864. E/C/c53.3 BCARS.

Crease, Sarah. "Diary of a Trip to Cariboo, Kamloops and New Westminster, Sept.1–Dec.7, 1880. A/E/C86 BCARS.

Currie, Vera Baker, Manuscript, "Susie", the life and times of Cecilia Elmore Baker. 1867–1958.

Darlington, Esther, Ashcroft, BC Manuscript, "The Fabulous Fanny Faucault." 1988.

DeWees, Dick. Transcribed tapes, August 1977. Accession #142. Horsefly Historical Society, Horsefly, BC.

Douglas, James, Private papers, 1860. Bancroft Library, Berkeley, California.

Evans, Chad. Thesis. "Theatre In The Cariboo". Barkerville Historic Park. Barkerville, BC, 1980.

Evans, Captain John, "Diary", "British Columbia Mining Adventure, 1862–1864." Add. Mss.2111 BCARS.

Guillod, Harry, Reminiscence, "Journal of a Trip to Cariboo." 1862. E/B/G94A. BCARS.

Gurney, William H., Reminiscence, "My First School, Cariboo Style." 1971. BCARS.

Hargreaves, Katherine G. Reminiscences. E/E/H221 BCARS.

Hills, Bishop George, "Diaries", 1860–1862. Anglican Provincial Synod of BC Archives. Vancouver, BC.

Johnston, W. Alvin, Manuscript, "Birchbark to Steel."

H. Albert Johnston family, Quesnel, BC.

LeBoudais, Louis. "Harry Jones Story." Add. Mss. 676, Vol.7. BCARS.

LeBourdais, Louis. Add Mss 361, Letters of Harry Jones, 1925–1936. BCARS.

Lyne, William Jr 1890–1891. Account books, blacksmith. Add. Mss. 417.BCARS.

McColl, Sergeant William. "Diary", September 26–November 23, 1861.
*   C/AB/30.6/M13. BCARS.*

McKinlay, Duncan, "Memoirs", Vertical Files, BCARS.

McMicking, Robert B., "Diary", 1862. Special Collections Library, U.B.C., Vancouver, BC.

McMurphy, Sergeant John, "Diary", May 1862–August 1863. E/B/M221 BCARS.

Moberly, Walter, "History of the Cariboo Wagon Road". Vancouver, BC Art,
*   Historical and Scientific Association of Vancouver. 1908.*

Moffat House, Alexandria, BC "Diaries" 1891–1940s. Originals, Moffat family,
*   Private collection.*

Roeder, Henry, "Letters", E/B/R62cA. BCARS.

Rose, Frederick, Family history, ongoing geneological study. Private collection.

Ryder, Angus G., "Recollections of Four Years at the 59 Mile House, Cariboo Road.
*   1910–1914. Add.Mss.1069, BCARS.*

Sargison, George, "Diary", "A Trip To Williams Creek." December 1871. E/C/Sa7 BCARS.

Slater, Ethel. "A Town Is Born." Vertical Files, BCARS.

Voorhis, Ernest. "Historical Forts and Trading Posts of the French regime and of the
English Fur Trading Co's." NW971.F Vol.951. BCARS.

Wade & Co., Daybook, June, 1863–December 1864. Howay Collection. Special
*   Collections Library, U.B.C., Vancouver, BC.*

Walters, Glen, Transcribed tapes, July, 1977. Accession #1–6, Side 1,2. Horsefly
*   Historical Society. Horsefly, BC.*

Wardrop, J. R. "Gustavus Blin Wright, Colonial Entrepreneur." Victoria, BC 1876. BCARS.

Williams, Agnes, Transcribed Tapes, Sept. 1977. Horsefly Historical Society, Horsefly, BC.

Public Documents and Records

Colonial Government Correspondence, 1858–1880. BCARS.

Begbie, Matthew Baillie, Supreme Court Bench Books, 1858–1879. BCARS.

Begbie, M. B., Colonial Correspondence, GR. 1372, F142–E. BCARS.

Cariboo Government Agency Letterbook, GR216, 1864-1880. BCARS.

Nind, Philip H. Colonial Correspondence, F1255. BCARS.

Palmer, Henry Spencer. Report of a Survey from Victoria to Fort Alexander via North
*   Bentinck Arm., New Westminster, 1863. BCARS.*

Department of Public Works, Notes on the Road History of British Columbia,
*   1853–1918. BCARS.*

Colonial Secretary, Miscellaneous Official Correspondence. 1858–1900.BCARS.

BC Ministry of Provincial Secretary. Planning & Interpretation Division, Heritage
*   Conservation, Victoria, BC assorted historical material, including "Cottonwood*
*   House, a documented history." by Judy Stricker, 1982.*

List of Pre-empted Lands in Yale, Lillooet and Cariboo districts, 1859–1920. BCARS.

Lists of Certificates of Improvement, (Pre-empted Lands) 1865-1900. BCARS.

GR216, Mining Records 1860-1900. BCARS

Geological Survey of Canada, Report of 1874. University of British Columbia. Vancouver, BC.

Geological Survey of Canada. Memoir #149, Johnston & Uglow, 1925.

BC Department of Mines, Annual Reports, 1874–1940.

BC Department of Mines, Bulletin 34. Stuart Holland. 1954.

BC Land Titles, Victoria, BC Books of Mortgages and Conveyances, 1860–1868.

BC Dept. of Lands, Victoria, BC Legal Surveys Dept. Crown Grant Registry.

BC Dept. of Lands, Legal Surveys Dept. Victoria, BC.

British Columbia Directories, 1863–1900.

Published Maps

Western Union Telegraph, 1866. 3 Sheets. Drawn by J. C. White, from notes by
    J. Maclure. 17B8. 1866. Map Collection, Bancroft Library, Berkeley, Cal.

Pre-emptors Map, Quesnel Sheet, 1921. BC Dept. of Lands, Victoria, BC.

Palmer, Lieutenant H. S., Sketch of Part of British Columbia. To accompany Report of
    Feb. 21, 1863.

Palmer, Lieutenant H. S. Sketch of Forks of Quesnel. Sept. 4, 1862. Land Reserves.
    16T1, 17T1, Legal Surveys, Vault. Victoria, BC.

Bowman, Amos, 9 Maps of Cariboo Mining District for Geological Survey of Canada,
    1885, 1886. Little Snowshoe and Keithley Creek. Antler Creek. Lightning
    Creek. Williams Creek.

Begbie, Matthew B. Sketch of BC & Cariboo Country, 1861. Engineer's Camp,
    New Westminster, BC.

Begbie, Matthew B. Discovery Route over Snowshoe Plateau. from Begbie's notes.
    Drawn by J.B.Launders, Oct. 1869.

Newspapers

BC Mining Journal, later known as the Ashcroft Journal

British Colonist, later known as the Victoria Colonist and the Colonist

New Westminster British Columbian

British Columbia Gazette

British Columbia Tribune

Cariboo Sentinel

Mainland Guardian

The New Westminster Times

100 Mile Free Press

Quesnel Cariboo Observer

Toronto Mail

Vancouver Province or The Province

Williams Lake Tribune

Yale British Columbia Tribune

Kamloops Sentinel

Tape Recordings

Selected tapes from Aural History Dept.
    BCARS

Fred Pinchbeck. Tape No.FT17

Porter, Isobel. Tape No.495

Yorston, Janet. Tape No.380.

Author's Tape Recordings Private Collection

Barlow, Alex. Quesnel, BC 1982

Barlow, Anne. Quesnel, BC 1982

Beath, Charles. Quesnel, BC

Cook, Florence. Quesnel, BC 1982

Forbes, Molly. Lac La Hache. 1986

Hilborn, Gordon. Quesnel, BC 1976

Lyne, Georgina. Lac La Hache. BC 1983

Moffat, Roddy R. Alexandria, BC 1976

Petrowitz, Dolly. Williams Lake, BC 1977

Rankin, Gerald. Mary and Joan, Soda
    Creek, BC 1983

Rankin, Nellie. Morgan Creek, BC 1984

Rankin, Jim. Soda Creek, BC 1984

Watson, Jean. Quesnel, BC, 1978

Windt, Tom. Alexandria, BC 1980

Yorston, Jack. Australian Ranch, BC

Yorston, Katherine. Australian Ranch, BC

Index